T0158400

INCARCERATION
AND RACE
IN MICHIGAN

INCARCERATION AND RACE
IN MICHIGAN

GROUNDING THE NATIONAL DEBATE IN STATE PRACTICE

EDITED BY Lynn Orilla Scott and Curtis Stokes

Michigan State University Press | *East Lansing*

Copyright © 2020 by Michigan State University

♾ The paper used in this publication meets the minimum requirements
of ANSI/NISO Z39.48-1992 (R 1997) (Permanence of Paper).

Michigan State University Press
East Lansing, Michigan 48823-5245

Printed and bound in the United States of America.

29 28 27 26 25 24 23 22 21 20   1 2 3 4 5 6 7 8 9 10

LIBRARY OF CONGRESS CATALOGING-IN-PUBLICATION DATA
Names: Scott, Lynn Orilla, 1950– editor. | Stokes, Curtis, editor.
Title: Incarceration and Race in Michigan : grounding the national debate in state practice
/ edited by Lynn Orilla Scott and Curtis Stokes.
Description: East Lansing : Michigan State University Press, [2019]
| Includes bibliographical references and index.
Identifiers: LCCN 2018059546| ISBN 9781611863383 (pbk. : alk. paper)
| ISBN 9781609176143 (pdf) | ISBN 9781628953770 (epub) | ISBN 9781628963786 (kindle)
Subjects: LCSH: Criminal justice, Administration of—Social aspects—Michigan.
| Discrimination in justice administration—Michigan. | Corrections—Social aspects—Michigan.
Classification: LCC HV9955.M5 R33 2019 | DDC 365/.6089009774—dc23
LC record available at https://lccn.loc.gov/2018059546

Book and cover design by Charlie Sharp, Sharp Des!gns, East Lansing, MI
Cover art *Charlie Mack's Glove* by Martin Vargas

Michigan State University Press is a member of the Green Press Initiative and is
committed to developing and encouraging ecologically responsible publishing
practices. For more information about the Green Press Initiative and the use of
recycled paper in book publishing, please visit *www.greenpressinitiative.org*.

Visit Michigan State University Press at *www.msupress.org*

CONTENTS

FOREWORD

Charles Corley

This wonderfully crafted manuscript fills a void between academe, practitioners, and the incarcerated. It has been suggested that academic researchers are often far removed from the subjects of their research, whereas practitioners cannot articulate their practices in a manner that lends to replication, verification, and publication. Hence, a comprehensive understanding of crime, responses to crime, judicial processes, incarceration, and the aftermath of the prison experience is seldom attained.

This text adopts a socio-historical perspective and blends it with a social justice imperative that offers an insightful critique of our criminal justice system with a particular emphasis on corrections. The inclusion of demographic and criminal justice statistics, survey analysis, as well as published "best practices" research results intertwined with writings and artworks of the formerly incarcerated culminates in a humanistic perspective that compels the reader to question political influences on our system of justice in both Michigan and the United States.

The disadvantaged classes have historically been the focus of social control agencies, and this text explores and articulates experiences of persons of color relative to policing, the courts, and corrections, offering insights into challenges faced by various racial groups. The inclusion of perspectives of the formerly incarcerated adds a human dimension that reminds us that inmates are our fellow brothers and sisters whose prison experiences and trials do not end upon release.

In short, this text is a must-read for individuals who desire a more comprehensive understanding of the operation of corrections in the United States and the forces that impact it.

ACKNOWLEDGMENTS

This book is largely the result of its authors, who tirelessly wrote their chapters, and the artists who graciously gave us permission to reproduce their work. Criminal justice professor Charles Corley generously wrote the foreword. One of our ten race conferences, Race in 21st Century America: The Seventh National Conference, which occurred on April 20, 2011, is its background. Authors were invited locally and regionally, while others came from elsewhere, to participate in the conference. James Madison College (Michigan State University) is the primary sponsor of our race conferences, so we highlight as well our students, faculty, and staff for their various roles in the conferences since 1999, and we especially celebrate JMC for providing funding to support our book project, specifically Dean Sherman Garnett, Associate Dean Julia Grant, and our University Committee on Faculty Affairs. A special thanks to the University of Michigan's Prison Creative Arts Project for facilitating our contacts with the incarcerated and formerly incarcerated writers and artists represented in this book. Finally, we must also thank Randall W. Scott for the index, and the entire staff at Michigan State University Press, especially Julie L. Loehr, whom we have known and worked with for many years.

INTRODUCTION

For almost two decades, Americans have been increasingly aware of the problem of mass incarceration. Many people have become familiar with these startling facts: The United States has the highest incarceration rate in the world, incarcerating four to eight times as many people as other liberal democracies. We have 5 percent of the world's population but 25 percent of the world's prisoners.[1] Slowly, we seem to be reaching an agreement across ideological and party lines that reforms are needed to reduce our prison population. After decades of dramatic growth, in the last few years prison populations have stabilized and even declined a bit, although national trends obscure large local variations.[2] In the fall of 2018, the passage of the modest First Step Act by the U.S. Congress and the passage of the, also modest, Objective Parole Bill in Michigan, both with significant bipartisan support, suggest that this is an opportune time to educate the public and its representatives on what further steps must be taken to significantly reduce incarceration and improve the often dire conditions of confinement. This volume of essays hopes to deepen the understanding of the causes of mass incarceration while arguing for systemic changes in attitudes as well as laws and practices.

Even though there have been modest declines in the rate of incarceration recently, the numbers remain staggering and bear repeating. In 2018, there were almost 2.3 million people incarcerated in the United States, when you count state prisons, federal prisons, juvenile correctional facilities, local jails, Indian Country jails, military prisons, immigration detention facilities, civil commitment centers, and prisons in U.S. territories.[3] "The number of people in state or federal prisons rose from just under 200,000 in 1972 to over 1.56 million in 2014; the incarceration rate grew from 93 per 100,000 to 498 per 100,000 (peaking at 536 per 100,000 in 2008). Another 700,000 people are in county jails on any given day, more than two-thirds of whom have not been convicted of any crime and are simply awaiting trial."[4] To get a picture of the full reach of the criminal justice system, we need to look beyond just the number of people in prisons and jails. There are 70 million Americans with criminal records, 600,000 people released from prisons each year, 11 million people who cycle through local jails annually, and 4 million people on probation.[5]

It is ironic that much of this drive to incarcerate has taken place during a period of decreasing crime. Crime rates have been going down since the early 1990s. Our violent crime rate is now where it was in the 1970s, but our incarceration rate is five times higher. According to the standard narrative, mass incarceration began in the 1970s as a response to rising crime rates that began in the 1960s and continued for thirty years. Yet, rising crime rates, in and of themselves, do not explain our high incarceration rates, nor is there evidence that our high incarceration rate has been a significant factor in the decreasing crime rate beginning in 1992 and continuing. By comparing trends in U.S. crime rates and incarceration rates with those of several European countries, Michael Tonry has shown that there is no necessary correlation between the two rates.[6] The rise in crime rates in the sixties and seventies, peaking at about 1980 (prior to the crack epidemic in the United States), and then the sharp decline beginning in the 1990s has been remarkably similar in the United States and in many European countries; yet, the trends in incarceration rates have not. Incarceration rates either remained stable or in some cases fell in Europe even as crime rates rose. Increased incarceration was simply not seen as the solution to rising crime rates. Only in the United States did incarceration rates increase substantially and consistently over the past forty years. By the early 2000s we were incarcerating more than five times as many people as we were in the early 1970s. As Marie Gottschalk has pointed out, there is widespread agreement among experts "that changes in public policies—not dramatic changes in criminal behavior—propelled the decades long prison boom in the United States."[7] Tonry claims, "American imprisonment rates did not rise because crime rose. They rose because American politicians *wanted* them to rise."[8] Moreover, the politics of incarceration is not just a question of the rhetoric and policies of presidents, senators, and congressmen, but "many observers attribute the punitive extremes of the U.S. criminal justice system to the exceptional politicization of prosecutors and judges, who are . . . chosen in a partisan manner."[9] It's also true, of course, that American people elected those politicians, prosecutors, and judges and that being labeled "weak on crime" was seen as political suicide by Democrats and Republicans alike. So it is fair to say that our extraordinarily high incarceration rates have a lot to do with how we think about crime and criminals, even though that thinking is seriously flawed.

There is general agreement that mass incarceration is ineffective and costly, that our prisons are more warehouses than corrective institutions, and that many supposedly "color-blind" policies, procedures, and laws operating at all points in the criminal justice system have had a devastating impact on racial minorities and the poor. Although recent studies have shown that the gap between white and black incarceration rates has been on the decline, the gap is still huge. A 2016 study of racial disparity in state prisons found that blacks continue to be imprisoned at more than five times the rate of whites, and in five states the disparity is more than 10 to 1. In Michigan in 2014, blacks were imprisoned at nearly seven times the rate of whites, and 54 percent of people in Michigan prisons were black.[10] "Hispanics now constitute 35 percent of all federal prisoners, making them the largest ethnic or racial group in the federal prison system."[11] Latinos are also imprisoned at a higher rate than whites in state prisons, with especially high disparities in Massachusetts, Connecticut, Pennsylvania, and New York.[12] According to data released by the Department of Justice, American Indian youth are three times as likely to be held in a juvenile detention facility than white youth.[13] One driver of the overrepresentation of minorities in prisons is the disparity in sentencing: "Black and Latino offenders sentenced in state and federal courts face significantly greater odds of incarceration than similarly situated white offenders and receive longer sentences than their white counterparts in some jurisdictions. Black male federal defendants receive longer sentences than whites arrested for the same offenses and with comparable criminal histories."[14]

In her hugely influential book *The New Jim Crow: Mass Incarceration in the Age of Colorblindness*, Michelle Alexander shows that at all points in the criminal justice system, people of color have experienced especially harsh punishment: from arrest to charging, sentencing, imprisonment, and parole. This is most spectacularly evident in the war on drugs, which targeted black communities even while whites were using illegal drugs at a comparable rate. She tells us: "The stark and sobering reality is that . . . the American penal system has emerged as a system of social control unparalleled in world history. And while the size of the system alone might suggest that it would touch the lives of most Americans, the primary targets of its control can be defined largely by race."[15] Moreover, Alexander understands mass incarceration as not just rates of imprisonment but also as all of the collateral damage on communities and individuals that result from being branded "criminal." Policies that prohibit former felons from receiving needed government and educational assistance, from finding employment and housing, and, in many states, from voting, result in a "civil death" that continues long after the prisoner has been released. Alexander argues that mass incarceration, fed by the war on drugs, has created a new, cleverly disguised caste system, the "new Jim Crow." She writes:

> Today it is perfectly legal to discriminate against criminals in nearly all the ways that it was once legal to discriminate against African Americans. Once you're labeled a felon, the old forms of discrimination—employment discrimination, housing discrimination, denial of the right to vote, denial of educational opportunity, denial of food stamps and other public benefits, and exclusion from jury service—are suddenly legal. As a criminal, you have scarcely more rights, and arguably less respect, than a black man living in Alabama at the height of Jim Crow. We have not ended racial caste in America; we have merely redesigned it.[16]

Alexander concludes that ending mass incarceration will require a broad-based social movement that overturns the current public consensus supporting it.

Yet, significantly reducing prison populations in the United States will require more than ending the war on drugs. As Marie Gottschalk has pointed out, "Even if we could release all drug offenders today, without major changes in U.S. law and penal policies and practices, the United States would continue to be the world's warden." While drug offenders are one half of all federal inmates, they are only 20 percent of state inmates, which house the large majority of prisoners. It is also true that if we could wave a magic wand and get rid of the racial disparities in prison populations in the United States, we would still have an incarceration crisis in the country. While prison reform must address the historical and continuing legacy of racism, it also must address additional causes of mass incarceration if we are to substantially reduce prison populations and make prisons humane and rehabilitative institutions. In her 2015 book *Caught: The Prison State and the Lockdown of American*

Politics, Marie Gottschalk points to the limitations of current leading penal-reform strategies (reinvestment, recidivism, and reentry). She argues that "a durable reform movement ... has yet to coalesce," and any substantial reductions in prison populations will require a broad political movement that successfully challenges the punitive rhetoric that is based on the fallacy that excessive punishment is a significant factor in reducing and controlling crime.[17]

This anthology of essays, stories, and art on race and prisons is part of a series of books resulting from the biennial Michigan State University Race Conferences that began in 1999. At that time, some MSU faculty inspired by President Clinton's call for conversations on race in America (One America in the 21st Century, Forging a New Future: The President's Initiative on Race) began organizing race conversations, conferences that have been widely attended by faculty, students, and community members for almost two decades thanks to the support of James Madison College and other academic units. There have been ten MSU national race conferences so far, bringing to campus some of the most important scholars, public officials, and community leaders/activists representing racial, ethnic, gender, and ideological diversity to participate in an important conversation on the problem of race, ethnicity, and gender in America, and most recently sexuality. This collection of essays on "race and prisons" originated primarily from the 2011 conference on "race and the criminal justice system." It strives to reflect the spirit of the conference by representing multiple angles of vision, bringing together the perspectives of scholars, activists, and incarcerated and formerly incarcerated citizens. We agree with the claims of Michelle Alexander and Marie Gottschalk that significant changes to mass incarceration in the United States will require changes in the public consensus that has supported it. Such a change requires multiple forms of knowledge: we need social science research, political analysis, witnesses, and the voices and visions of those most directly affected to understand the causes, impacts, and solutions to mass incarceration.

The causes of mass incarceration are multiple; moreover, as our criminal justice system is highly decentralized, the remedies will vary from state to state, county to county, and city to rural community. It is a national problem driven by state and local policies. Thus, as you will see, while this book does address the larger national context, a number of articles focus on Michigan. In 2007, Michigan's prison population was at an all-time high of 51,500. By the end of 2017 it was just below 40,000. In the past three years, the prison population in Michigan has declined by more than 7 percent and recidivism is at a historic low of 29.8 percent.[18] Yet, these numbers hide some less positive trends. While Michigan saw an 8 percent decline in the men's prison population between 2009 and 2015, it incarcerated 30 percent more women over the same time period. The increase in women's incarceration rates in Michigan is consistent with what is happening in other states as well and has hurt efforts to reduce overall prison populations.[19]

Nationally, mass incarceration was driven not only by sending more people to prison, but sending them for significantly longer periods of time. While almost all states passed laws increasing the length of prison sentences over the past two to three decades, a PEW study from 2012 revealed that prisoners in Michigan serve longer sentences than in any other state.[20] In 2015 the Michigan Supreme Court struck down mandatory minimum sentences as unconstitutional (*People v. Lockridge*), restoring judges' discretion and allowing defense attorneys to better advocate for their clients, potentially making sentencing directly proportional to the crime. While this will help the problem going forward, it does not address the current excessive sentences some prisoners face and the aging prison population in Michigan. Further parole reform is needed to release prisoners at low risk of reoffending who have been held long past their initial eligibility for parole. Michigan is not only an outlier in the length of prison stay, but is one of only four states to automatically prosecute seventeen-year-olds as adults, and jail and imprison seventeen-year-olds in adult facilities. At the top of the agenda for prison reform advocates in Michigan has been legislation aimed at meaningful parole reform and efforts to "raise the age" of criminal responsibility to eighteen.[21] In addition, Michigan allows juveniles to be put in solitary confinement, and there are no regulations about how long a person can be placed in solitary. "In Michigan, any inmate can be put in confinement for any period and allowed to leave their cell for only one hour a day. Inmates in confinement are not allowed to make phone calls or visit with friends and family."[22]

In 2014 several organizations who have long worked in the area of criminal justice and prison reform came together under the auspices of the Michigan League for Public Policy to form a Collaborative to End Mass Incarceration. Some of the organizations involved include Safe and Just Michigan, Citizens for Prison Reform, the Michigan ACLU, the League of Women Voters, a number of church and faith-based groups, and groups that represent prisoners and former prisoners, such as Nation Outside and several chapters of the National Lifers of America. At this point the collaborative has over fifty member organizations and many more individual members. The collaborative is a way for the various prison reform groups to share information and support each other's legislative and educational efforts. They address a wide range of issues beyond the ones mentioned above, including prison conditions, policies around visitation, and generally making prisons more transparent to those outside.[23]

Political concern over mass incarceration has been around since the beginning of the new millennium, and reform efforts have had some bipartisan support over the past decade; yet substantial criminal justice reform that would result in a significant reduction in the overall prison population has been very difficult to achieve. Recent books, including John F. Pfaff's *Locked in: The True Causes of Mass Incarceration and How to Achieve Real Reform* (2017) and the previously mentioned *Caught*, by Marie Gottschalk, provide careful analyses of why criminal justice reform is so difficult, while suggesting ways forward. Pfaff argues that reformers should focus on, among other things, the role of prosecutors because incarceration growth is driven more by the number of people admitted to prison than any other single factor. Both Gottschalk and Pfaff argue that to substantially decarcerate we must change how we sentence people charged with violent offenses, a politically difficult task. At bottom the difficulty rests in public attitudes and myths about crime and criminals. Our very decentralized criminal justice system is not insulated from public opinion and is vulnerable to "moral panics," a term that sociologists use to describe periods when public passions take over, shaping decisions, laws, and policies. Moral panics occur in response to highly publicized crimes that are terrible but atypical and have led to laws and policies that have driven up incarceration, have little, if any, deterrent value, and have many unintended negative effects. It will be difficult to change our regime of harsh punishment until more Americans come to understand that it is not an effective deterrent to crime and that harsh punishment has exacerbated inequality and poverty, conditions that cause some types of crime to increase.

Anne-Marie Cusac argues that a cultural change took place in the 1970s in the United States, changing the way Americans came to view crime and criminals. She claims that prior to this period we separated criminal behavior from the person, but then, due to a number of cultural shifts, crime became increasingly attributed to criminal personalities.[24] Once criminal activity became viewed less as a behavior (that could be changed) and more as the result of a criminal identity that was not redeemable, then it was easy to justify harsher and longer punishment. These attitudes are especially powerful in how we treat violent crime. Pfaff has argued that "our attitude toward violent crime needs to change if we hope to end mass incarceration."[25] Even if the public believes otherwise, the data is clear that long sentences for violent crimes don't produce additional deterrence. Substantial decarceration will require changes in how we punish violent crime.[26]

Changing the public's view about the nature of criminal behavior and the relationship between crime and punishment is no easy task; ultimately it will require more than studies by legal scholars, criminologists, and political scientists, no matter how well-researched and persuasive. When people are branded with a criminal identity and hidden away from public view in institutions with very limited public access, it becomes all too easy to imagine them as fundamentally different, less worthy, less deserving of human rights than those on the outside. Gottschalk writes,

> Today, what happens in prison stays mostly in prison, making it harder to draw connections in the public mind between justice on the inside and justice on the outside. The ability to identify with an offender—or not—is a key predictor of why people differ in their levels of punitiveness. The invisibility of the millions of people behind bars has made it extremely difficult to alter the negative portrait that members of the general public have in their heads of people who have been convicted of a crime. They are simply prisoners and criminals. As such, they often are denied their humanity and denied any right to democratic accountability, much as slaves were in the United States.[27]

We need to see those most affected by our criminal justice system as more than numbers and statistics. We need to imagine the costs of our criminal justice system to include not just the cost of running prisons, but the costs being paid by those incarcerated, their families, and their communities. Thus, changing the public's view about the nature of criminal behavior will also require that our correctional institutions become more transparent and accessible to the public, and that communities should be meaningfully involved in efforts to rehabilitate offenders and restore harms caused by criminal behavior.

Perhaps no other organization in Michigan has encouraged outsiders to view prisoners as complex and talented human beings than the Prison Creative Arts Project (PCAP).[28] Founded in 1990 by Professor Buzz Alexander, distinguished professor emeritus of English at the University of Michigan, and currently under the direction of Professor Ashley Lucas, PCAP has evolved into one of, if not the largest prison creative-arts programs in the world, training students and volunteers to conduct theater and writing workshops in prisons, as well as juvenile and psychiatric facilities. Their annual *Michigan Review of Prisoner Creative Writing* and their outstanding annual exhibitions of prisoner art reach every prison in the state. The Annual Exhibit of Art by Michigan Prisoners is a juried art show that includes work by several hundred prisoner artists and brings in several thousand visitors each year. The mission of these exhibits and programs is to connect "inside and outside" communities, thus transforming perceptions of who incarcerated people are and facilitating the self-transformation of incarcerated people. The incarcerated and formerly incarcerated writers and artists represented in this book have been part of PCAP, and it is through that organization that we became aware of their work.

In the spirit of bringing together academic research with voices from the inside, this collection of essays, stories, and art aims to detail and build upon the impressive body of prison reform literature briefly discussed here. The historical legacy of slavery and racism is a big part of the story of harsh punishment in the United States. "Policing Black/Brown Communities inside/outside the United States: Neoliberalism and the Rise of the 'Carceral State' in the Twenty-First Century," by Professor Darryl C. Thomas, examines the policing of black and brown communities, through the lenses of the black radical tradition, critical political economy, and the "longue durée" to show the continuities and discontinuities across time framing our current crisis with the increased use of police violence and mass incarceration.

While Thomas paints the larger picture, the effects of this crisis on youth in Michigan is thoroughly explored in "Youth of Color and Michigan's Juvenile Justice System," by Michelle Weemhoff and Jason Smith, who use state and national research data to reveal the experiences of many youth of color in Michigan's juvenile justice system and to make recommendations for reducing racial disparities and improving outcomes for youth involved in the criminal justice system.

Incarcerated at seventeen, Martin Vargas entered the Michigan prison system as a "juvenile lifer" and spent forty-six years in Michigan prisons. He is the author of the short story "Basketballs Can Be a Bitch!," an understated though vivid description of the 1981 prison riot in Marquette Branch Prison. His artwork has been exhibited in PCAP's annual exhibitions since the 1990s, winning numerous awards. Six of his pieces are reproduced here: *Charlie Mack's Glove*, which is the cover of this volume; *The Puddle Jumper*; *My Wife My Life*; *Black Top Mourning*; *Painting His Way Home*; and *Veritas—The Lifer*. The last of these was presented to Supreme Court Justice Sonia Sotomayor when she came to speak at the University of Michigan.

Teachers and professors who provide educational services to inmates are an important conduit linking inside and outside communities, even though educational opportunities for prisoners became much more scarce after the 1994 Crime Bill ended Pell Grants for prisoners. "Behind Bars: The Current State of U.S. Prison Literature," by D. Quentin Miller, professor of English at Suffolk University Boston, claims that reading prison literature is essential to creating a humane society because it is key to understanding the relationship between the conditions of those outside the bars to those inside them. Beginning with his own experience teaching in a prison, he goes on to analyze the long history of American literature that has engaged with the experience of incarceration.

Phillip "UcciKhan" Sample, sentenced to prison at eighteen for 12 to 20 years, had been recently released from a Michigan prison when he attended the 2011 Race Conference from which this book derives its inspiration. In a panel on "Prison Narratives," Phillip opened the eyes and hearts of his audience with his spoken word poetry and candid discussion of his prison experience. Phillip's poem "A Sense of Solitary Confinement" reflects on the long periods he spent in solitary, experiencing some of the worst conditions in Michigan prisons. In the years since his release, he has published an autobiography, *The Passion of The Life (Pt. 1: The Life): The Life, Death & Resurrection of Phillip A. Sample*, and has worked as an assistant director for prison reenactments.

"Solo's Life Narrative: Freedom for Me Was an Evolution, Not a Revolution" is an as-told-to narrative edited by Megan Sweeney, associate professor of English language and literature at the University of Michigan. Sweeney met "Solo," an incarcerated fifty-six-year-old African American woman, while researching the role of reading in prisons. As access to books in prison has become increasingly restricted, Solo's narrative reminds us of the key role reading has played in prisoners' ability to understand, grow, and remain connected to the world outside prison walls.

Rand Gould, who has been incarcerated in Michigan since 1999, is the author of "Outside the Fences: The Rewilding of the Motor City Viewed from a Prison," an essay that describes the view from inside the Mound Correctional Facility a couple of years before that facility was closed. Gould is a prison activist who writes about conditions and policies in Michigan prisons.

The paintings *Detroit Rising* and *Sunsetting* are by Reuben Kenyatta, a veteran and formerly incarcerated citizen who is an art curator for the Prison Creative Arts Project. His work can be seen at the Wild Wolf Fine Arts Studio.

So often our understanding of the racial disparities in prisons is painted in black and white, yet we know that Latinos and Native Americans are also disproportionately affected by harsh punishment policies. "Criminal Justice, Disconnected Youth, and Latino Males in the United States and in Michigan," by Rubén O. Martinez, director of the Julian Samora Research Institute at Michigan State University, with Bette Avila and Barry Lewis, argues that the incarceration of Latinos and other minorities shows the influence of Michigan's punitive approach under the ideology of neoliberalism. The paper examines theories about the causes of the increased number of incarcerated Latino males in the criminal justice system and recommends changes in social policy to address these problems.

Aaron Kinzel gives us a window into Native American experience in prison in "Lox (The Wolverine): The Struggle to Express a Native American Identity in the Carceral State." Kinzel, both an academic and a formerly incarcerated person, blends his academic research with his firsthand experience to write a critical self-narrative exploring prison culture, convict identity, and civic engagement within the carceral state. Kinzel is currently a lecturer in criminology and criminal justice studies at the University of Michigan-Dearborn.

Carolyn Pratt Van Wyck and Elizabeth Pratt's "Mass Incarceration and Mental Illness: Addressing the Crisis" examines the policies and practices that have turned jails and prisons across the United States into holding places for people with serious mental illness. The conditions of confinement, including lack of medical treatment, use of restraints, and solitary confinement, are devastating for the incarcerated person, whose condition often worsens, and for the family members who have few options for helping their loved ones. The essay recommends specific changes in criminal justice policy as well as health policy interventions that can effectively treat mental illness, keep mentally ill people out of prison, and thus address a significant contributor to mass incarceration.

We conclude with Dennis Schrantz's "What Works in Prisoner Reentry: Reducing Crime, Recidivism, and Prison Populations." As former deputy director of the Michigan Department of Corrections, Schrantz led the creation and implementation of the groundbreaking Michigan Prisoner ReEntry Initiative, which contributed to substantial reductions in the prison population without an increase in crime by parolees. Schrantz argues that improvements to community supervision, a major expansion of human service resources for offenders, and a rethinking of probation and parole services are needed to end the era of mass incarceration. After outlining the scope of the problem—the challenges faced by the hundreds of thousands of people released from state and federal prisons and the literally millions released from local jails each year—Schrantz provides a history of modern reentry practices and goes on to explore in detail the successful reentry model used in Michigan. Evidence-based research has shown what works, but the challenge remains for agencies to have both the resources and the ability to apply this knowledge. Schrantz's essay concludes with a reminder that multiple approaches are needed to end mass incarceration, and that reform work and movement building must go hand in hand.

Finally, a note about the cover art of this book. We chose this painting by Mr. Vargas before we knew its story. The workman's glove hanging from the concertina wire struck us as an image that summed up the harsh and lonely story of prison life. But as with much of Mr. Vargas's work, it is both symbolic and personal; in fact, there is a specific story about a specific individual.

Here is what he wrote us about his inspiration for *Charlie Mack's Glove*.

I was in Marquette Branch Prison in 1981 and met a man named Charlie Mack. He was a few years older than me and though not necessarily a quiet person neither was he anti-social. Something intriguing about him was his work-outs. Weights, aerobics, or running; it was high intensity from the word go! He never got high or drunk nor was he in any way a bully. I got to know him some, but nobody really knows anybody in prison. I remember him telling me once with a sincere smile that although he was serving a natural life sentence he would never die in prison. That didn't mean much to me because almost everyone with a long sentence says something similar. Not long after the riot I wrote about in "Basketballs Can Be a Bitch!," those not considered high security risks were transferred to Huron Valley Men's Facility. Charlie Mack and I both made that list. I found out he was training so hard so that he would not die in prison, but not because he wanted to remain in good health. In 1982 he died after being shot not far from the prison compound. He made a daring escape over a building surrounded by concertina wire. This is what gave birth to his flag of honor, as I see it; one of his gloves had been caught in the razor wire and waved in the wind where he crossed over. That scene was engraved in my mind and that's how CHARLIE MACK'S GLOVE came about.

NOTES

1. John F. Pfaff, *Locked In: The True Causes of Mass Incarceration and How to Achieve Real Reform* (New York: Basic Books, 2017), 1.

2. Marie Gottschalk, *The Prison State and the Lockdown of American Politics* (Princeton, NJ: Princeton University Press, 2015), 266.

3. Peter Wagner and Wendy Sawyer, "Mass Incarceration: The Whole Pie 2018," *Prison Policy Initiative* newsletter, March 14, 2018, https://www.prisonpolicy.org.

4. Pfaff, *Locked In*, 2.

5. Peter Wagner, *Prison Policy Initiative, 2016–2017 Annual Report* (Northampton, MA: Prison Policy Initiative, November 2017), 2.

6. Michael Tonry, *Thinking about Crime: Sense and Sensibility in American Penal Culture* (Oxford: Oxford University Press, 2004), esp. chap. 2.

7. Gottschalk, *The Prison State*, 258.

8. Tonry, *Thinking about Crime*, 33.

9. Gottschalk, *The Prison State*, 264.

10. Ashley Nellis, *The Color of Justice: Racial and Ethnic Disparity in the State Prisons* (Washington, DC: The Sentencing Project, 2016), 3, https://www.sentencingproject.org. The Michigan statistics come from "ACLU of Michigan Releases Blueprint to Cut Prison Population by 23,000, Saving Taxpayers $1.8 Billion," American Civil Liberties Union of Michigan, September 4, 2018, https://www.aclumich.org.

11. Gottschalk, *The Prison State*, 4.

12. Nellis, *The Color of Justice*, 3.

13. "Fact Sheet: Native Disparities in Youth Incarceration," The Sentencing Project, October 12 2017, https://www.sentencingproject.org.

14. American Civil Liberties Union, "Racial Disparities in Sentencing: Hearing on Reports of Racism in the Justice System of the United States" (paper submitted to the Inter-American Commission on Human Rights, 153rd Session, October 27, 2014), 1, https://www.aclu.org/sites/default/files/assets/141027_iachr_racial_disparities_aclu_submission_0.pdf.

15. Michelle Alexander, *The New Jim Crow: Mass Incarceration in the Age of Colorblindness* (New York: The New Press, 2010), 8.

16. Alexander, *The New Jim Crow*, 2.

17. Gottschalk, *The Prison State*, 4, 5, 22.

18. Paul Egan, "Michigan Prison Closing after State's Inmate Population Drop," *Detroit Free Press*, January 29, 2018.

19. Alfonso Serrano, "Report: National Movement to Reduce U.S. Prison Population Has Largely Ignored Women," *Colorlines*, January 10, 2018, https://www.colorlines.com.

20. The PEW Center on the States, *Time Served: The High Cost, Low Return of Longer Prison Terms* (Washington, DC: PEW Center on the States, June 2012).

21. The Objective Parole law (House Bill 5377), which passed in September 2018, was supported by reform groups, although it was less than hoped for. It is estimated to reduce the size of Michigan's prison population by 1,800 to 2,400 in five years. "New Law Reforms Parole Guidelines in Michigan." WDIV ClickonDetroit. September 13, 2018, https://www.clickondetroit.com. For a list of organizations supporting legislation to raise the age of juvenile court jurisdiction, see Raise the Age Michigan, https://www.raisetheagemi.org.

22. Ray Wilbur, "Michigan Lags in Solitary Confinement Reform," *Capital News Service*, December 9, 2016, http://news.jrn.msu.edu.

23. The Michigan Collaborative to End Mass Incarceration maintains an extensive website on prison reform issues and initiatives as well as their organizational vision and membership at https://www.michigancollaborative.org.

24. Anne-Marie Cusac, *Cruel and Unusual: The Culture of Punishment in America* (New Haven, CT: Yale University Press, 2009).

25. Pfaff, *Locked In*, 229.

26. Ibid. See esp. chaps. 7 and 8.

27. Gottschalk, *The Prison State*, 274.

28. The Prison Creative Arts Project is a program of the LSA Residential College at the University of Michigan. Their programs and a calendar of their public events can be found at https://lsa.umich.edu/pcap/programs.html.

Policing Black/Brown Communities inside/outside the United States

Neoliberalism and the Rise of the "Carceral State" in the Twenty-First Century

Darryl C. Thomas

There has never been any time in the history of African Americans' presence in the United States, from the slavery era to the present, when peace and peaceful coexistence existed between the police and African American people. Nothing since slavery, including Jim Crow segregation, forced convict labor, lynching, restrictive covenants in housing, the shutout of blacks from the New Deal programs like Social Security and the GI Bill, or massive resistance to school desegregation, or the ceaseless efforts to keep African Americans from voting, has sparked the level of outrage by African Americans as when they have felt under violent attack by the police. During these episodes of police violence toward the black community, African Americans have abandoned traditional civil-rights strategies, such as bringing court cases and marching peacefully, and instead have resorted to violence in the streets, destroying property and attacking symbols of the state in response to violent behavior of the police toward black communities. Starting with Watts in 1965, Newark in 1967, Miami in 1980, Los Angeles in 1992, Ferguson in 2015, Baltimore in 2016, Charlotte in 2016—each of these cities went up in flames in response to police killing of a black man. The recent acquittal of police in the killing of black men in Minneapolis and St. Louis in 2017 resulted in protest across the United States and some cases of civil violence.[1]

Cathy Lisa Schneider notes that no attribute of a racially divided society is a more compelling symbol of racial supremacy or instills the message of subjugation more persuasively than police. The persistence of identity checks, the stop-and-frisks, the contempt and ruthless manner with which police address black and Latino youths, and worst of all, the utter freedom that allows the most racist and sadistic cops to commit gross violations of human rights and homicide: all of these constantly and painfully remind minority youths of their subordinate status. In unequal, racially divided societies, political elites depend on police to enforce categorical boundaries. Police violence further polarizes social relations around an "us/them" divide. If social movements, courts, or other institutions offer alternative paths to justice, no matter how limited, political violence can be avoided. Riots or political violence are the last resort of those who find all paths to justice blocked.[2]

Eric Wolf observes that all societies establish boundaries that define rights of membership, construct justificatory ontogenies for their cadres, and lay down criteria for denying participation and benefits to groups deemed undesirable, undeserving, or deleterious.[3] Basically, state creation by definition involves the formation of unequal bounded categories—Frenchman/German, citizen/noncitizen, and national and non-national. Hence, extreme categorical inequality occurs when hegemonic groups conquer less powerful groups and force them into submission. During and following the inception of such historical processes, members of the hegemonic groups justify their privileged position through master narratives of empire or nation building.[4] Categories simplify and facilitate exploitation (the expropriation of profits, labor power, and resources) and opportunity hoarding (exclusion of others from access to valuable resources and opportunities). Categories constructed for the purposes of slavery, conquest, or colonialism can later be used to reinforce unequal systems of remuneration—establishing color bars or other barriers to upward social mobility. By the same token, Anibal Quijano and Ramon Grosfoguel and V. Chloe S. Geora emphasize "colonialities of power" in which social practices are implicated in relationships among people even after colonial relationships have been eradicated.[5] Over time, the police departments are perceived as an occupying army. Police community relations deteriorate, and trust between citizen and the state is lost.

Policing and Mass Incarceration

The standard narratives on the origins of mass incarceration cite President Ronald Reagan's infamous "War on Drugs" (in the 1980s) as the key factor behind the growth in black conviction and imprisonment. Nevertheless, Elizabeth Hinton contends that the growth of the mass incarceration regimes should be understood as the federal government's reaction to demographic transformation of the United States in the 1950s, including the achievements of the African American civil rights movement and the tenacious threat of urban rebellion.[6] From the First World War to the Vietnam War, more than 6 million rural African Americans escaped the exploitation and terror of the Jim Crow South and moved to the Northeast, Midwest, and the West Coast in a mass exodus that transformed the nation. Black civil rights activists and labor leaders began organizing at the start of the migration and eventually propelled President Franklin D. Roosevelt to desegregate the defense and government industries as a result of A. Phillip Randolph and the Brotherhood of Sleeping Car Porters' threatened March on Washington. The black efforts during the Second World War to seek a double victory against fascism at home and abroad, and their unrelenting call for integration eventually led the U.S. Supreme Court to endorse desegregation of Southern public schools in the 1954 *Brown v. Board of Education* decision. Increasingly, proponents of civil rights began to adopt the tactics of Gandhi promoted by Dr. Martin Luther King and began to engage in a strategy of civil disobedience—direct action—through marches, sit-ins, and public protests, challenging Jim Crow segregation laws. Still, Southern governors and law-enforcement officials categorized these actions, such as Rosa Parks's refusal to sit in the black section of the bus, as "criminal" acts committed by "hoodlums," and civil rights marches as "street mobs" that were attempting to undermine law and order.[7] As black citizens continued to move to the urban North amid the escalating civil rights movement, the ongoing exodus of primarily white middle-class residents from cities to suburban areas required new approaches to the problems municipalities faced, with a tax base in decline side by side with a growth of a black population in urban areas.

Starting in the early 1960s, the federal government began struggling with problems associated with remedying racial discrimination, ending poverty, and fighting crime in American cities, and these issues were crucial to domestic programs. Most African Americans were barred from participation in Aid to Dependent Children (ADC), the GI Bill, and many other social welfare programs associated with the

New Deal, making the Kennedy administration's total attack on delinquency one of the federal government's first reactions to the impact of the Great Migration in American cities. Cities with a high concentration of black population came under the scrutiny of the Kennedy administration as the President's Committee on Juvenile Delinquency and Youth Crime in 1961 targeted urban black youth for increased surveillance. Anxieties about managing crime in black urban neighborhoods, however, limited the range of possibilities of New Frontier and Great Society alike. Elizabeth Hinton asserts that federal policymakers and officials did acknowledge unemployment and subpar urban school systems as some among many factors contributing to both poverty and crime. Nevertheless, incidents of collective violence during the second half of the 1960s moved liberal sympathizers away from structural critiques of poverty and support for community action programs.[8] One of the outcomes of the Watts Rebellion in August 1965 was the developing consensus among policymakers, federal administrators, law-enforcement officials, and journalists who perceived crime as a specific problem associated with black urban youth. These actors concluded that the best way to suppress disorder and lawlessness on the nation's streets was through intensified enforcement of the law in black urban neighborhoods, where contempt for authority was extensive. After 250 separate incidents of urban civil disorder—euphemistically referred to in the literature as riots—that occurred in 1968, nearly half of them in the aftermath of Dr. Martin Luther King Jr.'s assassination in April, President Johnson signed the Safe Streets Act in June.[9]

During the 1970s, the discourse on "law and order" and crime captured the national imagination. The Bronx became a national symbol of urban decay, and out of the ashes of despair sprung the hip-hop music genre. All over America, the movement of factory jobs to the Third World exacerbated the conditions set in motion by Nixon's aggressive domestic and foreign policy agenda. Increasingly, as employment, tax bases, and economic opportunity shrank, both federal and state governments began to shift their interest from education and infrastructure to the eradication of crime, expanding police budgets and triggering the passage of punitive laws such as the notorious 1973 Rockefeller Drug Laws in order to calm the national fears about crime. The demonization of blackness was critical to this discourse on crime. White fears accelerated in the shadows of Black Power, defeat in Vietnam, the post-Watergate discontent, the economic stagflation of the decade, the Iranian hostage crisis of 1979, and the widespread perception that America was in decline.[10] African Americans in urban spaces emerged as an "enemy of the state," and later the Latino/a and Muslim populations joined them. The historical condemnation of blackness provides a rationale for aggressive and sometimes violent policing.

Policing Black and Brown Communities

Police forces across the United States have been given the task of surveillance, monitoring, and protecting middle and upper classes from a growing population of poor black/brown communities excluded from experiencing the benefits of the American dream, globalization, and neoliberalism. One of the results of this new situation has been the growth of mass incarceration of African American and Latino (black/brown) populations in the United States. At the same time, there has been a surge of police killings of unarmed black suspects. To date, few police officers are actually convicted in these cases. The recent acquittal of a Minnesota police officer in the killing of Philando Castile also reflects other cases where officers have faced similar charges but not convictions. Other examples may be found in Cleveland, Pennsylvania, and Tulsa, Oklahoma, where police officers have been found not guilty of manslaughter. Elsewhere, including Cincinnati and South Carolina, jurors have deadlocked on charges after a fatal shooting and failed to deliver a verdict at all.[11]

Starting in the 1980s the U.S. prison population increased more than 500 percent. Although its population is less than 5 percent of the world's population, the United States holds roughly 2.3 million people, including 1.6 million in state and federal prisons and over 700,000 in local jails and immigration detention centers. America passed the point of negative return on incarceration rates long ago. Per head, the incarceration rate in the United States has risen sevenfold since the 1970s; it now locks up seven times as many people as France, eleven times as many as the Netherlands, and fifteen times as many as Japan.[12] At any one time, one American adult in thirty-five is in prison, on parole, or on probation. Approximately one-third of African American men and one in six Hispanic men can expect to be locked up at some point in their lives, and one in nine black children has a parent behind bars.[13] No country imprisons as many people as the United States does, or for so long. The American criminal justice system is particularly punishing toward blacks and Latinos, who are imprisoned at six times and twice the rates of whites respectively. According to a recent *Economist* report, the system is riddled with drugs, abuse, and violence.

Ta-Nehisi Coates notes that from the mid-1970s to the mid-1980s, incarceration rates in the United States doubled, from 150 per 100,000 to about 300 per 100,000. From the mid-1980s to the mid-1990s, it doubled again. By 2007, it had reached a historic high of 767 people per 100,000 before reaching a modest decline to 707 people per 100,000 in 2012. In absolute terms, American's prison and jail population from 1970 until today has risen sevenfold, from 300,000 people to 2.2 million. Currently, the U.S. incarceration rate—which accounts for people in prison and jails—is roughly twelve times the rate in Sweden, eight times the rate in Italy, seven times the rate in Canada, five times the rate in Australia, and four times the rate in Poland. America's nearest competitor is Russia—with the autocratic Vladimir Putin locking up about 450 people per 100,000. At the same time, China has about four times the American population, yet American jails and prisons house about half a million more people. According to an authoritative 2014 report by the National Research Council, the current American incarceration rate is unprecedented by historical and comparative standards.[14]

Over the last couple of years alone, policing of black and brown communities resulted in significant civil rights violations that gained national and international attention. On April 25, 2015, a twenty-five-year-old African American male was stopped on the streets of Baltimore, forcibly taken into custody, and thrown, screaming in pain, into a police van. Later, he arrived at the University of Maryland R. Adams Crowley Shock Trauma Center in a coma from which he was never revived. He died one week later from a fatal spine injury after also experiencing complete cardiopulmonary arrest. His spine was 80 percent severed at the neck. As Jeffrey C. Isaac has observed, Freddie Gray never made it to prison. His incarceration began and terminated in the back of the police van. The Freddie Gray death at the hands of Baltimore police officers came only months after the controversial August 14 fatal shooting of Michael Brown, an unarmed African American teenager in Ferguson, Missouri; the September 14, 2014, fatal shooting of Tamir Rice, a twelve-year-old African American child, in Cleveland, Ohio; the April 5, 2015, fatal shooting of Walter Scott, an unarmed African American man with a broken taillight, in North Charleston, South Carolina; and the list goes on. The number of African American males as well as females who have been killed by police has increased with regularity, and the language of justice and injustice has become part of the discourse around human rights and democratic legitimacy.[15] The high American incarceration rates and the increase in police killings of unarmed African American suspects have raised questions about "American Exceptionalism."

Similarly, there are the policies associated with the practice of extraordinary rendition by which the United States sends terrorist suspects for interrogation in countries with a history of torture; unfortunately many of those receiving countries are in Africa—both north of the Sahara and in the Horn of Africa. President Obama only began to correct these injustices during his second administration. African countries with both Muslims and Christian citizens are still reportedly performing American dirty work. Good relations between Africa's Christians and Muslims are endangered by the policy of extraordinary rendition. It is also related to the growth and development of the "carceral state," blurring the lines between domestic and foreign affairs.[16]

The militarization of policing may be connected to the increase usage of deadly force in urban areas. In recent years the police mobilization of armored vehicles, automatic weapons, and military-grade Kevlar vests have been linked to the 1967 creation of the SWAT unit in Los Angeles with the Watts Revolt and the so-called War on Drugs of the 1980s, as well as the current "War on Terror" supported by the post-9/11 Department of Homeland Security. The militarization of the police may undermine democracy, freedom, and liberty of ordinary citizens as they contest public officials over access to public space. The introduction and usage by the police of paramilitary tactics and doctrines may also blur the lines between domestic and foreign policy. The show of force by the police in minority communities after the police killing of a person of color may have a lethal impact on police/community relations.[17]

After decades of persistent prison growth, the prison population has reached a plateau during the past five years. There are several factors contributing to the reduction in the prison population, ranging from the financial crisis of 2009 to the widening budget pressures many states are facing, particularly the larger ones such as California, New York, and Texas, which have led to efforts to cut the growth in their prison populations. At the same time, reform in the sentencing regime by Eric Holder, former President Barack Obama's attorney general from 2009 to 2015, may explain the modest decline in federal prison numbers. The rising and untenable fiscal costs of incarceration, combined with a growing belief that the system is racially biased and extremely punitive for drug and nonviolent offenders have drawn increasing opposition to sentencing laws from across the ideological spectrum.[18]

In spite of partisan acrimony and gridlock that permeates Washington and statehouses, politicians and interest groups on both the left and the right—including the American Civil Liberties Union, Americans for Tax Reform, the Tea Party–based

FreedomWorks, and the ultraconservative Koch Industries—are working jointly to reduce prison populations and revamp sentencing laws.[19] According to the Gallup Poll, the proportion of Americans who worry "a great deal about crime and violence" has fallen dramatically since 2001, although it has ticked up slightly from its previous low. In November 2014, California voters passed a ballot initiative designed to keep some nonviolent criminals out of prison.[20] In 2015, there were approximately 598,200 fewer people under the supervision of the adult correctional system as compared to 2007. Side by side with the decline in incarcerations, the rates along racial lines are also diminishing. Basically, there were 68,700 fewer African Americans in prison in 2015 in comparison to 2009.[21] The percentage of black people went from 36.6 percent of the total incarcerated population in 2009 to 33 percent in 2015. The incarceration rate for African Americans in 2000 hovered around 2,183 per 100,000 U.S. residents. By 2015, the rate had declined to 1,745 per 100,000.[22] Similarly, the *Washington Post* reports that since 2000 there has been a 47 percent drop in the incarceration rates of African American women and a 22 percent drop in the rate of African American males.[23]

However, the expanded prison system has built itself into the fabric or structure of American society. Even with a political appetite and a public mood conducive to reform, a comprehensive reduction will be difficult at best. Stakeholders and major actors include judges, district attorneys, state and county politicians, police forces, prison-guard unions, federal agencies, and private firms that build and run prisons. All have contributed to the rise of mass incarceration, and in fact, many benefit from it. As Rebecca U. Thorpe has suggested, in rural parts of America prisons are now the biggest employers in many towns and nonmetropolitan sectors of America.[24] Yet, both political parties increasingly regard mass imprisonment as problematic and were embracing policies that emphasize nonpunitive alternatives before the 2016 U.S. presidential election cycle resulted in Donald Trump's ascension to the presidency. Similarly, the U.S. Supreme Court increasingly evaluated massive imprisonment as both cruel and inhumane.[25] Although the internment rates may be declining, the use of deadly force by the police and the increase of police killings has intensified, entrenching the power of the carceral state through massive surveillance of black and brown communities.

Convict Lease System and Lynching as Prelude to Mass Incarceration

Conflicts between African Americans and the police have a long history. Slave patrols, which officially began during the 1700s, were the forerunners of the modern men and women in blue. Slave patrols started in South Carolina and spread to other slaveholding states and colonies. Slave patrol emerged as the enforcement arm of the slave codes. Slave codes were the laws that regulated the life of the slave, including where and when they could gather, what activities they were prohibited from engaging in, and the type of punishment they could receive for violating these codes. Patrollers, who generally were white slaveholders, observed and controlled all aspects of slave life. Laws characteristically permitted any white person between the age of sixteen and sixty to serve as a slave patroller. Basically, slave patrols were employed to search slave cabins, keep slaves off roadways, and ensure there were no gatherings of slaves. Patrollers could also exact punishment. Essentially, slave patrollers were the first distinctively American form of policing and the first publicly funded police agencies.[26]

Drawing on a massive historical archive, from the slave insurrections in the sixteenth century through the Black War/Civil War, down to the modern civil rights/Black Power movements, Cedric Robinson, in his trail-blazing publication *Black Movements in America*, contends that black Americans have developed a political culture of resistance. Basically, hundreds of thousands of slaves and free blacks participated as Union soldiers and civilians and a few served as Confederate soldiers, while many more were pressed into support services for the rebels. Later, efforts of loyalist blacks won the limited emancipation provided by Lincoln, then made applicable to all by Congress with the Thirteenth Amendment adopted on January 1, 1865. In further acknowledgment of their service during the Civil War, African Americans were granted citizenship. With the assassination of Lincoln in 1865, blacks had avoided exile as advocated by those championing exile and other forms of colonization. But, as Reconstruction sputtered and finally was undermined, the majority of blacks descended into a new bondage, the American apartheid orchestrated by federal and state officials. Seven years after the conclusion of the war, the pendulum swung away from liberty.[27] Robinson observes that the original Northern objectives of the Civil War—to appropriate the human capital and the natural resources of the South—had been reestablished. For more than 150 years, the struggles for freedom and equality were fought against the social compulsions of a fiercely racist culture as revealed in the Draft Riots in New York, where agents of greed provoked fear in the white laboring classes. The parade of black sacrifice in the Black War that was the Civil War and the wars that were to follow provided no lasting relief for blacks, nor any enduring justification for their freedom, or national resolve for racial justice. Rejection, however, did not kill the desire.[28]

Following the departure of federal troops from the South in 1877 and the dearth of authority to enforce the rights provided in the new amendments, Southern states would begin to take action to reclaim the mantle of their former powers, passing laws to erode the substance of the hard-won liberties enumerated in the new amendments. Over the course of the next 150 years, the undoing of civil rights and restoration of the economies of enslavement would continue unabated, as evidenced in the United States today, which has seen more black inmates imprisoned under the policies of mass incarceration than were enslaved in over four hundred years of American slavery. Wesley Kendall has noted that the distorted constitutional foundation of the modern mass-incarceration policies can be revealed in the isolated expression that is employed in both post-slavery amendments: "except."[29]

The Thirteenth Amendment, which sought to forbid all systems of slavery in America, states: "Neither slavery nor involuntary servitude, *except* as punishment for crime whereof the party shall have been duly convicted, shall exist within the United States, or any place subject to their jurisdiction." Kendall contends that the punishment clause of this amendment, also referred to as the "prison labor exception clause," laid the initial groundwork for a new Southern strategy—a tactic employed to reproduce a system of labor exploitation of slaves, which some scholars today consider worse than slavery. The courts in the United States held that although slavery was impermissible under any circumstances, "involuntary servitude" for a crime was allowable under law. Hence, the exception would be utilized throughout the South, enabling the imprisonment of thousands of former slaves.[30]

Kendall identifies the second foundation of the Southern strategy, hidden in plain sight within the Fourteenth Amendment, which was enacted to grant former slaves the right to vote. This amendment held that voting rights could not be abrogated or abridged, "*except* (as for punishment) for participants in rebellions or other crimes." This amendment would be later employed by Southern white-controlled state legislatures to weaken the emergent black voting bloc. During the Reconstruction era, Southern whites considered the black electorate that voted predominantly for the Republican Party and their Southern white supporters (scalawags) as a competitive threat to white establishment authority, and acted to remove blacks from the voting rolls en masse in order to dilute their collective power at the ballot box. These actors introduced a variety of schemes, from the poll tax and literacy examination to the grandfather clause to disenfranchise African Americans and dilute their voting power.[31]

Robinson notes that conservative Southern whites were in no way passive spectators of the interventions by the Union Army, the Freedmen Bureau, abolitionist volunteers, and recently freed former slaves. Paradoxically, the organization of Southern white mob violence, through the instruments of the Ku Klux Klan, the Knights of the White Camellia, the White Brotherhood, the White League, and similar secret societies, bolstered radical reconstruction for a short while, rescuing it from an increasingly lax Congress. Reacting to a surge in violence between 1868 and 1871, the Congress was forced to give artificial respiration to the administration of martial law imposed on the former Confederacy in 1867. By unloosing murder, rape, beating, arson, and mayhem upon the members of the Union League, the Klan sought to intimidate black and white Republicans from participating at the polls, destroy Republican political influence, terrorize Republican officeholders, sabotage the juridical and physical protections of blacks secured by the Freedmen Bureau and the Union Army, and hinder the development of black economic independence. In two years, the Klan slaughtered 20,000 men, women, and children. The incalculable rapes of black women, the murder of black women and children, the violent expulsion of elected officials, the killings and intimidation of voters, and even robbery made a mockery of the official creed of race purity and allegiance to the Constitution.[32]

At this juncture, the Black Codes, passed initially in Mississippi in 1865 and followed by state legislators throughout the South, criminalized the behavior of blacks in an effort to force them back on the plantation. Black Codes became a mechanism to subvert the contracts that blacks and plantation owners were required to negotiate in the post–Civil War era. Kendall notes that crimes such as "loitering" and "vagrancy" targeted an essentially migrant, jobless population of unemployed former slaves seeking work. Citing the Thirteenth Amendment exceptions permitting involuntary servitude for crimes committed by freedmen, states fiercely incarcerated former slaves, corralling them into state institutions. At this time, unemployment itself became a crime, with an 1865 statute in Mississippi ordering all African American workers to enter into labor contracts with white farmers by January 1st of every year or face arrest and incarceration. Kendall notes that one of the immediate results in the enforcement of the Black Codes criminal statutes was the explosion in black prisoners, which quickly exceeded the Southern white prison population for the first time in history. The overflow of prisons eventually led to the return of the black prison population as a new class of coerced workers in Southern plantations, many returning to work for their former owners. Du Bois conceptualized slavery and the slave trade as the pivotal foundation of the modern capitalist world system and redefined the "mere slaves" as "coerced workers" and the anchors of this economic system. According to Du Bois, black workers had freed themselves through the "general strike," that is, withholding their labor in the fields and through a vision of abolition democracy.[33] These "coerced workers" created a multiracial class alliance with poor whites that transformed the "terms of order" establishing the new Reconstruction governments throughout the South, where the first were last and the last were first. Reconstruction governments also gave the ballot to poor whites, who had been denied rights because of their lack of access to property. These new regimes also abolished the whipping post, the stocks, and other forms of barbaric punishment. In his most influential work, *Black Reconstruction*, Du Bois elaborated on the continuing development of racial capitalism with the rise of the second wave of colonialism in Africa and Asia. He argued that the colored people on a global scale perform the work and supply the mineral resources for Europe, making possible the wealth of the white world while being discriminated against on the basis of color.[34] Du Bois contended that the wealth of the United States and indeed of the Atlantic world was created by slave labor on plantations that were the most modern machines of this period and the forerunners of the twentieth century's factories.[35]

Further, Kendall opines that the enforcement of the Black Codes led to a new system of labor exploitation known as "convict leasing" in which state prisons would rent inmates to local businesses.[36] Hence, convict leasing became the antecedent to contemporary privatization of prisons. Southern states moved quickly to implement a convict lease system that enabled plantation owners and white businesses to purchase the services of black prisoners not only for agricultural and railroad work, but also for coal mining and steel forging. Kendall notes that the police, judges, and local officials conspired to keep arrest and conviction rates high and sentences excessively long and in sync with demand and the business cycle. Most of these leased prisoners were black. Mortality rates for convict prisoners in the South were unsurprisingly high; the mortality rate for prisoners leased to railroad companies in Arkansas was 25 percent, and an astonishing 45 percent in South Carolina. The overall mortality rate for Southern inmates was eight times higher than that of their

Northern counterparts. Eventually, efforts of the American Federation of Labor and other organized labor unions were successful in securing legislation to abolish this form of prison labor through the Hawes-Cooper Convict Labor Act of 1929 and the Ashurst-Sumners Act of 1935, which, combined with the federal New Deal, imposed statutory restrictions on the use of prison labor, signing the death warrant for convict leasing until its resurrection though contemporary private prisons.[37]

Lynching and Black Criminality

Perhaps the most infamous instrument of black oppression to predate contemporary mass incarceration was lynching. Between 1882 and 1968 there were 4,743 incidents of death by lynching in America, with the period between 1882 and 1902 reporting the most intense activity, according to the Department of Records and Research at Tuskegee Institute. The largest totals were in the states of Mississippi (581), Georgia (531), and Texas (493).[38] At this critical juncture, the federal government did not keep tally of these horrific incidents of mob violence confronting African Americans, and it wasn't until recently that the U.S. Senate apologized for its failure to enact any federal legislation outlawing this form of injustice and mob violence.[39] In addition, lynching, as defined narrowly (an illegal death at the hands of a group acting under the pretext of serving justice), did not include the wide-ranging forms of terrorism—rape, beating, torture, mutilation, arson, threats, and general mayhem—that all-embracing sphere of trepidation around black men, women, and children.[40] Fear of lynching propelled black outmigration from the South, resulting eventually in a major demographic shift in the U.S. black population.

Ida B. Wells emerged as one of the critical opponents of lynching and defenders of blacks against charges of criminality. She published three pamphlets—*Southern Horrors: Lynch Laws in All Its Phases* (1892), *A Red Record: Tabulated Statistics and Alleged Causes of Lynching in the United States, 1892–1893–1894* (1894), and *Mob Rule in New Orleans* (1900). Wells recites the sadism of lynching and disproves the conventional justification for lynching: black rape of white women. More often, she makes the case for "white Delilah seducing Black Samson." She attributed to lynching the imprimatur of barbarism driven by commerce and the determination to disenfranchise the black male.[41] Wells drew attention to the ongoing sexual violence committed against black women during and after slavery, and the unacknowledged duplicity of the lynching hysteria. She unmasked the double bind of racial and sexual exploitation revealed in the figurative and literal dehumanization and obliteration of black bodies.[42] For the most part, Ida B. Wells's campaign against lynching was largely ignored in both the North and the South; therefore she took her cause abroad to England to awaken American cousins to the barbarity of lynching. Wells's trip to England inspired the formation of anti-lynching societies, plans among newspapers as well as reformers to send investigators to America, and campaigns of letter writing to Southern and Northern newspapers, churches, and federal and state public officials. Robinson also notes that she had a larger ambition beyond ending the barbarism of lynching: the launching of a civilizing mission that would bring the rule of law and economic rights for blacks and women alike.[43]

The Great Migration and Demonizing Black Criminality

Starting in the 1960s, a broad political consensus mobilized the War on Crime, and much later, the War on Drugs. Government surveillance began targeting low-income neighborhoods in urban areas where African Americans were residing in increasingly larger numbers, bringing with them an upsurge in crime and a breakdown in law and order. Both liberal and conservative legislators and policymakers were very concerned that collective urban violence would become a permanent feature in American society, and they could not envision prevention and crime control outside of creating a more central role for law enforcement in urban communities. In his groundbreaking book *The Condemnation of Blackness*, historian Khalil Gibran Muhammad addresses the growing relationship between race and crime among policymakers, social scientists, and police departments from the Civil War era to the present.[44] He contends that when a white person commits a crime it is regarded as an individual or personal failure, but when a black person commits a crime it is viewed as an indication of broader failings of African Americans in general. Thus his work draws attention to the presence of implicit bias in policing black communities. John F. Pfaff states that these biases need not be conscious, as is made clear by the extensive literature on implicit bias, which draws attention to the numerous way people—white and black alike—exhibit unconscious bias toward minorities.[45] Muhammad demonstrates how these biases lead to the conclusion that these communities require boundaries or limits in order to reestablish order.

Elizabeth Hinton notes that in the decades following Emancipation, scholars, policymakers, and social welfare reformers had analyzed the contrasting rates of black incarceration as empirical evidence of the criminal nature of the African

American people. These beliefs were reinforced by the publication of the 1890 census and the prison statistics, and it laid the foundation for popular and scholarly discourse about African Americans as a dangerous population. Coming just twenty-five years after the Civil War and evaluating the first generation removed from slavery, the census data indicated that African Americans represented 12 percent of the U.S. population but 30 percent of its prisoners. Nevertheless, historian Khalil Gibran Muhammad's intervention through the introduction of his critical concept—a statistical discourse—explains how black crime is employed in the popular and political imagination, and how this data deeply influences ongoing debates about racial differences that reinforce social Darwinism. Muhammad observes that statistical discourse justified the expansion of the American prison system and harsh sentencing practices, informed decisions surrounding capital punishment (particularly in the Deep South), and endorsed racial profiling.[46] Although the problems revolving around crime among poor whites and immigrants concerned elected officials and academics, they were often explained by socioeconomic factors rather than biological characteristics, and by the Second World War, Irish, Italian, Polish, Jewish, and other European ethnic groups had, for the most part, shed their association with criminality. The perception that crime and violence were a genetics problem among citizens of African American descent has a long history in American academic circles. Considered as objective truth and statistically indisputable facts, ideas of black criminality justified both structural and everyday racism. These ideas also authorized the lynching of black people in the Southern states and the bombing of African American homes in the North (read Tulsa, Oklahoma) and institutions in the urban North before the Second World War—actions that were defended as preserving public safety.[47] In the aftermath of the First World War era, social scientists rejected the biological racism but created a new statistical discourse revolving around black criminality that had a greater impact on national policies. W.E.B. Du Bois addressed many of these issues and contradictions in his celebrated empirical study titled *The Philadelphia Negro*.

The Philadelphia Negro: Black Criminality and the Color Line Global/Local Nexus

In nineteenth-century industrial America, the greatest scientific discoveries and technological innovations that unleashed the full potential of fossil fuels and set the United States on course to be the world's leading manufacturer and first modern superpower or emerging hegemonic power also created devastating economic suffering, disease, and death among coal miners, canal diggers, railroad workers, and men, women, and children who populated factories across the country. Khalil Gibran Muhammad observes how inequality in the shape of unprecedented wealth and rampant poverty called into question the basic principles of a liberal society that all individuals possessed the sacred right to pursue their dreams based on their own aptitudes and drive.[48] During this same period, the implementation of the Jim Crow racial regime proceeded swiftly, and the lynching of blacks escalated. The American eugenics movement was consolidating its power by the second decade of the twentieth century as it developed the structural and conceptual infrastructure for its mission. The movement drew its inspiration from the English scientist Francis Galton, who is credited with developing in 1901 the science of eugenics, which could identify the fittest human beings. In his view and that of his followers, a superior race of human beings could be produced through proper breeding and sterilization. Hence, upper-class Western whites were discovered to be the superior stock of humans who deserved to be propagated through breeding across generations, because they met the strenuous standards of social Darwinism, whereas Africans and people of African descent did not, given their alleged innate biological and cultural inferiority. Social Darwinism and eugenics reinforced racial capitalism through the new waves of colonialism in Africa and Asia and the new Jim Crow regime in the United States.[49]

W.E.B. Du Bois published his infamous *The Philadelphia Negro: A Social Study* in 1899, and it was the first major scientific study of African American urban life in America. Du Bois employed empirical analyses of the Seventh Ward in Philadelphia, the home of the largest black urban community at this point in time. He performed a house-to-house canvass of the Seventh Ward, conducting extensive interviews with all families in the ward, including surveys, archival data, and ethnographic data from participant observation. As Aldon D. Morris notes, Du Bois emerged from this study as the first number-crunching, surveying, interviewing, participant-observing, and field-working sociologist in America. He provided a class analysis of this community and a comparative perspective, examining it in relation to European immigrants. He also traced the migration of blacks to Philadelphia from slavery to the late nineteenth century, examining the complex ways in which they developed an urban community in a large Northern city. Du Bois concluded that one could not understand black urban development without knowledge of these actors' participation in slavery in America. He contended that a comparative analysis was required if social scientists were to understand how and why blacks were designated as inferior. He compared the growth of the Philadelphia African American community with the city's European immigrants, demonstrating an equivalent stage of development. He paid attention to the sociology of work, providing an occupational analysis drawing attention to stratification and social mobility in the black community, and he refused to conceptualize this community as a mere imperfect fabrication or imitation of their white counterpart. Du Bois paid attention to the class dynamics within the black community, from the racial aristocracy to the underdeveloped bottom tenth. At the same time, Du Bois examined the plight of black women and the unique challenges they faced in the labor market. Du Bois examined gender relations in this community along with demographic and population changes, including health issues, paying attention to mortality and morbidity rates. He analyzed population turnover and the issue of ethnic succession that pervades contemporary studies of urban politics.

Du Bois also examined the impact of white supremacy on the black population, the pushing out of blacks from the service sectors as immigrants from Europe arrived in the City of Brotherly Love, undermining the job prospects for blacks. He argued that the color line was a social divide structuring inequality between the haves and have-nots, and that it was an oppressive system operating on a global scale limiting the social mobility of people of color in the colonial world as well as the United States.[50] Du Bois also examined black crime, which had climbed sharply, stating that it was related to social conditions rather than to biological and social degeneracy as white social scientists claimed. He attributed the rise in crime to forces related to white supremacy or the color line at home and abroad. He interrogated both his qualitative and quantitative analysis, making sure that he had ironed out all contradictions and mere correlations. His work unmasked the demonization of the black criminal that became so pronounced and also an integral part of the fabric of American life. He examined how urban space was utilized and the role of elites and power brokers in determining the use of this space, anticipating contemporary urban scholarship on the role of the business community and entrepreneurs in determining the use of urban space.[51] Nevertheless, Du Bois's magnum opus on the development of black urban communities was basically ignored by mainstream social scientists, including sociologists. Du Bois basically launched the subfield on black criminology through this work, placing this issue in a larger sociological context of the color line domestically and globally as it relates to African Americans and other Third World populations inside and outside the United States. Du Bois also made connections between the urban and rural population, showing how the political economy of rural areas influences urban black community formation, drawing attention to the spatial dimension of urban development.

The Death Penalty/Presumption of Guilt

Bryan Stevenson has drawn attention to the presumption of guilt that black males face in their encounters with the police and the criminal justice system. He draws special attention to the 1930s and the 1940s, when most of the capital punishment cases were predominantly African Americans facing court-ordered execution, which outpaced lynching in the South around the same time period. Basically, two-thirds of those executed were African Americans, and the trend continued: as the African American population declined to 22 percent of the Southern population between 1910 and 1950, African Americans constituted 75 percent of those executed in the South in those years. Starting in the 1940s and the 1950s, the NAACP's Legal Defense Fund (LDF) launched a major initiative challenging the American death penalty, which was most active in the South, as racially biased and a violation of the U.S. Constitution.[52] Eventually they won in *Furman v. Georgia* in 1972, when the U.S. Supreme Court struck down Georgia's death penalty statute, holding that "it still closely resembled self-help vigilante justice and lynch law," and "if any basis can be discerned for the selection of these few to be sentenced to death, it is constitutionally impermissible on the basis of race."[53] Southerners decried the decision and rewrote their death penalty statutes in light of the U.S. Supreme Court decision.

In 1976, in *Gregg v. Georgia*, the Supreme Court upheld the demand for Georgia's new death penalty statute and reinstated America's death penalty, surrendering to the demand that legal execution was needed to avoid vigilante mob violence. In the 1987 case of *McCleskey v. Kemp*, the U.S. Supreme Court considered statistical evidence proving that Georgia decision-makers were more than four times as likely to enforce the death sentence for killing a white person than for killing a black person. Accepting the data as accurate, the Court accepted racial bias in sentencing as "an inevitable part of our criminal justice system" and upheld Warren McCleskey's death sentence because he had failed to identify a "constitutionally significant risk of racial bias in his case." Still, African Americans make up less than 13 percent of the national population, but nearly 42 percent of those currently on death row in America are black, and 34 percent of those executed since 1976 were black. In most of the states where researchers have completed studies examining the relationship between race and the death penalty, the results reveal a pattern of discrimination based on race of the victim and race of the defendant, or both.[54]

Recall that W.E.B. Du Bois contends that American foreign policy and approach to world politics is a mirror image of its domestic policy, challenging the idea of "American Exceptionalism" as a benevolent force for good in the international system. Du Bois contends that a nation whose white citizens could not treat their black neighbors with equity, justice, and equality could not develop a foreign policy involving relationships reflecting equality and justice with two-thirds of the people of the world who are people of color.[55] The problem of the color line that Du Bois spent most of his academic, professional, and activist life in efforts to resolve and explain has remained at the center of American and global life since the seventeenth century. The emergence of black criminality can also be traced back to the color line. Given the thoroughness of racial disparities in the United States, African Americans and Latinos are not afforded the same level of public safety as Euro-Americans. This is not only a violation of their civil rights/human rights; it is also a violation of the Fourteenth Amendment to the U.S. Constitution—guaranteeing equal protection under the law. Increasingly, the police forces around the United States as the street-level bureaucrats that represent the "state" are breaking the social contract between the American government and black/brown communities throughout the nation. It is important for the police to restore public trust in policing regimes.

Mainstream Narratives on Mass Incarceration

The mainstream narrative on the rise in mass incarceration and prison population in the United States has its origins with the "War on Drugs" under the Nixon administration. According to this interpretation, the first state laws to introduce mandatory sentencing for drug crimes were enacted in New York in 1973, under Governor Nelson Rockefeller. Next, during the presidency of Ronald Reagan in the 1980s, both the federal government and many states initiated much tougher penalties for dealing crack cocaine than for dealing powder cocaine, a shift that enforced racial bias in sentencing. Between 1980 and 1990, the proportion of offenders in prison whose primary offense was drug-related climbed from under 8 percent to almost 25 percent. In addition, Loïc Wacquant traces the growth of the prison-industrial complex to the flight of low-skilled manufacturing jobs that made black labor expendable in the 1960s and the 1970s, reinforcing similar analyses by Samuel Yvette, Sidney Willhelm, and William J. Wilson Jr.[56] These patterns of global/local economic restructuring coincided with declining commitments to the social safety net and revived efforts to deregulate markets and undo social policies. Since the 1970s, policymakers have enacted new laws that criminalize behavior likely to flourish in urban communities plagued by economic isolation and joblessness, including harsh criminal penalties for the sale and possession of narcotics, as well as anti-panhandling and anti-loitering ordinances. Meanwhile the crack-cocaine epidemic produced more punitive policies across the board: (1) three-strike laws requiring 25-year-to-life sentences for a third offense including a drug violation or petty theft; (2) 10-, 20-, and 30-year minimum sentences for violent, gun-related, and drug offenses; and (3) laws enacted by several states permitting the prosecution of juveniles as adults. All of these activities have been directly and indirectly aimed at the urban communities where African Americans and Latinos make up the significant demographic factor. These new laws also occurred at the same time that civil rights and Black Power movements were challenging America as the "Jim Crow Nation."

Starting with the Kennedy administration in the 1960s and continuing to the present Trump administration, police departments across the United States have increased their decision-making and discretionary powers to detain suspects even when they may lack evidence that a crime has taken place. Both parties in the U.S. Congress have supported this growth in discretionary power. After the passage of the 1964 Civil Rights Act, the Voting Rights Act of 1965, and the Immigration Act of 1965, the Republican Party adopted a "law and order" agenda and intensified its efforts to rein in what it often referred to as the urban crisis plaguing American cities, targeting black and brown communities for special attention by law-enforcement agencies. President Bill Clinton was able to wrest away the Republican Party hegemony on this issue during his bid for the U.S. presidency in 1992. Afterward both parties coalesced in their efforts to reduce crime and increase the discretionary powers of police. In 1994, then president Bill Clinton signed a crime bill. The measure paid to put more cops on the beat, trained police and lawyers to investigate domestic violence, imposed longer prison sentences, and provided money for extra prisons. This action by President Clinton and the U.S. Congress reflected the punitive mindset of the American people; nevertheless, what they did not know was that the soaring murder and violent crime rates had already begun a downward turn.[57]

In recent years, the U.S. Supreme Court through key judicial decisions has also increased the discretionary powers of the police. In *Terry v. Ohio* (1968), the Court ruled that police can stop and frisk an individual without probable cause. In the *City of Los Angeles v. Lyons* (1983), the Court's decision immunized police departments from reviews of widespread policies like chokeholds by arguing that the plaintiff didn't have standing because he couldn't show that he would be subject to a repeat violation. In addition, that decision overturned a lower court decision that ordered the Los Angeles Police Department (LAPD) to cease using chokeholds unless the officer was threatened with death or serious injury. Thus, the Supreme Court provided a measure of protection to police officers involved in deadly encounters. In *Whren v. United States* (1996), the Court ruled that officers might use minor violations as a ruse to seek evidence for more serious criminal misconduct. Police discretionary powers were further enhanced in *Heien v. North Carolina* (2014). In this case the Court ruled that a police officer's reasonable mistake of the law can provide the individualized suspicion required by the Fourth Amendment justifying a traffic stop. This case added another layer of ambiguity to the boundaries of policing.[58]

Starting in the 1990s crime rates began to decline. By 2000 they were diminishing precipitously. A recent comprehensive study by the Brennan Center for Justice at New York University Law School, published in February 2015, found that at most 12 percent of the fall in property crime in the 1990s could be attributed to more people in prison—and that there might be no effect at all. In addition, two big states, California and New York, have done well enough to suggest new models for other states to use in order to reduce prison growth and reduce incarceration rates. In California, the imprisoned population has declined by 51,000, over 30 percent since 2006. The State of New York's prison population has been declining since 1999, and it is 25 percent smaller than what it was. In both states, the reforms that have been implemented have not included changes to the laws but rather adjustments to the way in which the entire system from arrest to release is organized. These states offer alternatives to high incarceration rates that are pervasive throughout the United States in the twenty-first century.

The case for change is real, and the outrage of black and brown citizens at police killings of unarmed suspects across the United States has prompted a new look at the criminal justice system that treats these actors differently from their white counterparts, violating their human rights and raising questions about how and why police departments routinely employ lethal force when they encounter African Americans and Latinos. A new social movement has emerged—Black Lives Matter—addressing the lack of accountability on the part of police departments across the United States. America's policing regime has attracted the attention of people around the world, and the recent killing of an Australian woman, Justine

Damond, by a Minneapolis Police Department officer in July 15, 2017, has drawn attention to the seriousness of police use of lethal weapons in policing and surveillance of the public. Let us examine parallels and differences between the Rodney King and Ferguson incidents and their impact on policing communities of color in the twenty-first century.

From Rodney King to Ferguson and Beyond

Prior to 2014, the American news media paid scant attention to police violence as a policy issue, but we have witnessed a sea change in coverage by both the media and the U.S. government at the local, state, and national levels. African Americans are calling for greater accountability of police departments, particularly with the increased media attention to police killings of unarmed African American men and women. These events have spawned Black Lives Matter as a new social movement drawing attention to the violation of African Americans' and Latinos' human rights and the social contract between citizens and the state. The narrative of Rodney King, a young African American brutally beaten by Los Angeles police in 1991 in an incident captured on a bystander's video camera, provides a relevant parallel to the recent event revolving around Ferguson and Michael Brown. Rodney King was the victim of clear and life-threatening, unnecessary force, but he survived his attack during a year when hundreds of Americans died by police force. The video camera captured the beating and the excessive use of force against Rodney King. This event captured the imagination of Americans as they viewed the video, followed by the acquittal of three Los Angeles police officers of state criminal charges.[59] Nevertheless, the Rodney King case endured for approximately two decades as a dangerous and historically significant episode rather than as a representative example of a persistent general problem. The perception of police's use of lethal force that increased in the wake of the Michael Brown shooting in Ferguson, conversely, quickly grew to include an entire list of fatalities and locations. As Franklin Zimring notes, Michael Brown was soon sharing the killings headlines with Freddie Gray of Baltimore, Tamir Rice in Cleveland, Walter Scott of North Charleston, South Carolina, and the earlier death of Eric Garner of Staten Island. These infamous incidents included shootings, chokeholds, brutal restraints, and the delay in transport of the arrestee. It is no longer about Darren Wilson and Michael Brown. At this critical juncture, there are so many police departments that have become implicated in this national problem revolving around policing and the decisions to employ deadly or lethal force that it is no longer about the local police in Ferguson, Cleveland, New York City, or North Charleston, South Carolina.[60]

Black Lives Matter and other such movements have transformed this issue into a civil rights/human rights issue for the twenty-first century in a manner that surpasses the Rodney King event more than fifteen years ago. Policing and police killings of black and brown citizens is no longer a local issue just confronting local communities in Ferguson, Missouri, or Staten Island, New York. Police killings have emerged as a national issue as Americans assess how policing in ordinary situations such as checking for traffic violations or car registration results in police homicides, and how citizens with mental illness have encounters with police forces that often result in fatalities regardless of race or gender. This approach to policing is associated with the "broken windows" regime popularized by the New York City Police Department under police chief William Bratton. Political scientist James Q. Wilson and criminologist George L. Kelling coauthored an article for *The Atlantic* that launched this new policing regime, and it offered a critique of American policing that emphasized solving big crimes while allowing minor crimes like panhandling, graffiti, and small-scale drug deals to fester.[61] They employed the analogy of a broken window that if left unrepaired would eventually lead to increases in crime, chaos, and disorder. They found that the sight of one broken window in both poor and wealthy neighborhoods led to more broken windows, because an unrepaired window conveys the message that people in the community do not care. Hence, if property is unattended, disrespect and disorder follows.[62]

According to Bratton, the NYPD that he inherited operated similarly to most American law-enforcement agencies, that is, in a reactive manner. It functioned primarily to apprehend criminals, not to prevent crime from occurring in the first place. Implicitly at this time, police departments operated on the assumption that crime was caused by societal problems that were resistant to police intrusions. On the contrary, Bratton believed that a constructive police presence could deter crime, and on his watch along with his successor's there was a measurable decline in crime lasting well into the new century. There were roughly 1,500 homicides in New York in 1982, while the number of murders was 304 in 2015. Nevertheless, crime went down in other major cities that did not employ the "broken windows" approach to policing. Bill de Blasio through his recent hiring of William J. Bratton as his police chief has continued the "broken window" policing regime.[63] The jury is still out or undecided on the relationship between the "broken windows" approach to policing and the decline in crime rates. What the evidence does suggest is that the two—high crime rates and disorder—are related to high levels of unemployment, lack of social resources, and concentrated areas of low income, all root causes of both high crime and disorder. Hence, investing economically in these communities rather than targeting for intensified arrests would effectively reduce crime. Community engagement remains a missing element in most police departments' approach to the "broken window" regime. Regardless of the evidence, the NYPD and other police departments have departed from including community engagement in their policing equation, focusing almost exclusively on aggressive policing of minor crimes. This divorce of community engagement from policing intensifies fear of crimes, corrodes community-police relations, and delegitimizes police in the eyes of black and brown communities, stoking fear of criminals and the police.[64]

Nevertheless, the police use of deadly force is on the rise at the same time we are witnessing a gradual decline in incarceration rates. Between 2012 and 2015, black incarceration rates went down 5 percent while police killings increased by 2.2 percent. Between 2005 and 2014, black people accounted for 24 percent of the arrest-related deaths and 17 percent of the arrested population. Hence, there is more of a racial disparity when it comes to arrest-related deaths than those arrested.[65] The data available for arrest-related deaths comes from sources such as the Bureau of Justice Statistics, the Federal Bureau of Investigation (FBI) Report on Justifiable Homicides by Law Enforcement, and nongovernmental organizations such as Fatal Encounters and KilledbyPolice.net, as well as news sources such as *The Guardian* and the *Washington Post*. Both newspaper outlets report an increase in the use of lethal force, resulting in the increased number of African American males killed in 2016. The reported number of blacks killed by the police is at best an estimate. The Department of Justice refuses to make data collection mandatory. The numbers that are reported are just a mere fraction of the total number of blacks dying from these fatal encounters with the police. Jurors are very reluctant to convict police in these cases and would rather not second-guess police with reference to these deadly encounters. The Justice Department reports that African American men are more likely to be killed by black rather than white cops. Another study in 1998 found that the "black officer kills black suspect" rate was 32 per 100,000 black officers, and the "white officer kills black suspect" rate was 14 per 100,000 white officers. Hence, an officer of the same race committed approximately 65 percent of the justifiable homicides.[66]

The U.S. Department of Justice investigation of the Philadelphia Police Department uncovered serious issues regarding police of color and threat-perception failures—cases in which officers mistakenly believe an unarmed suspect actually has a weapon. The threat-perception failure for white officers and black suspects was 6.8. For black officers and black suspects, the threat-perception failure rate was 11.4 percent. For Latino police officers and black suspects, the threat-perception failure was 16.7 percent. Latino officers were more likely to mistakenly think a black suspect was armed, followed by African American officers. White officers were least likely to shoot an unarmed black person.[67] This report confirms many African Americans' belief that police departments have declared war on their communities, and contributes to the distrust of cops in general.

Fundamentally, police brutality is rampant across America and so predictable that increasingly small and medium-sized cities are purchasing insurance to pay people who have experienced some form of police abuse. On the other hand, large cities self-insure, that is, they set aside a certain amount of money for this purpose. On this issue, Paul Butler raises a moral hazard—police departments might be less inclined to encourage officers to act responsibly because the cost of brutality is included in their budget.[68]

In recent years, the war on terrorism has profoundly impacted the militarized tactics of the police. There has been a dramatic shift from a defensive and controlling posture to prevention, proaction, reaction, deterrence to intelligence, and events to eventualities. Daniel Kato notes that it is not enough to lock people up after they have committed a crime. They now need to stop perpetrators before they have the chance to act. These new norms are being ushered in by the new spatial transformation in urban spaces. There is a mixture of push and pull factors that at once attract affluent people into urban areas and push poor people, particularly people of color, out of urban areas: the deindustrialization and gentrification of the central city, for all the tragic human dislocations, has eliminated many of the things that made affluent people want to move away from it during the twentieth century.[69] Short of control or restraint of the traditional ghetto, "the specter of blackness and increasingly brownness is heightened." Kato observes that as black people were gradually intruding on areas that had previously been havens for white flight, they were seen as more than just criminals that committed unlawful crimes, but threats that symbolize existential dangers. The changing geographies of race in this new era reinforces the previous discourse on black criminality. New policing seeks to monitor and control the increasingly fluid boundaries separating gated communities from infringement by black and brown communities.[70] The spatial connection between urban and suburban communities draws attention to the spatial issues and policing.

At this juncture, more research is required to deal with the increased deployment of police to address societal problems associated with globalization, gentrification, and even mental illness, contributing to post-traumatic stress or syndrome experienced by many police officers engaged in increased surveillance and policing of black and brown communities. Police are the new street-level bureaucrats representing the state and at times undermining the social contract between African Americans and the American society. Police departments should require psychological tests, including stress tests, to make sure officers are capable of adequate self-control. Police departments need to develop a continuum regarding preliminary steps to de-escalate their encounters with black and brown communities before making the commitment to employ lethal force in situations that do not require the use of deadly force. American society needs to address the historical relations with the African American communities and work toward social justice and transformation.

NOTES

1. Paul Butler, *Chokehold: Policing Black Men* (New York: The New Press, 2017), 2.
2. Lisa C. Schneider, *Police Power and Race Riots: Urban Unrest in Paris and New York* (Philadelphia: University of Pennsylvania Press, 2014), 4.
3. Eric Wolf, *Envisioning Power: Ideologies of Dominance and Crisis* (Berkeley: University of California Press, 1999), 273.
4. Schneider, *Police Power and Race Riots*, 5.
5. Ibid.
6. Elizabeth Hinton, *From the War on Poverty to the War on Crime: The Making of Mass Incarceration in America* (Cambridge, MA: Harvard University Press, 2016), 11.
7. Wesley Kendall, *From Gulag to Guantanamo: Political, Social and Economic Evolutions of Mass Incarceration* (London: Rowman & Littlefield, 2016), 21.
8. Hinton, *From the War on Poverty*, 12.
9. Ibid., 16.
10. Sohail Daulatzai, *Black Star, Crescent Moon: The Muslim International and Black Freedom beyond America* (Minneapolis: University of Minnesota Press, 2012), 91.
11. "Minnesota Officer Acquittal in Killing Philando Castile," *New York Times*, June 16, 2017.

12. *The Economist*, May 27–June 7, 2017, 13.

13. *The Economist*, June 20–26, 2015, 11.

14. Ta-Nehisi Coates, "The Black Family in the Age of Mass Incarceration," *The Atlantic* (October 2015): 60–84.

15. Jeffrey C. Isaac, "The American Politics of Policing and Incarceration," *Perspectives on Politics* 13, no. 3 (September 2015): 609.

16. Daulatzai, *Black Star, Crescent Moon.*

17. Ibid., 181–84.

18. Rebecca U. Thorpe, "Perverse Politics: The Persistence of Mass Imprisonment in the Twenty-first Century," *Perspectives on Politics* 13, no. 3 (September 2015): 618.

19. Ibid.

20. *The Economist*, June 20–26, 2015, 23.

21. Daniel Kato, "Carceral State 2.0? From Enclosure to Control and Punishment to Surveillance," *New Political Science* 39, no. 2 (June 2017): 201.

22. Bureau of Justice Statistics 2015.

23. Kato, "Carceral State 2.0?," 201.

24. Thorpe, "Perverse Politics," 619.

25. Kato, "Carceral State 2.0?," 201.

26. Katheryn Russell-Brown, "Making Implicit Bias Explicit: Black Men and the Police," in *Policing the Black Man*, ed. Angela J. Davis (New York: Pantheon Books, 2017), 139–40.

27. Cedric J. Robinson, *Black Movements in America* (New York: Routledge, 1997), 81.

28. Ibid., 82.

29. Kendall, *From Gulag to Guantanamo*, 48.

30. Ibid., 49.

31. Ibid.

32. Robinson, *Black Movements in America*, 86–87.

33. Jordan T. Camp, *Incarcerating the Crisis: Freedom Struggles and the Rise of the Neoliberal State* (Oakland: University of California Press, 2016), 24.

34. Darryl C. Thomas, ed., *The Theory and Practice of Third World Solidarity* (Westport, CT: Praeger, 2001), 24.

35. Anthony Bogues, *Empire of Liberty: Power, Desire and Freedom* (Hanover, NH: Dartmouth College Press, 2010), 55.

36. Kendall, *From Gulag to Guantanamo*, 50.

37. Ibid., 50–51. See David Oshinsky, ed., *Worse Than Slavery: Parchman Farm and the Ordeal of Jim Crow Justice* (New York: The Free Press, 1996).

38. Robinson, *Black Movements in America*, 105.

39. *Washington Post*, June 14, 2005.

40. Robinson, *Black Movements in America*, 105.

41. Ibid., 107.

42. Khalil Gibran Muhammad, *The Condemnation of Blackness: Race, Crime, and the Making of Modern Urban America* (Cambridge, MA: Harvard University Press, 2010), 61.

43. Robinson, *Black Movements in America*, 108.

44. Muhammad, *The Condemnation of Blackness*.

45. John F. Pfaff, *Locked In: The True Causes of Mass Incarceration and How to Achieve Real Reform* (New York: Basic Books, 2017), 146.

46. Muhammad, *The Condemnation of Blackness*.

47. Hinton, *From the War on Poverty*, 19.

48. Muhammad, *The Condemnation of Blackness*, 24.

49. Aldon D. Morris, *The Scholar Denied: W.E.B. Du Bois and the Birth of Modern Sociology* (Berkeley: University of California Press, 2015), 18.

50. Ibid., 49.

51. See W.E.B. Du Bois, *The Philadelphia Negro: A Social Study* (New York: Schocken Books, 1967); Aldon D. Morris, *The Scholar Denied*, 45–54; and David Levering Lewis, *W.E.B. Du Bois: A Biography* (New York: Henry Holt and Co., 2009), 128–51.

52. Bryan Stevenson, "A Presumption of Guilt: The Legacy of America's History of Racial Injustice," in *Policing the Black Man*, ed. Angela J. Davis (New York: Pantheon Books, 2017), 3–30, 19.

53. Ibid.

54. Ibid.

55. Mark Ledwidge, *Race and Foreign Policy: The African American Foreign Affairs Network* (London: Routledge, 2012), 6.

56. Loïc Wacquant, *Punishing the Poor: The Neoliberal Government of Insecurity* (Durham, NC: Duke University Press, 2009); Samuel Yvette, *The Choice: The Issue of Black Survival in America* (Laurel, MS: Cottage Books, 1982); Sidney Willhelm, *Who Needs the Negro?* (Hampton, VA: U.B. & U.S. Communications System, 1993); William J. Wilson, *When Work Disappears* (New York: Vintage Books, 1997).

57. "20 Years Later, Parts of Major Crime Bill Viewed as Terrible Mistake," *NPR—Morning Edition*, September 12, 2014, 1–10.

58. Kato, "Carceral State 2.0?"; Butler, *Chokehold: Policing Black Men*, 4–5, 82–83.

59. Franklin E. Zimring, *When Police Kill* (Cambridge, MA: Harvard University Press, 2017), 12.

60. Ibid., 14.

61. George Kelling and James Q. Wilson, "Broken Windows," *The Atlantic*, March 1982.

62. Marc Lamont Hill, *Nobody: Casualties of America's War on the Vulnerable, from Ferguson to Flint and Beyond* (New York: Atria Books, 2016), 39.

63. Ibid., 44.

64. Ibid., 45.

65. Kato, "Carceral State 2.0?," 203.

66. Butler, *Chokehold: Policing Black Men*, 34.

67. Ibid.

68. Ibid., 55.

69. Kato, "Carceral State 2.0?," 213.

70. Schneider, *Police Power and Race Riots.*

Youth of Color and Michigan's Juvenile Justice System

Michelle Weemhoff and Jason Smith

eorge Stinney Jr. was only fourteen years old in 1944 when he was arrested, convicted, and executed for a crime he did not commit.[1] According to police reports, Stinney, an African American boy, was said to have confessed to murdering two young white girls in their small South Carolina town. The confession, which was later determined to be coerced, was countered with the fact that Stinney had been with his sister during the time of the murders. His trial lasted only three hours, and his attorney, who had never represented a criminal defendant, called no witnesses nor cross-examined the contradicting testimony of the police officers. The all-white jury took only ten minutes to convict Stinney, then placed him in jail where he was not permitted to see his family. Only six weeks after his conviction, Stinney was put to death by electrocution, sitting atop a phonebook as his childish 5'1", ninety-five-pound frame was too small for the shackles of the electric chair.[2]

Unfortunately, the tragic miscarriage of justice that befell George Stinney remains palpable for thousands of youth of color nationwide in today's juvenile justice system, who are more likely to be arrested, detained, adjudicated, or tried as adults compared to their white peers.[3] In Michigan, youth who identify as black, Latino, Asian, and American Indian account for nearly 30 percent of the state's youth population, yet they represent up to 70 percent of the youth in the justice system.[4] Girls of color represent the fastest growing segment of youth entering the court system and those subsequently detained, primarily for status and nonviolent offenses.[5] At the deepest stage of the justice system—imprisonment—the racial disparity gap is most apparent; black youth are five times more likely to be incarcerated than white youth, and Latino youth are twice as likely to be incarcerated than whites.[6]

The complex problem of racial and ethnic disparity in the juvenile justice system is interwoven with our nation's historic and systemic racism, as well as misguided policies and practices that exacerbate the unequal treatment of youth of color in trouble with the law. Using both state and national research data, this chapter will provide an overview of the experiences of many youth of color in Michigan's juvenile justice system, and will highlight effective models for reducing racial disparities and improving outcomes for all justice-involved youth.[7]

The Creation of the Juvenile Justice System

Michigan's juvenile justice system was established in 1907, only a few years after the first juvenile court was created in Chicago in 1899.[8] While the juvenile court was originally developed to be a "helping system," its informal nature often led to youth being arrested without a warrant, interrogated without parental notification, not being advised of their legal rights, and being indeterminately incarcerated. Under the doctrine of *parens patriae*, the state was granted parental authority over justice-involved youth through age sixteen, allowing judges to exercise broad discretion, individual philosophies, and sometimes their own racial or cultural biases when issuing court orders.[9] This frequently led to youth with very similar offenses receiving dramatically different treatment or sanctions based on which judge heard their case.[10]

Youth of color were overrepresented in the caseloads of the early juvenile courts, remained in detention longer, and were prohibited from rehabilitative services that were accessible only to white youth.[11] Between 1904 and 1910, a period that saw thousands of black families migrate to northern U.S. cities to escape the Jim Crow South, the rate of incarceration doubled for black boys and nearly tripled for black girls.[12] In Midwestern states, including Michigan, black boys and girls were ten times more likely to be incarcerated than their white peers.[13] The majority of black youth incarcerated during this period were placed in adult prisons, despite the fact that many had committed nonviolent offenses, and were subjected to punishment ordinarily given to adult offenders, such as convict leasing, chain gangs, and penal farms.[14]

Period of System Reform

While the informal structure of the juvenile justice system continued for the first fifty years of its existence, the system's procedures for handling the cases of court-involved youth were eventually challenged and reformed. In the 1960s and 1970s, a series of U.S. Supreme Court decisions affirmed youths' rights to due process and other legal protections.[15] In 1974, the federal government instituted the Juvenile Justice and Delinquency Prevention Act (JJDPA) requiring the separation of children from adults in jails and prisons, as well as prohibiting the detention and confinement of youth who commit status offenses—behaviors not considered illegal if engaged in by an adult—such as running away, skipping school, or drinking alcohol.[16] The JJDPA also added a core requirement in 1992, reauthorized in 2018, that mandates all states to assess and address disproportionate minority contact (DMC) at nine decision points in the juvenile justice system—from arrest to detention to confinement.[17] Unfortunately, the language within the JJDPA that required states to address DMC is vague and failed to articulate clear guidelines, leading to little enforcement of any standards and slow progress in driving down disparities.[18]

Tough on Crime Era

In 1989, race became a focal point in the highly publicized case of New York's "Central Park Jogger," in which a woman was violently sexually assaulted and nearly died in the park. The teenage defendants, four black and one Latino, were prosecuted and incarcerated as adults under New York's harsh sentencing laws, each serving between 6 and 13 years in prison.[19] All five boys were later cleared of the charges when the real attacker came forward; however, the rhetoric surrounding their trial gave rise to the myth of the "super-predator," characterizing youth of color, in particular, as "remorseless, lacking conscience and empathy, and capable of committing the most heinous acts of violence."[20] Despite declining crime rates, these inaccurate perceptions sparked a national shift to "get tough" on youth crime.[21]

By the turn of the century, nearly every state in the nation enacted laws that made it easier for youth to be arrested at school, prosecuted and convicted as adults, and sentenced to adult jails and prisons. Michigan's policies are among the harshest, giving prosecutors discretion to bypass the juvenile courts entirely and prosecute children as young as fourteen years old as adults for certain offenses, some of which require adult sentencing.[22] The state also created "designated proceedings" in which a child *of any age* can be tried and convicted as an adult but receive a blended sentence, combining a juvenile disposition and an adult sentence. These policies have particularly impacted youth of color and exacerbated existing racial disparity at every level of the justice system.

The sweeping policies of the 1990s contradict the significant body of research on adolescent development that has emerged over the last twenty years, proving that youth are very different than adults. Using new technologies, scientists have shown structural and functional changes in the human brain during one's teenage years, which does not fully complete development until one's mid-twenties.[23] These physiological changes, coupled with typical psychosocial development, contribute to a youth's likelihood to engage in risky and impulsive behaviors, lesser ability to exercise sound judgment or understand long-term consequences, and susceptibility to peer pressure. However, research has also revealed that most young people desist, or "age out" of, delinquency, even when no intervention is offered.[24] This compelling research set the stage for a series of recent U.S. Supreme Court decisions that clearly distinguished youth from adults, including a ban on the juvenile death penalty and mandatory life sentences for youth.[25]

The country is now experiencing a steady, forty-year overall decline in youth arrests, which has resulted in a dramatic 47 percent reduction of the number of young people being incarcerated nationwide. However, racial disparities in youth confinement and arrest rates have actually increased by 15 percent nationally, with Michigan's disparity gap between black and white youth confinement rising by a startling 73 percent over the past decade.[26]

Vulnerable Lives: The Link between Trauma and Justice Involvement

The causes of racial disparity in the justice system cannot be fully articulated without first acknowledging the link between the intersecting issues of exposure to violence, behavioral health needs, and chronic trauma.[27] Over 90 percent of justice-involved youth have experienced a traumatic event in their childhood, two-thirds have a diagnosable mental health condition, and one-quarter experience substance abuse.[28] While maltreatment does not necessarily cause delinquency, it does increase the likelihood of arrest by as much as 60 percent, and heightens other risk factors associated with justice involvement, such as drug and alcohol abuse, mental health conditions such as depression, post-traumatic injuries, educational delays, unplanned pregnancy, and suicide.[29] Often termed "crossover youth," children who are concurrently involved with both the child welfare system (because of abuse or neglect) and juvenile justice system (as a result of a delinquency charge) are more likely to remain in care longer and experience numerous out-of-home placements, and are often truant or perform poorly at school.[30]

In Michigan, approximately 33,000 children are found to be abused or neglected each year, and nearly a third are placed in foster care.[31] Black youth account for half of those who are removed from their homes as a result of maltreatment and are less likely than white youth to be reunited with their families, be adopted, or achieve permanency.[32] Beginning in 2006, the state of Michigan faced a class-action lawsuit, *Dwayne B. v. Snyder*, on behalf of youth in foster care, citing violations such as excessive lengths of stay, frequent moves among multiple placements, and inadequate care while in state custody.[33] In an effort to achieve compliance with the settlement agreement for the lawsuit, the state significantly reduced the length of stay of youth in foster care, expedited reunification and adoptions, and created the Michigan Coalition for Race Equity in Child Welfare and Juvenile Justice to review the impact of child welfare policies and programs on families of color. As a result of the coalition's work, two thousand state employees participated in cultural diversity and awareness training, and the state has begun working in targeted counties to drive down disparities and implement culturally competent trainings and programs.[34]

Additionally, systems integration models, like the Crossover Youth Practice Model and Systems of Care, are proving to be highly effective at coordinating multiple child-serving systems and addressing the intersections of trauma, behavioral health needs, and child welfare involvement while diverting youth from the justice system.[35] Over the past five years, the Saginaw MAX System of Care, for example, has served nearly three hundred youth with emotional and behavioral challenges, the majority of whom are youth of color who presented with conduct or delinquency problems, poor school performance, or disruptive behavior. After participating in Systems of Care, 77 percent of students maintained or improved school attendance and performance and most reduced feelings of depression, anxiety, withdrawal, and acting-out behaviors.[36]

Girls and LGBTQ Youth in the Justice System

Girls are twice as likely as boys to experience complex trauma (five or more adverse childhood experiences), frequently involving physical or sexual violence victimization.[37] However, rather than being viewed as victims, girls who are sexually exploited or trafficked are often criminalized as a result of their abuse and funneled into the justice system.[38] Girls as well as youth who identify as lesbian, gay, bisexual, transgender, or questioning (LGBTQ) most frequently enter the justice system as a result of status offenses, which are often symptomatic of underlying problems at home or school. While girls represent only 28 percent of court cases overall, they account for 53 percent of runaway cases nationally.[39] Even though the JJDPA prohibits the detention of youth charged with a status offense, like running away, girls of color represent the highest rate of confinement for technical violations of probation that stem from status offenses.[40] Once confined, LGBTQ youth, many of whom are girls of color, are seven times more likely to experience sexual victimization than their heterosexual peers.[41]

The Victimization of Young Men of Color

Among the entire U.S. population, black youth and young men ages sixteen to twenty-four are at the greatest risk of violent victimization, including homicide, which is the leading cause of death for this group.[42] Unfortunately, there are few services for victims of crimes like robbery and assault (the most common offenses experienced by youth of color) that provide culturally relevant support within the context of concentrated poverty, familial incarceration, chronic illness, and the lack of access to basic needs and services.[43] Without appropriate treatment, black and Latino boys are three to four times more likely to experience post-traumatic stress than their white peers, which can have significant long-term implications for their health, educational attainment, employment, and safety.[44]

While most of the violence experienced by youth of color is inflicted by their peers,[45] they are sometimes victimized by the individuals tasked with protecting them from harm—the police. In 2014, Michael Brown, an unarmed black eighteen-year-old young man from Ferguson, Missouri, was shot and killed by a white police officer. The circumstances surrounding Brown's death brought national attention to long-standing issues of mistrust between communities of color and local law-enforcement agencies, and highlighted the disproportionate use of lethal force against youth of color during interactions with police officers. In 2015, black males between the ages of fifteen and thirty-four were killed at a rate five times higher than white men of the same age.[46] These often avoidable, violent encounters have only exacerbated racial tensions and raised questions about discriminatory policing practices.

Disparities at Arrest

Given the vulnerabilities and trauma disproportionately endured by youth of color, it is not surprising to learn that they have an increased risk of coming into contact with local law enforcement. Nationally, over half of all black males in the United States have at least one arrest by the age of twenty-three, compared to 38 percent of white males in the same age range.[47] In Michigan, black youth disproportionately account for 40 percent of all juvenile arrests.[48] While the circumstances leading to a youth's arrest vary on a case-by-case basis, there is a strong argument that police practices targeting communities of color, combined with racial bias, play a major role in disparate arrest rates.[49]

Following the death of Michael Brown, the U.S. Department of Justice launched an investigation, which ultimately discovered that "Ferguson law enforcement practices are directly shaped and perpetuated by explicit and implicit (unconscious) racial bias." The report detailed how Ferguson officers more frequently stopped black residents, and although black residents make up 67 percent of Ferguson's population, they represented around 90 percent of vehicle stops, citations, and arrests.[50] While this particular precinct may be an extreme example, studies examining unconscious racial stereotypes by law-enforcement officers have found that when "primed" with cues that invoke race, black youth were judged as older or more adult-like, more culpable for their crimes, and deserving of harsh punishment.[51]

While the targeting of persons of color by police increases racially disproportionate contact, there is also evidence indicating that it reduces crime only minimally. Research on "stop and frisk," a law-enforcement tactic meant to deter illegal behavior through the use of random searches (or "pat-downs") of individuals suspected of committing a crime, has shown that young black and Latino men are targeted for the majority of police encounters. However, an extremely low percentage of the individuals stopped and searched were found to be participating in illegal activity (e.g., possession of weapons, illegal substances).[52] As a result, the use of "stop and frisk" seems to harm more than it helps, by increasing the number of negative interactions between youth of color and the police. Research further indicates that individuals who are stopped and frisked are less likely to call the police when they or others are harmed.[53]

Statewide, law-enforcement agencies have increasingly recognized the need to address racial bias and improve relationships with communities of color. In 2015, the City of Grand Rapids, Michigan, developed a twelve-point plan that included training officers in cultural competency, requiring all police officers to wear body cameras, changing hiring models to increase the number of minority and women officers, and conducting an independent study of why residents of color are arrested more than white residents.[54] Likewise, in February 2016, Michigan State University's (MSU) police department created a new Inclusion and Anti-Bias Unit, with the goal of improving relationships with the university's diverse student body. Facilitated by faculty of MSU's Psychology Department, campus police officers, neighboring police departments, and staff from the Michigan Attorney General's Office will be regularly trained on how explicit and implicit bias may affect their work, and learn strategies for reducing the impact of bias in their interactions with community members.[55]

Law-enforcement agencies are also creating new opportunities to partner more directly with the communities they serve in order to build trust and improve public safety. In Detroit, Michigan, the police department's Neighborhood Police Officer Program seeks to improve communication by encouraging one-on-one contact between community members and the officers assigned to the program.[56] At the state level, programs like Advocates and Leaders for Police and Community Trust (ALPACT), sponsored by the Michigan Department of Civil Rights, bring local law-enforcement officials, community leaders, and faith-based organizations together to encourage community dialogue around public safety, police-community relations, racial profiling, and incidents where police used lethal force.[57]

Racial Disparities in School-Based Arrests

Racial disparities among youth arrests extend beyond law-enforcement encounters in the community. Today, youth are more likely to be arrested at school than they were a generation ago.[58] The increase in school-based arrests is due in part to the passage of the federal Gun-Free Schools Act in 1995, mandating expulsion of students who possess a "dangerous weapon." Incentivized by federal funding tied to the Gun-Free Schools Act, Michigan and many other states enacted and expanded "zero tolerance" laws that increased the penalties for students who are caught with a weapon on school grounds.[59] While the goal of such laws is to improve school safety by reducing violent behavior, they are often subjectively applied to noncriminal behaviors, such as disruptive conduct, disturbance of the peace, or insubordination. Although these behaviors were historically resolved by school staff, students with behavior issues are now frequently referred to school-based police officers, known as "school resource officers," substantially increasing the risk of arrest.[60]

The shift toward criminalizing student misbehavior, often referred to as the "school-to-prison pipeline," has disproportionately affected students of color, particularly black and Latino youth, who experience much higher rates of suspension, expulsion, and school-based arrests than white students.[61] While the teachers, administrators, and school resource officers tasked with student discipline are, more often than not, acting with good intentions, various research studies have shown that the nationwide racial disparities in school-based arrests cannot be solely attributed to higher rates of misbehavior by students of color, and that the implicit racial bias of school authority figures is a likely contributing factor.[62]

Increasing concerns over the "school-to-prison pipeline" have prompted some schools to train administrators, teachers, and even students to resolve conflicts using restorative justice models, like peace circles and victim/offender conferencing, aimed at engaging all parties in repairing the harm caused by problem behavior.[63] For example, in 2014, Ann Arbor, Michigan's Skyline High School created "Skysquad," a group of students trained in restorative circles to resolve student conflicts. Since Skysquad's launch, the team has completed over one hundred restorative circles, resolving issues that might have otherwise resulted in school fights, suspension, expulsion, or arrest.[64] According to the federal Department of Education, the use of restorative practices has resulted in a 20 percent decline in suspensions nationally; however, racial disparities still persist.[65]

School resource officers and local police departments nationwide are beginning to adopt new strategies to divert youth from formal court involvement. For example, a number of Michigan police departments are utilizing youth-focused Crisis Intervention Teams (CIT-Y) to train officers, both in schools and in the community, to identify the symptoms of mental health needs and de-escalate situations before an arrest is necessary. Students can then be diverted away from the formal justice system by linking them to mental health services and treatment.[66] Michigan policymakers have also reached out to the School District of Philadelphia in Pennsylvania to learn about their diversion model, in which school-based police officers divert youth with low-level misdemeanor offenses (e.g., disorderly conduct, graffiti, bullying) to agencies that offer family-based social services. During the 2014–2015 school year, the School District of Philadelphia, whose current student body is 51 percent black, saw a steep 54 percent decline in school-based arrests.[67]

Unfair and Inequitable Access to Justice

Racial disparity in the justice system is amplified once a petition is filed by the prosecutor and a case goes to court.[68] Among the 34,000 delinquency cases in Michigan's juvenile courts each year, youth of color are less likely than white youth to be diverted or placed on community probation and more likely to be placed in detention while awaiting a hearing, adjudicated (found responsible for the offense), and transferred to the adult system than their white peers.[69]

As with law enforcement, the perceptions and decisions made by prosecutors, judges, probation officers, and even defense attorneys may be influenced by structural racism and implicit bias.[70] Research studies have shown that court officials responsible for determining the use of detention before adjudication were more likely to perceive a white youth's behavior as a product of negative environmental influences (e.g., family conflict, negative peers, issues at school), while the behaviors of black youth with similar offenses and histories were perceived as negative personality traits (e.g., uncooperative, lack of remorse) that increase the likelihood that they will reoffend.[71] Another study found that prosecutors implicitly treated what should be viewed as normal adolescent behavior as criminal activity "warranting law enforcement intervention" more often for youth of color.[72]

A Broken System of Public Defense

Although young people are entitled to an attorney if they cannot afford one, Michigan's public-defense delivery system has been characterized as one of the worst in the nation, ranking 44th in state public-defense spending.[73] Inadequate funding forces attorneys to take on unmanageable caseloads, with no maximum limits or regulations, in order to make it financially worthwhile. As a result, youth often have little or no time to meet with an attorney prior to their hearing. In addition, a lack of statewide requirements for ongoing legal education means that many attorneys have limited or no training or experience in handling delinquency cases, yet are allowed to represent youth nonetheless. The lack of resources also limits access to investigators, experts, or specialists in adolescent development, special education, mental health, or other peripheral issues. As a result of these systemic failures, youth are more likely to waive their right to counsel, make poor decisions regarding their cases, and sink deeper into the system.[74]

Disparities in Sentencing and Plea Agreements

For serious crimes, youth receive longer sentences than adults for comparable offenses, and the rate at which youth are offered plea bargains differs significantly by race. Youth accused of a homicide offense involving a white victim were 22 percent less likely to receive a plea agreement than instances in which the victim was a person of color.[75] There also appears to be inconsistencies in the severity of sentences across county lines. The Michigan counties of Oakland, Calhoun, Saginaw, and Kent, for example, were less likely to offer pleas compared to the state average.[76] Even when presented with a plea offer, young people are often less likely to accept pleas, which could, in part, be related to their immaturity, less-developed reasoning abilities, or lack of understanding about the legal proceedings.

Juvenile Life without Parole Sentencing

Disparities in sentencing are most striking when youth are facing the ultimate punishment—life in prison without the possibility of parole (JLWOP). Michigan accounts for the second largest number of JLWOP cases nationally, with black youth in Michigan receiving JLWOP sentences at ten times the rate of white youth. Among the nearly 350 individuals currently serving JLWOP sentences in Michigan, the majority (69 percent) are people of color.[77] Most of these youth were represented by public defenders, of whom a shocking 38 percent have been publicly sanctioned or disciplined by the State Bar of Michigan for egregious violations or ethical misconduct, compared to 5 percent of attorneys overall.[78]

In 2012, the U.S. Supreme Court ruled in *Miller v. Alabama* that mandatory sentences of juvenile life without parole are unconstitutional for youth under age eighteen. A subsequent ruling in *Montgomery v. Louisiana* affirmed that the *Miller* ruling applies retroactively, making all Michigan JLWOP cases eligible for resentencing or parole based on new guidelines that require consideration of the youth's maturity, family circumstances, and role in the offenses. As of April 2018, cases are still in the process of being resentenced.

Dangers of Detention and Incarceration

At the height of the "tough on crime" movement in the mid-1990s, Michigan incarcerated over 3,700 youth in juvenile facilities every year, primarily for nonviolent offenses such as property offenses, truancy, incorrigibility, and technical violations of probation.[79] While placement rates have declined significantly—estimated to be 1,683 youth placed in 2014—the rate of disparity has dramatically increased by 73 percent over the past decade.[80] Today, 65–75 percent of youth in detention and out-of-home placement are youth of color.

It is widely recognized that the experience of confinement can be traumatic, dangerous, and ineffective.[81] Youth can be sent to placements that are hundreds of miles away from family and friends, both in Michigan and sometimes out of state. The only state-operated facility for girls is located in Escanaba, Michigan, a seven-hour drive from Detroit, where most of the families reside. Once in placement, the youth, most of whom already have histories of trauma or mental health conditions, may be further traumatized by exposure to threats, violence, restraints, and seclusion.[82] Procedures such as using handcuffs, shackles, and personal searches deprive a young person of autonomy and privacy and can trigger feelings of victimization.

In 2004, an investigation by the U.S. Department of Justice found that Michigan's largest secure facility, the W.J. Maxey Boys Training School, had routinely violated children's constitutional rights by depriving them of medical, mental health, and educational programs.[83] Michigan facilities received further scrutiny after a 2009 report by the Bureau of Justice Statistics revealed that 27 percent of youth respondents in the state-operated Shawono Center reported sexual victimization by staff or other youth—ranking it within the top five worst in the nation. Sexual victimization was also reported by 23 percent of youth respondents from W.J. Maxey Boys Training School, which has since been closed.[84] The state has now closed eight of its ten public facilities and now contracts with forty-eight private nonprofit facilities to house the majority of committed youth.

Because juvenile justice is primarily managed at the county level in Michigan, local courts are responsible for the supervision and treatment of adjudicated youth. At its peak, Michigan's largest counties were spending over $150 million for out-of-home placements, only to have two-thirds of those youth return to custody within six months.[85] Many counties have since found that serving youth in the community through the use of diversion, counseling, court-ordered community service, wraparound case management, specialty courts, and evidence-based programs, such as Multi-Systemic Therapy, is far more cost-effective and produces better outcomes.[86]

Most notably, Wayne County, Michigan (home to Detroit), became an early pioneer of fiscal realignment, redirecting funds for out-of-home placement toward developing one of the nation's most renowned community-based juvenile justice models. The Wayne County model includes the establishment of a Juvenile Assessment Center, which conducts comprehensive risk and needs assessments on every youth, and contracts with five local Care Management Organizations (CMOs), where all adjudicated youth are assigned to receive comprehensive case management services. Wayne County's model prioritizes diversion for the lowest-risk youth, diverting more than five thousand kids since its inception, and, through numerous partnerships, links youth with myriad local services. As a result, the number of out-of-home placements have decreased by over 50 percent, costs have plummeted by nearly $70 million, and recidivism has dropped from 56 percent in 1998 to 13 percent in 2015.[87] Smaller counties have also realigned their resources toward evidence-based programs offered in their local community and have achieved similarly impressive results.[88]

While this progress is encouraging, the state as a whole continues to struggle with collecting data and is unable to consistently track the aggregate number of youth in detention and out-of-home placement, their demographics, offenses, lengths of stay, or recidivism rates. This lack of coordinated data collection makes it impossible for the state to accurately assess racial disparities to determine if out-of-home placements are truly being reserved as a last resort, and to compare interactions at various decision points. Research shows that long lengths of stay have no impact on reducing recidivism, so it is particularly important for jurisdictions to monitor progress and, ideally, limit out-of-home placements to three to six months.[89]

Youth Incarcerated in Adult Correctional Facilities

From 2003 to 2013, over 20,000 youth under age eighteen were convicted as adults in Michigan, with over half of them incarcerated in adult jails or prisons. The majority of these youth were seventeen years old—since Michigan remains one of four states to automatically treat seventeen-year-olds as adults—and were convicted of nonviolent offenses. Black youth were sentenced to prison almost three times more frequently than white youth with similar offenses, and were far less likely than whites to receive community-based sanctions, such as probation, fines, or community service. Among youth who were transferred to the adult justice system, 59 percent were black, despite comprising only 18 percent of the total youth population.[90]

Research consistently shows that is it dangerous to confine youth with adults. Youth in adult jails and prisons are more likely to be physically and sexually victimized by other prisoners as well as by staff, held down with restraints, and placed in solitary confinement "for their own safety," where the resulting isolation can exacerbate mental health conditions and increase the risk of self-harm and suicide.[91]

In 2012, the U.S. Department of Justice issued federal guidelines in accordance with the Prison Rape Elimination Act (PREA) that required youth under eighteen to be housed separately from adults, noting that isolation should be minimized.[92] However, in 2013, a class-action lawsuit was filed against the State of Michigan, alleging physical and sexual violence and degrading treatment against youth incarcerated in Michigan prisons, and failure to comply with the PREA standards.[93] The lawsuit also claims that the Michigan Department of Corrections does not adequately supervise youth or properly train and monitor the staff who oversee their care.

The growing concerns about youth in prisons prompted the Michigan legislature to convene a legislative work group in 2015 to identify policy solutions aimed at reducing youth incarceration. The resultant bill package included proposals to raise the age of juvenile court jurisdiction to eighteen, remove all youth from adult jails and prisons, and restructure funding such that it encourages the use of community-based programs. Many other states, and even other countries, have employed these strategies with impressive results.[94] Connecticut and Illinois, for example, have reduced their out-of-home placement rates and are spending less after raising the age to eighteen, with an estimated cost savings of $3 for every dollar spent to implement the policy change.[95] Policymakers in both of those states have now proposed raising the age to twenty-one, and, in Connecticut, are considering alternative services for young people up to age twenty-five.

Lifelong Consequences

Juvenile adjudications and convictions in adult court can have lifelong consequences. Despite popular belief, juvenile court records are not necessarily private or sealed from public access. Even if the adjudication is set aside and the record is made non-public, some government and law-enforcement agencies can see it, and courts may use it when considering any subsequent sentence in the future.[96]

Based on the offense, young people with a record may also be prohibited from accessing federal financial aid, serving in the military, receiving driver's or professional licenses, finding or maintaining employment, and may have their parental rights terminated or their entire family evicted from public housing.[97] A number of Michigan communities are responding to these barriers by encouraging employers to remove or "ban the box" on employment applications indicating whether someone has a previous conviction. While these efforts are intended to create pathways for people to succeed, some evidence suggests that they actually exacerbate hiring disparities between equally qualified white and black applicants.[98] Without widespread efforts to combat racial inequity across all segments of society, many of the same disadvantages that initially drive young people into the system may fuel generational cycles of crime.

Recommendations

Despite the historical, political, and cultural barriers that drive youth of color into the justice system, numerous efforts are underway to eliminate disparate treatment in Michigan and nationally, as well as improve equity and lifelong outcomes for youth of color. The following recommendations outline some of the steps that states and local jurisdictions can take to better understand racial disparities in their own jurisdictions, and design policies, systems, and practices that are developmentally appropriate, trauma-informed, gender-responsive, and culturally competent.

First, states must improve data collection and analysis to better understand the prevalence and underlying causes of racial disparities as well as monitor trends and improvements. In order to identify disparities, states and local jurisdictions must ensure that they effectively collect, analyze, and report aggregate data related to race and ethnicity. The information obtained should be based on the youth's self-identification and disaggregated to ensure that ethnic groups are not undercounted. Additionally, uniform definitions should be established for each justice system contact point (i.e., arrest, petition, adjudication, etc.) and across child-serving systems, schools, and law enforcement. By using a statewide data-collection system, states can better track the demographic data of all justice-involved youth and use it to design interventions for specific youth populations or decision points. It is important that staff and resources are allocated to monitor the data collection/analysis and track progress made toward reducing disparities. The federal government could support states in these efforts by strengthening the JJDPA's requirements and funding incentives to address disproportionate minority contact.

Next, political and community leaders must ensure that policies are equitable and disparities are addressed. Tackling the issue of racial disparity in the justice system requires leadership and commitment from policymakers, multisystems stakeholders, law enforcement, and the youth and families who are most impacted by the justice system. Several states have convened DMC work groups to ensure that racial and ethnic disparities are being tracked, monitored, and addressed effectively.[99] The DMC Steering Team in Ramsey County (St. Paul), Minnesota, for example, instituted a number of policy changes after identifying practices that overwhelmingly impacted youth of color. In particular, they eliminated a discretionary practice that allowed probation officers to detain youth for up to forty-eight hours without the court's permission; ended automatic detention of low-risk youth who failed to appear in court; and created graduated sanctions in order to reduce detention as a result of technical violations. As of 2012, Ramsey County reduced its total detention population by 68 percent.[100]

In addition to monitoring trends, state leaders should also proactively consider whether new justice policies will have disparate impact on communities of color. A number of states, notably Iowa, Connecticut, Oregon, and Minnesota, have developed racial impact statements to assist policymakers in assessing any potential negative impacts on communities of color for justice-related policies prior to legislation being passed or enacted.[101]

Eliminating discretion is one of the most effective ways to reduce biased decision-making. Objective assessments and structured decision-making tools, in particular, can help lessen the impact of unconscious bias and inform decisions to connect youth with appropriate services.[102] Because many of these tools were initially normed on white male populations, it is important to scrutinize the findings for measurement bias, in which the tool may predict reoffending differently among racial groups simply based on the types of questions asked.[103] As with other data collection methods, these findings, too, should be consistently monitored to identify trends or disparities.

Training is also critical for all personnel who interact with youth (e.g., police, probation officers, lawyers, jurists, facility staff, and cross-system staff in child welfare, schools, and behavioral health agencies) to ensure that staff have the tools to understand cultural influences, attitudes, and beliefs, and are able to interact respectfully and appropriately with youth of color and their families and communities. The training should include techniques for responding to and de-escalating tense situations, as well as explore the personal biases of trainees that may lead to unconscious, disparate decisions when working with certain racial or ethnic groups. Research has shown that the most promising interventions are those that focus on intentional strategies to overcome bias as well as exposure to individuals who defy stereotypes, known as "counter-stereotypical exemplars."[104]

Child-serving systems, schools, and law enforcement should coordinate their efforts to prevent and divert youth from the justice system, given the strong link between trauma exposure, mental health, and justice involvement. This includes implementing culturally relevant and trauma-informed approaches to identify problem behaviors that are manifestations of trauma or mental health symptoms, and addressing the underlying issues causing the delinquent behavior, while preventing retraumatization. This is particularly important for girls and LGBTQ youth, for whom special attention is needed to ensure that they are not being detained for status offenses. Ultimately, the detention of status offenders for technical violations of probation should be prohibited.

The majority of youth can and should be served in community-based programs rather than in out-of-home placements or adult jails and prisons. While many jurisdictions reserve community-based interventions for low-risk youth, there is strong evidence that high-risk youth can also benefit from interventions while remaining at home.[105] Large-scale systems reform efforts that promote the use of community-based alternatives across numerous states—such as the Annie E. Casey Foundation's Juvenile Detention Alternatives Initiative (JDAI) and the MacArthur Foundation's Models for Change DMC Action Network—have increasingly used these types of interventions to reduce racial and ethnic disparities.

Although justice-involved youth of color have multiple pathways and unique experiences within the justice system, the common thread that binds them together is the fact that they are still youth. Decades of research have overwhelmingly affirmed that developmentally appropriate programs and services are far more effective at reducing the risk of reoffense and improving long-term outcomes than incarceration.[106] In recent years, there has been a nationwide effort to reduce the prosecution of youth as adults, housing them in adult prisons, or sentencing them to life without the possibility of parole. Further, increased investments in prevention, diversion, and community-based models have saved states hundreds of millions of dollars, reduced crime, and improved youth well-being. These policy shifts drive the field as a whole in a positive direction, but it is up to us to ensure that such improvements are applied equitably, so that youth of color, and indeed all young people, are protected, valued, and given real opportunities to thrive.

NOTES

1. In 2014, the case of George Stinney was vacated, essentially clearing his name.
2. D. Cassens Weiss, "Murder Conviction of Boy, 14, Is Tossed 70 Years after His Execution; Judge Cites Bad Lawyering," *American Bar Association Journal*, December 18, 2014; M. R. Jones, "Too Young to Die. The Execution of George Stinney, Jr.," in *South Carolina Killers: Crimes of Passion* (N.p.: History Press, 2007), 38–42.
3. J. Rovner, *Disproportionate Minority Contact in the Juvenile Justice System* (Washington, DC: The Sentencing Project, 2014); P. Soung, "Social and Biological Constructions of Youth: Implications for Juvenile Justice and Racial Equity," *Northwestern Journal of Law and Social Policy* 6, no. 2 (2011): 428–44.
4. The term "youth of color" broadly refers to youth populations under age eighteen who identify as a race or ethnicity other than white. According to the U.S. Census Bureau (2013), the total Michigan youth population includes 18 percent who identify as black/African American, 7 percent who identify as Hispanic/Latino, 3 percent Asian/Pacific Islander, and 1 percent American Indian or Alaska Native. The authors recognize that these categories do not encompass every racial and/or ethnic group or subpopulation by which youth self-identify. For example, Michigan's sizable Arab American population is categorized as "White/Caucasian," so is notably unrepresented in the data picture. See also Michigan Committee on Juvenile Justice, *Michigan Disproportionate Minority Contact Data*, 2013, http://michigancommitteeonjuvenilejustice.com.
5. J. Nanda, "Blind Discretion: Girls of Color and Delinquency in the Juvenile Justice System, *UCLA Law Review* (2012); Office of Juvenile Justice and Delinquency Prevention (OJJDP) Policy Guidance, "Girls and the Juvenile Justice System," 2015, https://rights4girls.org/wp-content/uploads/r4g/2016/08/OJJDP-Policy-Guidance-on-Girls.pdf.
6. Burns Institute, "Unbalanced Juvenile Justice" (2016), http://data.burnsinstitute.org.

7. This chapter primarily focuses on black youth, who represent the largest proportion of youth of color in Michigan. It is not intended to discount or ignore the experiences of other racial or ethnic groups or subpopulations within any group. More research is needed to explore the unique pathways and challenges encountered by youth from each racial and ethnic group.

8. Act 6 of the Special Session and Act 323, of 1907; In re Mould, 162 Mich. 1 (1910); W. T. Downs, *Juvenile Law and Practice* (St. Paul, MN: West Pub. Co., 1983), supra note 1 at sect. 1.12.

9. R. Weisheit and D. Alexander, "Juvenile Justice Philosophy and the Demise of *Parens Patriae*," in *Criminal Justice in America: Theory, Practice, and Policy*, ed. Barry W. Hancock and Paul M. Sharp (Upper Saddle River, NJ: Prentice Hall, 1996), 321–32.

10. J. Butts and O. Mitchell, "Brick by Brick: Dismantling the Border between Juvenile and Adult Justice," in *Boundary Changes in Criminal Justice Organizations*, ed. C. Friel (Washington, DC: U.S. Department of Justice, 2000), 167–214.

11. G. K. Ward, "Color Lines of Social Control: Juvenile Justice Administration in a Racialized Social System, 1825–2000," *Dissertation Abstracts International* 62, no. 10 (2001); J. Bell and L. Ridolfi, *Adoration of the Question: Reflections on the Failure to Reduce Racial and Ethnic Disparities in the Juvenile Justice System* (San Francisco: W. Haywood Burns Institute, 2008); J. Bell, *Repairing the Breach: A Brief History of Youth of Color in the Justice System* (Oakland, CA: W. Haywood Burns Institute for Youth Justice Fairness and Equity, 2016).

12. G. K. Ward, "Color Lines of Social Control."

13. Ibid.

14. Ibid.

15. The first landmark case to address youths' constitutional rights was *Kent v. United States*, 383 U.S. 541, 86 S.Ct. 1045 (1966), in which the U.S. Supreme Court ruled that youth must be afforded a due process hearing before being waived to adult court. In the case of *In re Gault*, 387 U.S. 1, 87 S.Ct. 1428 (1967), the Court further ruled that juveniles have the right to reasonable notification of the charges, the right to effective legal counsel, the right to confront and cross-examine witnesses, the right to protection against self-incrimination, and the right to remain silent. In the case of *In re Winship*, 397 U.S. 358, 90 S.Ct. 1068 (1970), the Court ruled that if the youth faces the possibility of incarceration, the proof must be beyond a reasonable doubt. See also Office of Juvenile Justice and Delinquency Prevention, National Report Series, *Bulletin: Juvenile Justice: A Century of Change* (Washington, DC: U.S. Department of Justice, Office of Justice Programs, 1999), https://www.ncjrs.gov.

16. Juvenile Justice and Delinquency Prevention Act of 1974, Pub. L. No. 93–415, 88 Stat. 1109 (codified as amended at 42 U.S.C. § 5601 et seq. (2002)).

17. The JJDPA language in 1992 required that states track disproportionate minority confinement for short- and long-term facilities. It was expanded during the 2018 reauthorization to provide clear direction to states and to plan and implement data-driven approaches to ensure fairness and reduce racial and ethnic disparities, to set measurable objectives for disparity reduction, and to publicly report such efforts. Act 4 Juvenile Justice, *Overview of the Juvenile Justice Reform Act of 2018* (Washington, DC: Act 4 Juvenile Justice, 2018), http://www.act4jj.org/sites/default/files/resource-files/JJDPA%20 Reauthorization%20Summary%20December%202018.pdf.

18. M. Lieber and N. Rodriguez, "The Implementation of the Disproportionate Minority Confinement/Contact (DMC) Mandate: A Failure or Success?," *Race and Justice* 1 (2011): 103–24.

19. N. Byfield, *Savage Portrayals: Race, Media and the Central Park Jogger Story* (Philadelphia: Temple University Press, 2014).

20. J. Howell, "Superpredators and other Myths about Juvenile Delinquency," *Preventing and Reducing Juvenile Delinquency: A Comprehensive Framework* (Thousand Oaks, CA: Sage Publishing, Inc., 2009); J. Pizarro et al., "Juvenile 'Super-Predators' in the News: A Comparison of Adult and Juvenile Homicides," *Journal of Criminal Justice and Popular Culture* 14, no. 1 (2007).

21. Brief amici curiae of Jeffrey Fagan et al. (January 17, 2012), Miller v. Alabama, 567 U.S. (2012).

22. Michigan Compiled Laws § 764.1f; § 712A.4(1); § 712A.2d; § 712A.2(a)(1); § 791.233; § 380.1311.

23. E. Scott and L. Steinberg, *Rethinking Juvenile Justice* (Cambridge, MA: Harvard University Press, 2008).

24. E. Mulvey, *Highlights from Pathways to Desistance: A Longitudinal Study of Serious Adolescent Offenders*, OJJDP Juvenile Justice Fact Sheet, March 2011, https://www.ncjrs.gov.

25. Roper v. Simmons, 125 S. Ct. 1183 (2005); Graham v. Florida, 130 S. 2011 (2010); J.D.B. v. North Carolina, 131 S. Ct. 2394 (2011); Miller v. Alabama, 567 U.S (2012); Montgomery v. Louisiana, 577 U.S. (2016).

26. The Sentencing Project, *Policy Brief: Racial Disparities in Youth Commitments and Arrests* (Washington, DC: The Sentencing Project, 2016).

27. Michigan Advisory Committee on the Overrepresentation of Children of Color in Child Welfare, *Equity: Moving toward Better Outcomes for All of Michigan's Children* (Lansing:

State of Michigan, Department of Human Services, 2006); Michigan Coalition for Race Equity, *Key Findings and Recommendations of the Michigan Race Equity Coalition* (Lansing: Michigan Coalition for Race Equity, 2014); M. Harris and H. Benton, "Implicit Bias in the Child Welfare, Education and Mental Health Systems" (Oakland, CA: National Center for Youth Law, July 2015).

28. Justice Policy Institute, *Healing Invisible Wounds: Why Investing in Trauma-Informed Care for Children Makes Sense* (Washington, DC: Justice Policy Institute, 2010); J. Shufelt and J. Cocozza, *Youth with Mental Health Disorders in the Juvenile Justice System: Results from a Multi-State, Multi-System Prevalence Study* (Delmar, NY: National Center for Mental Health and Juvenile Justice, 2006); Mental Health and Juvenile Justice Collaborative for Change, *Better Solutions for Youth with Mental Health Needs in the Juvenile Justice System* (Delmar, NY: National Center for Mental Health and Juvenile Justice, 2014).

29. National Juvenile Justice Network, *A House Divided No More: Common Cause for Juvenile Justice Advocates, Victim Advocates, and Communities* (Washington, DC: National Juvenile Justice Network, 2014); Justice Policy Institute, *Healing Invisible Wounds*; National Child Traumatic Stress Network, Justice System Consortium, *Helping Traumatized Children: Tips for Judges* (Los Angeles: National Center for Child Traumatic Stress, 2009); R. L. Listenbee and J. Torre, National Task Force on Children Exposed to Violence, *Report of the Attorney General's National Task Force on Children Exposed to Violence* (2012), https://www.justice.gov/defendingchildhood/cev-rpt-full.pdf; Janet Wiig and Cathy Spatz Widom, with John A. Tuell, *Understanding Child Maltreatment and Juvenile Delinquency: From Research to Effective Program, Practice, and Systemic Solutions* (New York: CWLA Press, 2003).

30. Center for Juvenile Justice Reform and Robert F. Kennedy Children's Action Corps, *Addressing the Needs of Multi-System Youth: Strengthening the Connection between Child Welfare and Juvenile Justice* (Washington, DC: Georgetown University, 2013).

31. Alicia Guevara Warren, *Kids Count in Michigan Data Book 2016: Child and Family Well-Being in Michigan, Its Counties and Detroit* (Lansing: Michigan League for Public Policy, 2016).

32. Michigan Advisory Committee on the Overrepresentation of Children of Color in Child Welfare, *Equity: Moving toward Better Outcomes.*

33. Dwayne B. v. Snyder (2006), filed by Children's Rights, a nonprofit organization, against the governor of the state of Michigan and the director of the Department of Human Services (DHS) on behalf of all children who are now or will be in the foster care custody of DHS. The parties settled the case in 2008 and the court approved the first Modified Settlement Agreement and Consent Order (MSA) in 2011. http://www.childrensrights.

org/class_action/michigan.

34. Child Welfare Improvement Report, Michigan Department of Human Services, pursuant to Sec. 582 of Public Act 190 of 2010, http://www.michigan.gov/documents/dhs/Sec-582_364723_7.pdf.

35. The Crossover Youth Practice Model is currently being piloted in Oakland, Berrien, Genesee, and Wayne Counties in Michigan. Systems of Care, funded by the federal Substance Abuse and Mental Health Services Administration, has been implemented in six jurisdictions in Michigan, including the counties of Wayne, Ingham, Saginaw, Kalamazoo, Kent, and a regional site in Chippewa, Mackinac, and Schoolcraft Counties in partnership with the Sault Ste. Marie Tribe of Chippewa Indians and Bay Mills Ojibwa Indian Community. See N. Taylor and C. B. Siegfried, *Helping Children in the Child Welfare System Heal from Trauma: A Systems Integration Approach* (Los Angeles: National Child Traumatic Stress Network Systems Integration Working Group, 2005); Center for Juvenile Justice Reform and Robert F. Kennedy Children's Action Corps, *Addressing the Needs of Multi-System Youth.*

36. Saginaw MAX System of Care, Monthly Evaluation Summary, January 2016.

37. Center for the Study of Social Policy, *Fight for Our Girls* (Washington, DC: Center for the Study of Social Policy, 2016).

38. M. Saada Saar, R. Epstein, L. Rosenthal, Y. Vafa, *The Sexual Abuse to Prison Pipeline: The Girls' Story* (Washington, DC: Human Rights Project for Girls, Georgetown Law Center on Poverty and Inequality, Ms. Foundation for Women, 2015).

39. A. Irvine, "We've Had Three of Them: Addressing the Invisibility of Lesbian, Gay, Bisexual, and Gender Non-Conforming Youths in the Juvenile Justice System," *Columbia Journal on Gender and Law* 19, no. 3 (2010); S. Hockenberry and C. Puzzanchera, *Juvenile Court Statistics 2011* (Pittsburgh, PA: National Center for Juvenile Justice, 2014).

40. National Juvenile Justice Network, *Addressing the Intersection of Gender and Racial Disparities* (Washington, DC: National Juvenile Justice Network, 2016).

41. A. J. Beck, D. Cantor, J. Hartge, and T. Smith, *Sexual Victimization in Juvenile Facilities Reported by Youth, 2012* (Washington, DC: U.S Department of Justice, Office of Justice Programs, Bureau of Justice Statistics, 2013), http://www.bjs.gov; C. Gilbert and H. Hussey, *Young, Queer, and Locked Up: LGBT Youth in the Adult Criminal Justice System*, Campaign for Youth Justice Voices, blog (June 18, 2015), http://campaignforyouthjustice. org.

42. D. Sered, *Young Men of Color and the Other Side of Harm: Addressing Disparities in Our Response to Violence* (New York: Vera Institute of Justice, 2014).

43. J. Rich, T. Corbin, S. Bloom, L. Rich, S. Evans, and A. Wilson, "Healing the Hurt:

Trauma-Informed Approaches to the Health of Boys and Young Men of Color," *Center for Nonviolence and Social Justice, Drexel University School of Public Health and Department of Emergency Medicine* 9 (2009); J. Truman, L. Langton, and M. Planty, *Criminal Victimization* (Washington, DC: U.S. Department of Justice, Office of Justice Programs, Bureau of Justice Statistics, 2012).

44. Sered, *Young Men of Color and the Other Side of Harm.*

45. Federal Bureau of Investigation, *Uniform Crime Reports: Crime in the United States* (Washington, DC: U.S. Department of Justice, Federal Bureau of Investigation, 2012).

46. "The Counted: People Killed by the Police in the United States," *The Guardian* online, June 1, 2015, http://www.theguardian.com/us-news/ng-interactive/2015/jun/01/the-counted-police-killings-us-database.

47. R. Brame, S. Bushway, R. Paternoster, and M. Turner, "Demographic Patterns of Cumulative Arrest Prevalence by Ages 18 and 23," *Crime & Delinquency* (2014), DOI: 10.1177/0011128713514801.

48. Michigan State Police, Michigan Crime Incident Reporting, Statewide Arrest Totals 2012: Arrests by Age, Sex, and Race (2013) https://www.michigan.gov/documents/msp/StatewideArrests_433547_7.pdf; Michigan Committee on Juvenile Justice, Michigan Disproportionate Minority Contact Data, 2013, https://michigancommitteeonjuvenilejustice.com/michigan-data/socio-demographic-data.html.

49. T. R. Tyler, J. Fagan, and A. Geller, "Street Stops and Police Legitimacy: Teachable Moments in Young Urban Men's Legal Socialization," *Journal of Empirical Legal Studies* 11 (2014): 751–85.

50. U.S. Department of Justice Civil Rights Division, *Investigation of the Ferguson Police Department*, March 4, 2015, https://www.justice.gov/sites/default/files/opa/press-releases/attachments/2015/03/04/ferguson_police_department_report.pdf.

51. B. Lowery and S. Graham, "Priming Unconscious Racial Stereotypes about Adolescent Offenders," *Law and Human Behavior* 28, no. 5 (2004): 483–504; P. A. Goff, M. C. Jackson, B. A. L. Di Leone, C. M. Culotta, and N. A. DiTomasso, "The Essence of Innocence: Consequences of Dehumanizing Black Children," *Journal of Personality and Social Psychology* 106, no. 4 (2014): 526.

52. ACLU Foundation of Massachusetts, "Black, Brown and Targeted: A Report on Boston Police Department Street Encounters from 2007–2010," https://www.issuelab.org/resources/25157/25157.pdf; A. Gelman, J. Fagan, and A. Kiss, "An Analysis of the New York City Police Department's 'Stop-and-Frisk' Policy in the Context of Claims of Racial Bias," *Journal of the American Statistical Association* 102, no. 479 (2007): 813–23.

53. J. Fratello, A. F. Rengifo, and J. Trone, *Coming of Age with Stop and Frisk: Experiences,*

Self-Perceptions, and Public Safety Implications (New York: Vera Institute of Justice, 2013).

54. M. Vande Bunte, "$1.5 Million Grand Rapids Police Plan Starts Putting Body Cams on Cops This Spring," MLive.com, January 13, 2016.

55. "New MSU Police Unit Focuses on Anti-Bias, Inclusion," *MSU Today*, February 8, 2016; R. J. Wolcott, "At MSU, Training Police on Microaggressions and Bias," *Lansing State Journal*, February 10, 2016.

56. "Editorial: Detroit Community Policing Cutting Murders," *Detroit News*, October 13, 2016.

57. J. Oosting, "Michigan Police Shootings Have Prompted Anger, Not Violence, as Leaders Build Relationships," MLive.com, May 8, 2015, http://www.mlive.com/lansing-news/index.ssf/2015/05/michigan_alpact_terrance_kello.html. ALPACT is anchored in Detroit, Grand Rapids, Flint, Saginaw, and Benton Harbor.

58. G. Fields and J. R. Emshwiller, "For More Teens, Arrests by Police Replace School Discipline," *Wall Street Journal*, October 20, 2014.

59. Currently, there are bills within the Michigan Legislature that would amend the state's zero tolerance laws to provide more discretion to schools when deciding to suspend or expel a student. See Gun-Free Schools Act of 1994, 20 U.S.C. §§ 7151 et seq.; Michigan Public Act 328 of 1994, Section 380.1311 of the Michigan Compiled Laws.

60. U.S. Department of Education, National Center for Education Statistics, 1999–2000, 2003–2004, 2005–2006, and 2007–2008 School Survey on Crime and Safety (SSOCS), 2000, 2004, 2006, and 2008; The Advancement Project, *Education on Lockdown: The Schoolhouse to Jailhouse Track* (Washington, DC: Advancement Project, 2005).

61. Dignity in Schools, *Campaign Fact Sheet: What Is School Pushout?* (Washington, DC: Dignity in Schools, 2015).

62. J. Nance, *Over-Disciplining Students, Racial Bias, and the School-to-Prison Pipeline*, 50 U. Rich. L. Rev. 1063 (2016).

63. The Advancement Project, *Restorative Practices: Fostering Healthy Relationships and Promoting Positive Discipline in Schools: A Guide for Educators* (Cambridge, MA: Schott Foundation, 2014).

64. L. Slagter, "Young Citizen Transforms School Culture through Restorative Justice," MLive.com, May 27, 2016.

65. U.S. Department of Education, Office for Civil Rights, "2013–14 Civil Rights Data Collection: A First Look" (Washington, DC: U.S. Department of Education, Office for Civil Rights, 2016).

66. "Gov. Rick Snyder: Mental Health Diversion Council Progress Report Implements Strategies to Help People, Communities," CSG Justice Center, September 4, 2014, http://www.michigan.gov.

67. "Testimony to the President's Task Force on 21st Century Policing," February 13, 2015 (testimony of Kevin Bethel), http://cops.usdoj.gov/pdf/taskforce/submissions/Bethel_Kevin_Testimony.pdf.

68. Michigan Compiled Laws, 712A.11(3).

69. The state reports the number of cases but not the number of people involved in those cases. It is assumed that the number of people is actually much lower since one person could have multiple cases within a single year. Michigan Committee on Juvenile Justice, Michigan Disproportionate Minority Contact Data, 2013; State Court Administrative Office, 2015 Court Caseload Report, Statewide Circuit Court Summary.

70. It is important to note that biased decision-making is only one possible explanation or factor contributing to racial disparities.

71. George S. Bridges and Sara Steen, "Racial Disparities in Official Assessments of Juvenile Offenders: Attributional Stereotypes as Mediating Mechanisms," *American Sociological Review* 63 (1998).

72. Z. Bell and A. Rasquiza, *Implicit Bias and Juvenile Justice: A Literature Review* (Washington, DC: National Center for Youth Law, 2014); K. Henning, "Criminalizing Normal Adolescent Behavior in Communities of Color: The Role of Prosecutors in Juvenile Justice Reform," *Cornell Law Review* (2012): 12–117.

73. National Legal Aid and Defender Association, "A Race to the Bottom—Speed and Savings Over Due Process: A Constitutional Crisis" (Washington, DC: National Legal Aid and Defender Association, 2008).

74. In July 2013, the Michigan Indigent Defense Commission was created and charged with collecting data for review of trial-level indigent defense services across the state; creating defense standards to ensure all systems meet constitutional obligations; and working with counties to implement plans to meet the new standards. In 2016, the commission proposed its first set of standards, addressing education and training of defense counsel, initial interview, investigations and experts, and counsel at first appearance and other critical stages; however, the proposed standards do not specifically address legal representation in delinquency cases.

75. D. LaBelle and A. Addis, *Basic Decency: An Examination of Natural Life Sentences for Michigan Youth* (Detroit: American Civil Liberties Union of Michigan, Second Chances 4 Youth, 2012).

76. Ibid.

77. Ibid.

78. Ibid.

79. M. Sickmund, T. J. Sladky, W. Kang, and C. Puzzanchera, "Easy Access to the Census

of Juveniles in Residential Placement, Detailed Offense Profile in Public and Private Facilities for Michigan, 2010," U.S. Department of Justice, Office of Juvenile Justice and Delinquency Prevention, 2011, http://www.ojjdp.gov/ojstatbb/ezacjrp. The OJJDP collected their data through self-reported surveys from all public and private licensed residential facilities in Michigan.

80. The Sentencing Project, Office of Juvenile Justice and Delinquency Prevention, *Census of Juveniles in Residential Placement* (Washington, DC: Office of Juvenile Justice and Delinquency Prevention, 2015).

81. R. Mendel, *No Place for Kids: The Case for Reducing Juvenile Incarceration* (Baltimore, MD: Annie E. Casey Foundation, 2011); B. Holman and J. Ziedenberg, *The Dangers of Detention: The Impact of Incarcerating Youth in Detention and Other Secure Facilities* (Washington, DC: Justice Policy Institute, 2010).

82. Ibid.

83. U.S. Department of Justice, "Findings Letter of the CRIPA Investigation of W. J. Maxey Training School," 2004, http://www.justice.gov/crt/about/spl/documents/granholm_findinglet.pdf.

84. A. J. Beck, P. Guerino, P. M. Harrison, *Sexual Victimization in Juvenile Facilities Reported by Youth, 2008–09* (Washington, DC: U.S. Department of Justice, Bureau of Justice Statistics, 2010).

85. D. N. Evans, *Pioneers of Youth Justice Reform: Achieving System Change Using Resolution, Reinvestment, and Realignment Strategies* (New York: Research and Evaluation Center, John Jay College of Criminal Justice, 2012).

86. K. Staley and M. Weemhoff, *There's No Place Like Home* (Lansing: Michigan Council on Crime and Delinquency, 2013); S. Fazal, *Safely Home: Reducing Youth Incarceration and Achieving Positive Youth Outcomes for High and Complex Need Youth through Effective Community-Based Programs* (Washington, DC: Youth Advocate Programs Policy & Advocacy Center, 2014); M. Lipsey, J. Howell, M. Kelly, G. Chapman, and D. Carver, *Improving the Effectiveness of Juvenile Justice Programs: A New Perspective on Evidence-Based Practice* (Washington, DC: Georgetown University Center for Juvenile Justice Reform, 2011); J. Butts and D. N. Evans, *Resolution, Reinvestment, and Realignment: Three Strategies for Changing Juvenile Justice* (New York: John Jay College of Criminal Justice Research and Evaluation Center, 2011).

87. National Association of Counties, *Issue Brief: County Leadership in Juvenile Justice Reform: Wayne County, Michigan* (Washington, DC: National Association of Counties, 2015).

88. Staley and Weemhoff, *There's No Place Like Home*.

89. J. Feierman, K. Mordecai, and R. Schwartz, *Ten Strategies to Reduce Juvenile Length of Stay*

(Philadelphia: Juvenile Law Center, 2015).

90. M. Weemhoff and K. Staley, *Youth Behind Bars: Examining the Impact of Prosecuting and Incarcerating Kids in Michigan's Criminal Justice System* (Lansing: Michigan Council on Crime and Delinquency, Michigan Department of Corrections, 2014); Michigan State Police, Michigan Incident Crime Reporting (MICR), 2014.

91. Ibid.

92. National Standards to Prevent, Detect, and Respond to Prison Rape: Final Rule, 77 Fed. Reg. 37,106, 37,196 (June 20, 2012), http://ojp.gov/programs/pdfs/prea_final_rule.pdf.

93. Summons and Complaint for Petitioner, John Doe v. Michigan Department of Corrections, No. 13-1196-CZ (22nd Mich. Cir., December 9, 2013).

94. V. Schiraldi and B. Western, "Time to Rethink the Age of Jurisdiction," *Translational Criminology* (Fall 2015).

95. S. Kollman, *Raising the Age of Juvenile Court Jurisdiction: The Future of 17-Year-Olds in Illinois' Justice System* (Springfield: Illinois Juvenile Justice Commission, 2013); R. A. Mendel, *Juvenile Justice Reform in Connecticut: How Collaboration and Commitment Have Improved Public Safety and Outcomes for Youth* (Washington, DC: Justice Policy Institute, 2013).

96. Michigan Compiled Laws, 712A.18e.

97. C. Gowen, L. Thurau, and M. Wood, "The ABA's Approach to Juvenile Justice Reform: Education, Eviction, and Employment: The Collateral Consequences of Juvenile Adjudication," *Duke Forum for Law and Social Change* 3, no. 1 (2011): 187.

98. A. Agan and S. Starr, "Ban the Box, Criminal Records, and Statistical Discrimination: A Field Experiment," U of Michigan Law & Econ Research Paper No. 16-012 (2016), http://dx.doi.org/10.2139/ssrn.2795795.

99. National Juvenile Justice Network, *Policy Updates: Reducing Racial and Ethnic Disparities in Juvenile Justice Systems: Promising Practices* (Washington, DC: National Juvenile Justice Network, 2014).

100. R. A. Mendel, *No Place for Kids: The Case for Reducing Juvenile Incarceration* (Baltimore, MD: Annie E. Casey Foundation, 2011); B. Holman and J. Ziedenberg, *The Dangers of Detention: The Impact of Incarcerating Youth in Detention and Other Secure Facilities* (Washington, DC: Justice Policy Institute, 2010).

101. N. D. Porter, *Racial Impact Statements* (Washington, DC: The Sentencing Project, 2014).

102. National Juvenile Justice Network, *Policy Updates: Reducing Racial and Ethnic Disparities in Juvenile Justice Systems: Promising Practices* (Washington, DC: National Juvenile Justice Network, 2014).

103. Most validated risk assessment tools today have been normed on white, African

American, and Latino populations.

104. Z. Bell and A. Rasquiza, *Implicit Bias and Juvenile Justice: A Literature Review* (Washington, DC: National Center for Youth Law, 2014).

105. Fazal, *Safely Home.*

106. National Research Council, *Implementing Juvenile Justice Reform: The Federal Role: Committee on a Prioritized Plan to Implement a Developmental Approach in Juvenile Justice Reform*, Committee on Law and Justice, Division of Behavioral and Social Sciences and Education (Washington, DC: National Academies Press, 2014).

Basketballs Can Be a Bitch!

Martin Vargas

I n May of 1981, after serving almost 10 years of a parolable life sentence, I was in Marquette Branch Prison, where, after news of a riot at the State Prison of Southern Michigan hit the yard, there was a tension so thick, everyone's senses were tuned up to maximum.

Sitting on ancient bleachers, "Fry" and I watched a basketball game that guys had been at for hours. Some were tired of playing and others were tired of losing. After one loss, "Poncho" angrily tossed the ball over a fence. A heavyset guard got the ball and the game resumed. Another game was lost and there went the ball again. This time when the guard goes after it, another guard nicknamed "Buffalo Soldier" tells him to leave it. "Bitch ass motherfucker" someone yells.

Buffalo Soldier orders everyone to disperse and a heated exchange ensues. This guard isn't about to let convicts have the last say, so he runs up to "M" and handcuffs him! M knows he's going to the hole, but keeps his cool and asks the guard to loosen the cuffs, which are on too tight.

Testiness plagues the crowd and the more humane guard says something about it not being that serious, almost getting M off the hook. "Bitch-ass police," someone yells, and Buffalo Soldier's riled up anew. While everyone runs off at the mouth,

"Big W" uncoils a punch that hits Buffalo Soldier from somewhere deep in Texas. Another punch is thrown and the shit is on.

Suddenly, Buffalo Soldier's getting pounded, and since everyone on the court would be implicated anyway, there was nothing to lose; several guys get their licks in too. When there's a lot against one, people just get in each other's way, so, even though he got smacked around some, Buffalo Soldier wasn't hurt so bad that he couldn't crawl out from under everyone's legs and haul ass towards the Control Center. Fry and I watched this new game, but ran for cover when a tower guard shot at the dull-yellow wall we leaned on. When paint chips scattered, we did too.

Why Buffalo Soldier did that is a mystery, since in minutes a loudspeaker would announce that yard was over and we would all return to our cells. The smoldering ambience present all week had not stirred until this incident ignited it, but in seconds, the pregnant strain erupted into a chaos so completely out of control that a thousand loudspeakers would not get us off the yard. Buffalo Soldier ran for home and safety while a herd of Captain Save-A-Ho's ran from the Control Center to rescue him.

Even though Marquette's prison yard is very small and not many guys knew what had just happened, the spirit of tension ignited an immediate fight-or-flight reaction from everyone. Those of us who did see knew that the anal-structured timeline of prison life had just received a laxative, and yard would not be over at the regularly scheduled time that day.

As they rushed the yard, confused guards confronted by an uncommonly aggressive environment had good reason to slow down. Many saw the odds stacked against them as they saw colleagues running from prisoners. Nobody carried weapons, but these quickly materialized. Everyone finds something suitable for defense if the time calls for it.

A concrete yard between the ball court and Control Center held dozens of small wooden tables spread every few feet; an unwritten rule allowed gambling. Hearing the commotion and watching guards gallop by, gamblers tossed tables in their way. I was told later that "Charlie Mack," a lifer who swore not to die in prison, smashed a table over a guard's head. Charlie was killed in a field in Ann Arbor during an escape attempt in 1982.

Gates maybe ten feet high stood between the gambling tables and Control Center. These gates, and a cell block leading to the arsenal, were immediately locked, inadvertently keeping guards from the area of safety they ran to. Unfortunate guards who fell while running towards that zone got a pretty good whooping—or bad, depending on whose side you were on. Some fought enraged convicts, but these fights were futile, and the guards were forced to retreat.

As these fiery minutes emerged, a convict was hit in the leg by a guard blindly shooting through the window of a shack used by yard workers to warm up in the winter. There was no reason to blindly shoot in there, but I suppose there was no reason to beat the shit out of Buffalo Soldier either. Anyway, thanks to some well-placed gunshots, guards safely regrouped behind locked gates, while everyone tried to figure out what the hell just happened—and thus began the riot I witnessed that made national news, in May of 1981.

I don't say it's right, but when the oppressed see oppressors weakening, retaliation is a given. Watch any news channel today and you'll see this too. A light appears in the eyes of those with grievances against authority. Grievances for abuse of power can be real or perceived—regardless, someone is pissed, and someone else is going to pay.

As all this was taking place, Fry and I took cover in a spot opposite to where the guards ran. As we crouched in a trough used to wash potatoes in decades past, we were kept immobile by bullets periodically digging into a wall behind us.

The trough ran the length of the building and was about two feet wide by as many deep. We hugged the wall nearest the shooter to minimize his aim. We weren't being targeted directly, but it's still a bitch when concrete lands close and bullets hit nearby walls. We watched the guard in the tower, and when his focus went elsewhere, we scampered off in separate directions and snatched up what weapons we could. I grabbed some lumber from a recently deceased card table, satisfied that it would do.

————————————

From age eighteen to twenty-three I was at Michigan Reformatory—known then as Gladiator School—and from two riots there, I learned what to do in these cases. There, and the first law of nature.

Lesson one in RIOT 101 is "Wear a disguise, stupid." Cameras are always rolling and you don't want to earn your fifteen minutes of fame cheesing at people watching a riot on the news. I geared up in a coat many sizes too big and, cutting holes in a blanket, draped that over me like a poncho. Sunglasses and stretch cap topped off a look you won't find in any fashion magazine. One never knows what will happen in a riot, but dressed this way and armed with a two-by-heavy, I felt less threatened in the yard.

The inmate store is where I found glasses, stretch cap, and food. They were just lying there, not belonging to anyone. Someone found the postage stamps, someone else found the tokens (money), others found televisions, cassette players, radios, and food of course.

"C.P." didn't lose sight of much that day and was one of the few with sense to keep the big picture in mind. Guys laughed as he rang up his "purchases" on the cash register and put the receipt in his pocket, but he laughed last when, the next day during a shakedown, he was allowed to keep everything he bought. He was just about the only one found "not guilty" of inciting to riot too. Apparently he asked, as a witness, the inspector who wrote over eighty misconducts for inciting to riot that night. This inspector wasn't in the yard that night, so when C.P.'s ticket reached the person reviewing misconducts, it had to be thrown out because nobody can write a ticket for something they didn't personally see.

Dressed in my riot suit, I went to the basement level of the store. Smoke and water were everywhere because someone had lit a fire and sprinklers rained water continuously. A dense cloud of smoke camped inside the flooded building and, to see where I was going, I had to duck-walk my ass a long time, and when I exchanged my wooden club for a knife lying on the floor, nobody cared. They were painstakingly trying to find a way through a severely rusted and locked steel gate. I discovered why the guys were so aroused by this opening, and also became intrigued.

The locked gate housed a treasure built in 1860, or whenever the prison was built—a drainage tunnel that went under the wall and led outside the prison. I don't know how they knew this, but didn't really care. I doubt there's a prisoner anywhere who hasn't thought of escape at one time or another, and I was glad to be in that mix. One good reason to be accepted by old-timers is that they know some cool-ass shit.

Smoke made it very difficult to breathe in there. We coughed a lot and teared up some, but if the locked-gate puzzle could be solved, there was a presumed road to freedom on the other side. Someone suggested cutting the steel with an acetylene torch in the maintenance building, and half a dozen heads bobbed in unison. So away we went, squatting low like a bunch of ducks, leaving a good wake of water and smoke behind us.

Getting the torch was a great idea, but as with most great ideas, someone's already thought of it. Coming out of the store and looking towards the maintenance building, we saw it burning too. Someone used the torch to light it—it wouldn't have been so bad, but whoever did it forgot to rescue the chained-up torch! That idea literally went up in smoke. We didn't return to where our envisaged freedom rested, but inhaled more smoke before parting ways. This smoke was way more tolerable, but it brought on munchies big time. Fortunately there was a cookout in the yard. Well, there was all this food in the butcher shop that, you know, didn't seem to belong to anyone.

Many people have a perception of prison riots, but they're not bad for everyone. Take the cookout for example: burgers and steaks with all the works were passed around, music played, and there was some pretty good herb and drink too. People partied peacefully and, until the cops came, everything was cool. Shit, we had our own Woodstock going on that night, but guards weren't having any of that. As we partied, they grouped up at the far end of the yard.

"OFF THE YARD!" they yelled through loudspeakers at one point. "CLEAR THE YARD AND RETURN TO YOUR CELLS!" "YOU HAVE A DIRECT ORDER TO DISPERSE! RETURN TO YOUR CELLS OR YOU WILL BE TICKETED FOR INCITING TO RIOT!" Nobody listened to their demands.

At least one helicopter added its own angry, buzzing protest to the hysteria already present in the night, though not like the movies where lights focus on one sinister scene and cellos play something deep and dramatic.

I once painted a self-portrait where, encased in a series of bubbles, I painfully struggled for freedom, and that's a good analogy to relate how I felt walking through the turbulence of that night. I meandered through a corridor of safety in the middle of a prison riot, and honestly felt protected by a warm and throbbing bubble. Weird, but true.

Fry was solid and everyone liked him. I knew he was okay but I hadn't seen him in a while, so I went to look for him. It was an excuse to see what was happening on that side of the prison. I took my time walking through the unfolding drama, and remember being awed by the immense rage, violence, and destructiveness of my colleagues.

Lesson two in RIOT 101 is "It's better to walk with a crowd than to run from it." Tough guys I knew got pretty fucked up for not following that rule. Some were only bruised, but others dripped blood from wounds made by pipes, hammers, or knives.

Randy and Mike were not brothers, but similar last names and looks made everyone think they were. I saw Randy on a gallery, fighting a couple of brothers, black not biological. On another gallery was Mike, fighting someone else. Or was it Randy? It was surreal. Some guys running amuck tried to fuck the one who was gay, but mistakenly ran up against the one who was not. That night must have been rough for both of them. If you're on your way to prison, "fight, fuck, or lock up" is a philosophy you should know, but you can't lock up in the middle of a riot.

Another guy not so lucky that night was an alleged white supremacist. Many guys disliked him, and a riot created a perfect opportunity to make that known. "T" and his crew busted him up in C Block, where Augie, Jamaica, and Louie B. locked. Apparently, he was only going to be robbed, but was left for dead after a ball-peen hammer left a pretty convincing hole in his head. Allegedly, Jamaica dragged him to a cell, put his own lock on the door, and this is what may have kept him alive.

Fry and friends were smoking weed when I got there, ironically watching the riot on TV—but nothing funny was going on in the next cell. When I drove up I saw a black mob gathered there, but not the fury they released against a white guy who once bragged about "killing niggers" in the streets. Not immediately visible either was the brutal gang rape that was taking place.

I went to get some food I had stashed earlier and saw the inevitable. Guards in their riot gear lined up shoulder to shoulder at the part of our yard they had previously run towards. They disturbed the peace by drumming batons on shields. Disguised in darkness, they weren't the same ones who, with fear in their eyes, danced through a card-table obstacle course earlier. I hate to admit it, but with demeanors completely changed, they looked impressive in their ever growing, tight-knit formation. They added their noise to the night, which ricocheted from darkened, smoldering buildings surrounded by silhouetted walls and towers.

With night's lights dancing sharply off their riot gear, they let us know that another phase of their training would be coming into play soon. They didn't rush the yard, but they looked sinister as hell and capable, and we knew they had recaptured the odds. Well, you can't smoke dope and cook burgers in any prison yard anyway, so the short-lived putsch neared its end, as does this narrative.

I will end by saying that the riot of '81, inside Michigan's highest security prison, was quashed—of course. Convicts, in some cases eight to ten, were jammed into any available cell. Early the next morning we were strip-searched, cuffed, and escorted to our assigned cells. Every prisoner was accounted for, after a slow and careful process, and eventually things returned to a semblance of normalcy. For a time, we settled into a lengthy detention time where only basic human rights were observed. No visits or phone calls for a couple of weeks; showers weekly, not daily; and sack lunches for meals. In the end, a prisoner was left with a bullet wound; a male guard was paraded up and down a gallery and raped; prisoners were raped, beaten, and left for dead; and probably millions of taxpayers' dollars were consumed in damages, all because of a stupid, unnecessary argument over a bitch-ass basketball.

Behind Bars

The Current State of U.S. Prison Literature

D. Quentin Miller

I write this essay from behind bars.

Imagine what the world looks like when your field of vision is crisscrossed by vertical iron lines segmenting space from floor to ceiling, and by horizontal lines cutting off any possibility of a better world above. My world is an elongated grid, cut into rectangles that distort rather than frame. It's impossible to see clearly.

I entered prison in 1996, a medium-security dump in Connecticut, built of brick and cinderblock and surrounded by the usual razor ribbon and barbed wire, lit up at night like a car dealership. I was twenty-nine years old. Scared.

I was told I couldn't bring in a pen because it could be fashioned into a weapon. The warden predicted that I would hear one sob story after another about how all of the guys I would meet behind bars would claim to be innocent. "*Con* artists," he chuckled. I was cautioned not to tell them where I lived, or whether or not I was married or had kids. I was given a body alarm and taught how to use it in case I felt threatened by any of the inmates.

Yes, the inmates. *Them*. I entered the prison world not as a convicted criminal, but as a teacher.

I've never been incarcerated. I claim to be "behind bars" to suggest that everyone is, yet only those who are locked up understand that they are. The bars distort the vision of anyone who tries to look through them in either direction. Most of the time, those of us behind the bars on the outside are reluctant to look. Reading prison literature forces us to do so. The bars aren't always helpful. Sometimes they frame their subjects in a limiting way. Sometimes they get in the way of the big picture. Invariably, though, reading prison literature makes us aware of the bars and of the way they symbolize our common condition.

By "our common condition," I am referring to the state of American culture in the twenty-first century, a state governed by the logic of an advertising/entertainment/news-media empire that has overwhelmed our collective capacity for creativity, humanity, and morality. In a world where journalism and entertainment are indistinguishable, prison and criminality function as shorthand that allows the general public to easily classify people marked by difference (usually expressed in terms of race, class, or mental health). Cop shows and prison dramas tend to depict "bad guys" in such crude, broad strokes that the viewer can easily recognize them and assume that they belong behind bars based on the way they look: no trial or even crime necessary. (The 2012 murder of Trayvon Martin in Sanford, Florida, is a clear example of how dangerous this situation can become: a seventeen-year-old black man wearing a hoodie sweatshirt and walking too close to the houses of the paranoid white middle class is assumed to be criminally dangerous, though he has committed no crime and is unarmed.) Our common condition in the twenty-first century involves a fear of those who look like the criminals who are paraded across TV and movie screens. Not coincidentally, these depictions are almost always of poor and dark-skinned people. Increasingly, they are also immigrants (a word often paired with the adjective "illegal," or even replaced by the plural noun "illegals").

In placing others (and thus selves) behind bars, contemporary "law-abiding" Americans are clearly acting on a desperate need to feel safe in a mediated world that constantly persuades them that they cannot be safe without taking action. Prison is a response to the base animal fear that causes people to believe that their enemies surround them and that those enemies will attack them at any moment unless self-protective strategies are put firmly in place. The prison-industrial complex, as Angela Davis has described it, has become so highly evolved that Americans tend not to question its purpose or efficacy. As citizens of the nation with the highest rate of incarceration (by far), Americans are complacent in our belief that we have done something right by developing this complex. And yet, we are surprised when it turns out that the neighborhood watch volunteer who gunned down hooded-sweatshirt-wearing Trayvon Martin is accused of murder, or that the middle-class, white graduate student in neuroscience is the one who opens fire at a movie theater in suburban Colorado, killing or wounding dozens, or that the rich guy at the country club named Bernie Madoff who offers benign financial advice is actually bilking people and foundations out of millions of dollars and sinking the U.S. financial system in the process. The truth is that we don't know a criminal when we think we see one. The truth is not only that safety is an illusion, but that the prisons we are so devoted to prevent us from progressing toward a society that upholds a coherent set of humane values.

It may seem hopelessly romantic, but I believe that the study of literature can renew our commitment to such values, and that reading prison literature is the best way to comprehend our relationship to the bars that divide us.

Defining Prison Literature

What is prison literature? Most broadly defined, it is any work of serious writing, imaginative or otherwise, that engages with the experience of incarceration. In terms of American literary history, it is nothing new. Consider that the following incidents all took place inside prison walls and became the occasion for writing:

- Malcolm X committed himself to reading, and joined the Nation of Islam.
- Henry David Thoreau served time for refusing to pay his taxes and gained insight into the nature of his society as valuable as any observation he recorded while communing with nature at Walden Pond.
- Hawthorne's Hester Prynne was locked up for her sexual transgressions and gave birth to her daughter Pearl.
- Martin Luther King Jr. wrote what was arguably the most rhetorically powerful open letter of the civil rights era.
- Melville's Bartleby, the forlorn scrivener who passively rebelled against the dehumanizing effects of the modern workplace, died.
- John Cheever's Farragut kicked his drug habit.
- Rebecca Harding Davis's despondent iron-mill worker Hugh Wolfe slit his wrists.
- Richard Wright's Bigger Thomas listened as his fate and that of his class and race were spelled out in greater detail than he imagined possible.
- Eugene O'Neill's Yank Smith—the "hairy ape" from the play of the same

title—finally learned how controlled he had been his entire life by the
system of capitalist industry that he had falsely thought he controlled.

And so on. These instances—some fictional, some historical—prove how central
the prison experience is to American literature from its "renaissance" in the
mid-nineteenth century on. And these are only examples from the established
canon of great works, the literature that most students of the American literary
tradition would encounter. A broader history of prison literature can be discerned
in the critical works of H. Bruce Franklin: the study *The Victim as Criminal and
Artist* (1978)[1] and the anthology *Prison Literature in 20th Century America* (1998).
In this latter work, Franklin contends that his studies in prison literature led him
to conclude that he "was not looking at some peripheral cultural phenomenon but
something close to the center of our historical experience as a nation-state. At least
from the viewpoint of the people creating these works, America is itself a prison,
and the main lines of American literature can be traced from the plantation to the
penitentiary."[2]

My own interest in the field has picked up where these two works by Franklin
leave off by focusing on contemporary prison literature. The essays in my edited
collection *Prose and Cons: New Essays on Contemporary U.S. Prison Literature* (2005)
introduce some of the scholars who remain active in the field today.[3] Peter Caster's
book *Prisons, Race, and Masculinity in Twentieth-Century U.S Literature and Film*
(2008), Joy James's *The New Abolitionists: (Neo) Slave Narratives and Contemporary
Prison Writings* (2005), Dylan Rodriguez's *Forced Passages: Imprisoned Radical
Intellectuals and the U.S. Prison Regime* (2006), Doran Larson's *Fourth City: Essays
from the Prison in America* (2014), and Judith Scheffler's *Wall Tappings* (1986; reissued
2002) are just a few of the many essential critical works published in recent years.[4]

It may sound crass to call prison literature an ever-expanding subfield of United
States literary history, but it's true, and our skyrocketing rate of incarceration since
the mid-1970s has created the conditions for this proliferation. The examples I list
above from canonical American literary history only serve to illustrate how prevalent the prison has always been in our nation's most studied works. As Rodriguez
argues, "Equally significant . . . are the unpublished, undercirculated, or heretofore
uncirculated texts produced by captive intellectuals who remain largely outside
the nonimprisoned public's . . . concern."[5] There is indeed so much writing that
could be called "prison literature" that the reader who wants to encounter more of
it might not know where to begin. I offer the following taxonomy not as a way of

diminishing this body, but rather to portion it into smaller sections so as to make the overall body less daunting.

Classifying Contemporary Prison Literature

In my attempt to peer beyond the bars that separate me from those on the other side, I have taught and written about a number of contemporary prison writers in a variety of contexts. I have found it useful to place contemporary prison literature—a period defined for my purposes by the sharp spike in the rate of mass incarceration since the early 1970s—into a few broad categories.

One category is literature by professional writers who have experienced prison secondhand, by becoming close to the incarcerated and attempting to reimagine their experiences from this proximate position. Truman Capote's *In Cold Blood* (1966) was the progenitor of this genre.[6] Capote famously traveled to Kansas to investigate the murder of a farming family by interviewing the accused killers. Norman Mailer's *The Executioner's Song* (1979) was another similar attempt to merge the novelist's imagination with the nonfictional details of an actual convicted criminal: Mailer subtitled it a "true life novel."[7] James Baldwin's personal involvement with a close friend and bodyguard named Tony Maynard, accused of murder in 1967, led him not only to devote much time and energy to Maynard's case, but also to pen a number of essays on the subject and one novel, *If Beale Street Could Talk* (1974), an overlooked masterpiece (recently made into a major motion picture) narrated from the point of view of a seventeen-year-old girl pregnant with the child of her incarcerated lover, who was wrongfully accused of raping another woman.[8] John Cheever's novel *Falconer* (1977), considered by many his finest extended work of fiction, is deeply involved with the prison experience based on his own work teaching in prison in the early 1970s.[9] John Edgar Wideman's *Brothers and Keepers* (1984) is one of the most poignant works by a novelist about the lives of prisoners because the subject is Wideman's brother, Robby, serving a life sentence after a botched robbery turned into murder.[10] Wideman's attempts to merge autobiography and biography and to blend his own voice with that of his brother result in a work that is powerful and original. Andre Dubus III worked as a prison guard before devoting himself to fiction. The title story of his collection *The Cage Keeper* (1995) is one example of the way these experiences changed his trajectory; his novels *House of Sand and Fog* (2001) and *The Garden of Last Days* (2008) both consider the prison experience toward their conclusions.[11] *The Prisoner's Wife* (1999), asha bandele's memoir, is a variation on this category since it was her first published work, but has led to a career that includes the publication of other memoirs, novels, and poetry.[12]

A second category of prison literature involves writers whose cases have been nationally famous and/or controversial, or whose public selves have been shaped to some degree by the prison experience. Malcolm X, Martin Luther King, and Eldridge Cleaver, to varying degrees, used their incarcerated status as a rhetorical platform to advance the struggle for civil rights and racial equality in the 1960s. Leonard Peltier, a Native American activist whose alleged involvement in the killing of FBI officers at the Pine Ridge Reservation in South Dakota in 1975 led to his lifelong incarceration, has been the subject of a widespread campaign to advocate for his freedom. His 1999 book *Prison Writings: My Life Is My Sun Dance* examines both the prison experience and the cultural circumstances that have led to his incarceration.[13] Kathy Boudin was convicted for the murder of a police officer in 1981 in conjunction with the Weather Underground and the Black Liberation Army. Her prison writings have included poetry and nonfiction and deal with the effects of incarceration on families. Mumia Abu-Jamal's controversial case has resulted in multiple books, notably *Live from Death Row* (1995) and *All Things Censored* (2000).[14] Angela Davis is perhaps the most familiar writer in this category, though her work has tended more toward cultural analysis and political activism than literature.

A third category is comprised of writers whose writing careers began in prison. The poet Etheridge Knight is the contemporary originator of this genre. Jimmy Santiago Baca may be the most prolific poet whose work is almost entirely concerned with the prison experience. "Monster" Kody Scott (aka Sanyika Shakur) published a memoir (*Monster* [1993]) in the aftermath of the Rodney King riots that addresses (somewhat bombastically and indelicately) the dangerous spread of gun violence and black-on-black crime in Los Angeles in the late 1980s and early 1990s.[15] A host of anthologies have been published that showcase the work of prison writing programs in the United States, notably Bell Gale Chevigny's collection *Doing Time* (1999), selected from twenty-five years of the PEN Prison Writing program.[16] Wally Lamb's edited collection *Couldn't Keep It to Myself* (2003) showcases prison writings by women.[17] Recently, R. Dwayne Betts has emerged as a young prison writer of great promise, having published both poetry and nonfiction, notably his 2009 memoir *A Question of Freedom*.[18] Doran Larson's *Fourth City* (2014), in his words, "presents the widest sampling to date of first-person, frontline witness to the human experience of mass incarceration in the United States."[19] Indeed, this volume contains more than seventy voices that would otherwise have remained "undercirculated," to use Rodriguez's phrase. In many ways the volume illustrates how diverse and supple a term like "prison literature" can be; Larson argues that the writers in his collection "are Americans whose lives and voices are as singular as any in the free world."[20] There are many websites and digital archives that further augment the amount of prison writing we can discover, including the American Prison Writing Archive, which continues the work published in Larson's book, and prisonwriters.com.

A fourth category has emerged by authors who encounter prisoners as I did: as educators or volunteer workers. This genre serves to examine the attempts of writers who, often reluctantly, enter prisons with a set of assumptions similar to those I describe above and test them. Books like Mark Salzman's *True Notebooks* (2003) or Robert Ellis Gordon's *The Funhouse Mirror* (2000) are perhaps most common: stories of writing teachers who enter prison, encounter students that they don't know how to teach, and make important adjustments that edify not only the prisoners they are teaching, but also themselves and the reader.[21] Sister Helen Prejean's work *Dead Man Walking* (1993) is a powerful account of her encounter with a death row inmate.[22] There are some interesting variations on this genre: Ted Conover's *Newjack* (2000) details a year he spent incognito as a prison guard at the infamous Sing Sing prison in order to write the book.[23] *Newjack* is poignant because Conover encounters not only inmates but also those in charge of regulating them, and the authorities and bureaucracies that control the guards. Avi Steinberg's *Running the Books* (2010) is a sometimes humorous account of a prison librarian who believes his investment in the lives of inmates is perhaps shallower than that of a traditional prison educator would be, but who is drawn in nonetheless to those lives and ultimately feels a deeper sense of self-worth than he had prior to his experience.[24]

These four categories cannot be said to encompass the full range of contemporary prison literature, but they do give an overview of certain trends available to the reader interested in pursuing this field. It would be advantageous to sample from all of these categories to benefit from multiple perspectives. I would suggest that there is no simple conclusion to be derived from studying prison literature this way: it is unlikely that the sensitive reader would come away from an encounter with prison literature with the desire to ban prisons altogether, or to advocate for a higher rate of incarceration than the current one, or to believe that prison sentences should be uniformly lengthened, shortened, made harder, made easier, etc. Prison literature yields no easy answers, which is why it is a good corrective to the advertising/entertainment/news-media industry I describe above.

I'd like to conclude with a brief analysis of one writer from each of the four categories I describe above: four writers whose works might serve as an introduction to the field of contemporary prison literature as I understand it in the context of race. One of the bars that distort vision is, of course, the bar of racialized thinking. Given the extreme disparity between races in prison populations, it is evident that the study of prison literature can help readers of all races gain an appreciation for the complexity of the intersection between race and incarceration.

Finding a Voice: John Edgar Wideman

Of the many books by professional writers who gain their insights through proximity to inmates, John Edgar Wideman's *Brothers and Keepers* stands out because of its personal confession combined with its intellectual intensity. Wideman tells the story of the divergence between his own path as a celebrated writer and educator and that of his brother Robby, sentenced for life after killing a man during a robbery. For Wideman, prison is more than a metaphor; he writes,

> Even as I manufactured fiction from the events of my brother's life, from the history of the family that had nurtured us both, I knew something of a different order remained to be extricated. The fiction writer was also a man with a real brother behind real bars. I continued to feel caged by my bewilderment, by my inability to see clearly, accurately, not only the last visit with my brother, but the whole long skein of our lives together and apart. So this book. This attempt to break out, to knock down the walls.[25]

He later writes, addressing his brother, "The problem was that in order to be the person I thought I wanted to be, I believed I had to seal myself off from you, construct a wall between us."[26] In these two passages, walls operate similarly to the way I described bars at the beginning of this essay: as barriers that can be circumvented through literature. Wideman attempts to break down the walls between himself and his brother even as he realizes that he has constructed them. Significantly, he also wants to "break out" as well as to knock down the walls, signaling a desire to escape the forces that have created his separation from his brother in the first place, and also indicating that he, too, feels imprisoned. The walls he perceives represent many things: the illusion of safety, the struggle to identify one's success against the failure of others, the denial of family, and the desire to bury problems or to lock them away rather than to confront them.

Wideman's book—difficult to classify generically—documents one man's attempt, specifically one *writer's* attempt, to understand the conundrum at the heart of the current culture of incarceration. What exactly separates Wideman from his brother besides their first names and birth order? What does race have to do with it? Wideman wonders if he was just lucky to have gotten off the path that landed Robby in prison. Like the narrator of James Baldwin's masterful story "Sonny's Blues" (1957), the older brother initially places himself at a remove from his beleaguered younger brother as a way to survive. Entering the prison to visit Robby functions for John Wideman the same way as entering the jazz club does for the narrator of Baldwin's story: there is a difficult reckoning that forces a confrontation, that thing to be "extricated" in the passage above, a truth that renders most societal distinctions illusory. Wideman writes, "Not even inside the walls yet and I can sense the paranoia, the curtain of mistrust and suspicion settling over my eyes. Except for the car jockey and a runner outside the guards' kiosk, all the trustees in the yard are black, black men like me, like you [Robby]. In spite of knowing better, I can't shake the feeling that these men are different. Not just different. Bad. People who are dangerous. I can identify with them only to the extent that I own up to the evil in myself."[27] This insight is a valuable lesson to anyone attempting to look with honesty upon the prison experience. "These men" who are "bad" and "dangerous" in Wideman's curtained eyes include his brother. Until this moment, they have not included himself, but the prison gets him wondering. Is it so simple to divide people into "bad" and "good" and separate them with iron and concrete?

Not for a novelist. One of the strengths of Wideman's book is his gradual willingness to turn off his own intellectual/analytical voice and to allow Robby to tell his own story in his own voice. Even during the book's composition, Wideman realizes the need for this shift; he writes, "The problem with the first draft was my fear. I didn't let Robby speak for himself enough."[28] Robby tells his own story in the final draft, and it comes through in an uneven flow, in his own idiom. Like all stories that are told rather than written, it does not progress fluidly, but circles back on itself, sometimes aware of the need to restart so the auditor can follow. Late in the book, Robby realizes that he hasn't yet gotten to an important plot point in his story, the attempt to escape the law; he says, "What time you have, Bro? Ain't told you nothing about running yet. Must be close to three hours, ain't it? Seems like we just started talking a minute ago. Wall clock says 1:50. I hate even looking at that damn thing. One-fifty is right, though, ain't it? Leaves us fifteen minutes if they give us a whole visit. You can be sure they won't stretch it. Not by a minute. Might cut it short an hour but you don't never get no extra minute."[29] By including Robby's voice this way, verbatim, John offers more than Robby's story as imagined by an outsider, even one as close as his brother. The reader feels the prisoner's unrelenting consciousness of time, his desperate need for human connection, his awareness that "they," the guards, are in full control of his freedom. John Wideman effectively knocks down the walls that he admits he has created by allowing Robby his creative freedom and by fulfilling his desire to tell his own story in his own voice, even though it might not turn out as coherent or as well designed as a story John might tell. The hybridity of *Brothers and Keepers* allows its author to move between perspectives, to examine his brother's story in the broadest and deepest terms imaginable, and to connect his own story to it. The book is also deliberately inconclusive, as are most great works of prison literature, which allows the reader to draw individual conclusions, or at least to raise additional questions about the nature of incarceration.

Defending Self and Nation: Leonard Peltier

Leonard Peltier, like Mumia Abu-Jamal, has been the subject of a grassroots campaign advocating for his freedom. For a time in the 1980s and 1990s, "Free Leonard Peltier" bumper stickers, posters, and T-shirts were common fixtures. His case has been controversial, fueled partially by Peter Matthiessen's book *In the Spirit of Crazy Horse* (1983) and Robert Redford and Michael Apted's documentary *Incident at Oglala* (1992), and by the fact that former U.S. attorney general Ramsey Clark has been Peltier's advocate for years.[30]

Prison Writings begins with a preface by Clark following an introduction by Chief Arvol Looking Horse, both of whom argue for Peltier's release. These introductions, along with Harvey Arden's "editor's note" and two appendices at the end—one a timeline of Peltier's life, the other a transcription of Peltier's pre-sentencing statement from his 1977 trial—frame the book in terms of Peltier's celebrated case. Yet what makes *Prison Writings* interesting is the author's persistent voice in which he addresses us, his readers, directly. His chapters are admittedly uneven and his rhetorical purpose shifts, but Peltier's voice is honest and clear. His primary role is to educate his reader as a patient but stern lecturer who forces us to consider injustice, to pay attention to the plight of Native Americans, and to contemplate the inhumanity that we participate in by supporting current incarceration methods. From the beginning, Peltier's book emphasizes the inhumanity of the contemporary prison; he writes, "The Hole—with which I've become well acquainted at several federal institutions these past twenty-three years, having become something of an old-timer myself—remains, in my experience, one of the most inhuman of tortures. A psychological hell." He paints his experience in broad strokes, occasionally leaving his depictions unfinished: "The days just happen to you. The nights you've got to imagine, to conjure up, all by yourself. They're the stuff of your nightmares." Unable to control his destiny, Peltier seems lost in a funhouse world where nothing makes sense; he writes, "The first thing you have to understand is that you never understand anything in here."[31] Prisons are the sadistic creations of madmen, in Peltier's eyes. His stated quest is to enlighten his reader about his own life and the lives of his people, but also to demonstrate how prison operates as a metaphor for the way those lives are marked by oppression.

Because the crime he is accused of involved the murder of two FBI agents, corrections officers are especially hard on Peltier. Other prison narratives tend to dwell on the menace of other inmates, but Peltier's is largely about the power exercised by prison guards and their bosses. There is even a glimmer of solidarity among Peltier and other inmates, but guards are universally evil: "They don't just take your freedom from you—which you'd think would be enough—but they demean and humiliate you, it seems, whenever and wherever possible. . . . I was fed cold, tasteless meals, denied exercise, visits from my family, even showers. At one jail a trustee told me they had been urinating in my food. When I shoved the food back through the slot in the door they shoved it back in and told me, 'Eat this or die, you piece of shit!'"[32] Following this second incident, a number of guards storm into Peltier's cell and threaten physical violence, but he manages to stare them down and avoid a physical confrontation. This response is consistent throughout the book: he has developed his spirit and mind to such a high degree that the physical circumstances of his incarceration—which are rough—do not break him. The Sun Dance ceremony, which acts as a touchstone throughout the book, is a metaphor for this principle as it involves ritualized, self-inflicted pain that the dancers overcome.

It is not surprising that the dominant note of Peltier's book is political, given his case. Yet the most interesting aspects of it as an example of prison literature are the moments of creative expansiveness, the snippets of poetry and philosophy that help him articulate his complex feelings. Toward the middle of the book he tells "a story in the form of a vision." He also incorporates tribal history and spiritual practices into his writings. He does not see any easy resolution to the problems that divide white people from Native Americans, but he realizes that prison is not the answer: "We need not courtrooms but schoolrooms, not jails and prisons but decent homes and jobs for the millions of every color—including many, many white people—who are being denied their human and civil rights every day of the week.... Democracy means difference, not sameness. Allow us our differences as we allow you yours. We don't conflict with each other; we complement each other."[33] Although idealized, this perspective is certainly one that the reader is likely to agree with, whether or not he or she has been persuaded of Peltier's innocence. It is only through an extended telling of his tale with poetic and visionary flourishes that Peltier has earned the right to stake this claim. What is fascinating is that he has arrived at this conclusion in spite of his decades of incarceration, not because of them.

New Kid on the (Cell) Block: R. Dwayne Betts

R. Dwayne Betts, in some ways, is a common type of incarcerated twenty-first-century American: first, he served time for a silly, unpremeditated crime, and second, he is a young black male. Betts had been a bright high school student who had never held a gun until the day he and his friends pulled one on a man sleeping in a car. The way he describes it, this carjacking was a lark, but it landed him in prison for six years. (Like Malcolm X's partner-in-crime Shorty, Betts initially thought his sentence was much longer because he didn't realize what the judge meant by "concurrent" sentencing).[34] Betts entered the prison complex before he was old enough to vote or legally smoke tobacco. His memoir *A Question of Freedom* is subtitled "A Memoir of Learning, Survival, and Coming of Age in Prison." The subtitle is more compelling than the main title, especially the chilling final phrase "coming of age in prison." His story is ultimately one of hard-earned success in a life that seemed destined for failure, but it serves to remind readers of the many others like Betts whose paths ended up leading them back to the revolving door of prison once released, if they ever managed to be released.

   A Question of Freedom is a rich work of prison literature for many reasons. The author's voice doesn't often resort to bombast, swagger, or overindulgence in the language of the underworld. Despite the author's transformation from a street punk to someone who improves his lot in prison and emerges to make positive contributions to society, the memoir doesn't have the occasionally sanctimonious tone of *The Autobiography of Malcolm X*. Betts doesn't play the blame game, or try to evoke our pity. He admits that he is responsible for his crime, and at his sentencing trial, after hearing his attorney's defense including the absence of Betts's father, blurts to the judge, "I have to say, your Honor, that I didn't do it because I didn't have a father in the house." His second chapter, though, is entitled "Things I Know and Don't Know about My Father." His abrupt speech to the judge is, like the memoir as a whole, refreshingly spontaneous and suspicious of easy answers. It also risks contradiction and doesn't always fulfill the reader's expectations. In this regard, he may be a product of his environment; he writes, "Prison blossomed contradictions." He sees his behavior as the result of a system designed not to rehabilitate, but to harden him or make him mad: "I lived in a world that had given up on sanity."[35]

Readers may have different opinions about whether they admire or even like Betts as he portrays himself in the memoir, but virtually all readers will agree that they should listen to him. We enter prison with him, conditioned by media images; after listing the ones that weighed on his mind as he was being hauled in, he admits, "I want to tell you that I could talk tough, that I was going over every way I knew to say fuck you. But I wasn't. . . . Every movie or book I'd ever read about prison bled with violence and I knew the list I was making in my head could go on forever. . . . I was getting ready to learn what it meant to lock your thoughts inside of yourself and survive in a place governed by violence, a place where violence was a cloud of smoke you learned to breathe in or choked on."[36] Experience will be his only teacher as he attempts to protect himself, physically and emotionally, from the dangers of the world he is about to enter.

He does encounter violence, and he reacts to it as any scared young man might: by attempting to fight back. After doing so, he is promptly placed in solitary, where he is even more profoundly alone with his thoughts. He flirts with religion and ideology as powerful systems that might help save him from the woes of prison life, but none of the systems he encounters or individuals he befriends truly seizes him. He lurches through his prison experience, making some admittedly bad choices as he tries to figure out a direction. His moment of salvation comes when someone—he never learns who—slides a copy of *The Black Poets*, edited by Dudley Randall, under the door of his cell. He writes, "For a moment, reading Etheridge Knight, I began to figure that I could fish for the gray in the lives around me and write the life that I didn't see in books. Etheridge Knight weaved prison's hurt into poetry, and for the first time I wanted to write a poem that wasn't for women. A poem that was for the dudes around me, carrying time like the heaviest albatross around their necks."[37] Cleverly ending this observation with an allusion to another poem—Coleridge's "Rime of the Ancient Mariner"—Betts understands poetry as a form of salvation, but not as a ready-made one. Reading Knight's prison poetry causes him to enter upon a journey that will be arduous, and that has no ending: to "fish for the gray in the lives around" him is to reject the notion that there are black or white answers to the lives they lead. Fishing is a hard, patient pursuit that only yields results sporadically. His pronouncement implies a level of commitment, though, that he has not demonstrated before this point.

The memoir opens with one of his own poems, "Shahid Reads His Own Palm," which is also the title poem of his 2011 collection. "Shahid" is Betts's prison alter ego, a name that means "witness." In reading his own palm, Shahid witnesses himself and divines his future. He speaks of his origins: four of the poem's five sentences begin with "I come from" (lines 1, 6, 13, 17). The poem tells essentially the same story that the memoir does, evoked through poetic imagery rather than analysis: a basketball becomes an "orange globe with black stripes in Bishop's left / hand" (9–10), and he extols the rush of smoking crack cocaine as "the way glass heats rocks into a piece of heaven" (18). The final montage of images—a bullet in an unfired gun, scrambled tofu, his trigger finger, and his girlfriend's eyelashes—are both tender and violent, chaotic and controlled. The poem ultimately reflects the state of a mind consumed with competing discourses.

One of the more moving chapters in the book details his fervent attempt to get published. In the process of doing so, he writes letters on the prison's typewriter to "every poet and novelist [he admires]." When one—the poet Tony Hoagland—writes back to him, he is inspired to continue his Sisyphean task; he writes, "Being in prison, I didn't expect to have the support of people I admired. And without that support I'm not sure rehabilitation can take place."[38] Hoagland's support is a cross between luck and persistence, and it is ultimately what saves Betts by affirming the worth of his creative impulses.

Interestingly, that chapter, "Most of the Way Home," is followed immediately by one called "The Color Line," which begins, "Prison was the first place where I was around blacks and whites, Asians and Hispanics on a regular basis." Part of his coming of age in prison involves a transformation from someone so fearful of white people that he victimizes a random white man into someone mature enough to judge others (and himself) as individuals. He observes how his experience in one medium-security prison "gave me room to break down certain walls for myself," namely, the wall of racial isolation and fear. He speaks of a budding friendship with a white inmate his own age named Justin. They discuss music and books. "One afternoon I told him he was the first white guy I'd talked to on a regular basis in my life. He looked at me and asked me if that shit was supposed to make him feel special. It wasn't." And yet, the reader is acutely aware of Betts's transformation. His own need in prison is to feel connected after his deep severance from his family, and this friendship with Justin begins to build a bridge between himself and others. Writing is a continuation of that bridge.[39]

Department of Incorrections: Ted Conover

The final category of prison literature I have described—works written by volunteers or prison workers—is dominated by white male writers. Issues of race are magnified as these writers realize their majority status in terms of power and control, and also find themselves, perhaps for the first time in their lives, in the position of being in the minority of a population. The dust jacket of Ted Conover's *Newjack: Guarding Sing Sing* features a black-and-white, grainy, magnified version of his corrections officer ID with his white face and his white uniform featured prominently, evoking a mug shot from another era. The first line of the book is: "Six-twenty a.m. and the sun rises over a dark place."[40] The intent of the opening line and of the book as a whole is not to interrogate or illuminate race as much as to examine the "dark place" that is prison and the power imbalance it highlights. Yet Conover's work ends up revealing realities about the larger world highlighted by the prison complex to the same degree that Wideman, Peltier, and Betts attempt to peer into the dark places of their own experience on both sides of the bars.

Like the other nonfiction works I have discussed here, *Newjack* does not fit easily into a generic category. It is ostensibly journalism, yet it includes elements of history, memoir, philosophy, sociology, and even fiction in the way it relies on dialogue. Other authors in this genre assume the role of the mentor, whether they initially reject it or not. Conover, incognito, enters the prison as someone who is universally loathed by the inmates by virtue of his uniform. This oppositional disguise opens up a wide space for creative inquiry.

Conover's project is to reveal the institutionalized madness that constitutes the so-called logic of the modern prison. He also wants to understand whether "even seemingly decent people could be corrupted by undue authority," especially him.[41]

As his experience continues, he finds it increasingly difficult to separate his mask from his true self and is appalled to see himself acting toward his young child at home as he would toward an inmate in Sing Sing.

Conover attempts to fit into his new role by doing what he assumes prison guards are supposed to do: enforce rules. One rule pertains to the size, shape, and composition of radio antennas inmates are allowed to have in their cells. On his rounds, Conover confronts an inmate who has an illegal antenna. He pointedly describes him in terms of age and stature—"a short, white-haired man in his sixties"—rather than in terms of race, but after their confrontation, the man's race becomes clear and meaningful; he says to Conover, "You didn't tell that guy down there to bring his [antenna] in, did you? The white guy?" This line of accusation escalates immediately: "'You're just picking on the black man, aren't you? Well, have a good time at your Klan meeting tonight,' he spat out." Conover regrets his petty enforcement of rules and notes that "power and authority were at stake in nearly every transaction" in prison. What should be clear to the reader is the truth of this statement in society in general. Conover is unaware that his supposedly neutral show of power in this situation has broader implications when viewed from the vantage point of a member of a racial minority. It takes the outburst of an inmate to shock him into a kind of understanding, even as he has attempted to divide the world into inmates and guards, or bad guys and good guys, rather than into racial categories.[42]

Final Sentences

Prisoners tend to refer to all non-incarcerated spaces as "outside." The freedom implied by that word makes it difficult to accept my claim at the beginning of this essay that I am writing from behind bars. Yet it's possible to feel free while being aware that we don't always see freely. The famous brother of an infamous and anonymous criminal, a man jailed for life for a crime he claims he did not commit, a teenager locked up as an adult on a charge too trivial to justify the sentence, and a reporter who learns what it is like to be in charge of people who hate him by virtue of his uniform are all able to change our angle of vision. The bars that we construct to protect ourselves are ultimately ways of separating ourselves. We may not be willing to take them down or even to unlock them temporarily, but the real trouble begins when we pretend they don't exist.

NOTES

1. H. Bruce Franklin, *The Victim as Criminal and Artist* (New York: Oxford University Press, 1978).

2. H. Bruce Franklin, *Prison Writing in Twentieth-Century America* (New York: Penguin, 1998), xxii.

3. D. Quentin Miller, *Prose and Cons: New Essays on Contemporary U.S. Prison Literature* (Jefferson, NC: McFarland, 2005).

4. Peter Caster, *Prisons, Race, and Masculinity in Twentieth-Century U.S. Literature and Film* (Columbus: Ohio State University Press, 2008); Joy James, ed., *The New Abolitionists: (Neo) Slave Narratives and Contemporary Prison Writings* (Albany, NY: SUNY Press, 2005); Dylan Rodriguez, *Forced Passages: Imprisoned Radical Intellectuals and the U.S. Prison Regime* (Minneapolis: University of Minnesota Press, 2006); Doran Larson, *Fourth City: Essays from the Prison in America* (East Lansing: Michigan State University Press, 2014); Judith Scheffler, *Wall Tappings* (New York: The Feminist Press, 2002).

5. Rodriguez, *Forced Passages*, 29.

6. Truman Capote, *In Cold Blood* (New York: Random House, 1965).

7. Norman Mailer, *The Executioner's Song* (Boston: Little, Brown & Co., 1979).

8. See especially Baldwin's essay *No Name in the Street* (London: Joseph, 1972); James Baldwin, *If Beale Street Could Talk* (New York: Dial, 1974). See D. Quentin Miller, *"A Criminal Power": James Baldwin and the Law* (Columbus: Ohio State University Press, 2012).

9. John Cheever, *Falconer* (New York: Alfred A. Knopf, 1977); Scott Donaldson, *John Cheever: A Biography* (New York: Delta, 1988), 262–63.

10. John Edgar Wideman, *Brothers and Keepers* (New York: Vintage, 1984).

11. Andre Dubus III, *The Cage Keeper* (New York: Dutton, 1989), *House of Sand and Fog* (New York: Norton, 1999), *The Garden of Last Days* (New York: Norton, 2008).

12. Asha Bandele, *The Prisoner's Wife* (New York: Scribner's, 1999).

13. Leonard Peltier, *Prison Writings: My Life Is My Sun Dance* (New York: St. Martin's, 1999).

14. Mumia Abu-Jamal, *Live from Death Row* (New York: Addison Wesley, 1995), and *All Things Censored* (Philadelphia: Seven Stories Press, 2000).

15. Kody Scott, *Monster: The Autobiography of an L.A. Gang Member*, reprint (New York: Grove Press, 2004).

16. Bell Gale Chevigny, *Doing Time* (New York: Arcade, 1999).

17. Wally Lamb, ed., *Couldn't Keep It to Myself* (New York: HarperCollins, 2003).

18. R. Dwayne Betts, *A Question of Freedom* (New York: Penguin, 2009).

19. Larson, *Fourth City*, 1.

20. Ibid., 5.

21. Mark Salzman, *True Notebooks* (New York: Vintage, 2003); Robert Ellis Gordon, *The Funhouse Mirror* (Pullman: Washington State University Press, 2000). See also Lamb's introduction to *Couldn't Keep It to Myself*.

22. Sister Helen Prejean, *Dead Man Walking* (New York: Vintage, 1994).

23. Ted Conover, *Newjack: Guarding Sing Sing* (New York: Random House, 2000).

24. Avi Steinberg, *Running the Books* (New York: Anchor, 2011).

25. Wideman, *Brothers and Keepers*, 18.

26. Ibid., 26.

27. Ibid., 46.

28. Ibid., 195.

29. Ibid., 236.

30. Peter Matthiessen, *In the Spirit of Crazy Horse* (New York: Penguin, 1992).

31. Peltier, *Prison Writings*, 5, 4, 7.

32. Ibid., 142, 152.

33. Ibid., 176, 207.

34. R. Dwayne Betts, *A Question of Freedom* (New York: Avery, 2010), 79.

35. Ibid., 78, 181, 182.

36. Ibid., 4.

37. Ibid., 165.

38. Ibid., 216.

39. Ibid., 221–23.

40. Conover, *Newjack*, 3.

41. Ibid., 50.

42. Ibid., 98.

A Sense of Solitary Confinement

Phillip "UcciKhan" Sample

SOLITARY: done alone without the company of other people. 2. secluded in a remote location, apart from others. 3. ZOOL: used to describe animals that live alone or in pairs rather than in colonies or social groups. 4. BOT: used to describe flowers that grow singly than as a cluster.

CONFINEMENT: restriction or limitations within the boundaries or scope of something.

---

american maximum facility—I was there
in utter north ice cold Michigan where
for 700 some odd nights—frozen time no space
I encountered—the same scenes, sounds, feelings, and tastes

1 hour in a cage—3 × 4 miniscule feet
escorted to and fro via dog type leash
if I shalt dare plod too fast—they'd tug
I've even seen—many get drug

my eyes
burn from the bland gray walls that speak with
urine they reek as they watch me sleep like freaks
I seen
brotha' man lose it and take his loose fit
jump suit and construe it noose like and use it.

I hear the music—groan from swollen bluish lips
as the teeth of the cuffs eat the flesh of his wrist
him talking to himself
him screaming for help
them slamming the locker doors and punching the floors to be felt
the feeling of being alone 12 hours away from home
is this distance a coincidence or conspiracy
how long?
will they keep me here
i fear and release tears as i
ponder dude over yonder whose been here for 15 years
oh dear
can you smell it
the gas
inhale it
choke
soak towel in toilet
oh pissy cloak my throat
stings as the chemicals linger
my peers having fits
it's mixed with the stench of shit as they
succumb to environment, fear, hopelessness, and rage and
take on the ways of monkeys who when caged they
wage wars with feces
a species of man reduced
no lie even I
strong mind
hath pondered the noose.

They ignore us when they walk past
they don't see us crying
they walk too fast
I seen his naked ass
when they took him to detention
another dimension of this hole
where was his clothes?

I've tasted food loaf
do you know what that is
some shit for a dog or a pig
ol'boy is just a kid
sorry for what he did
but it doesn't matter none
cruel and unusual
hopefully he doesn't do
what timothy souder done.

    *   *   *

Without the company of other people
secluded
a lonely animal
flower
limited
what will he do when freed
how will he see what will he hear, feel smell taste
and from memory can that time be erased?

We must not answer for beasts
nor flowers even
STOPMAX!!!
as we must answer for human beings.

———————————

Writing, in my opinion, is an extension of thinking. I have been a thinker my entire life; however, it took great tragedy before I truly began to desire to write about my thoughts. When I was eighteen years of age, I found myself facing life in prison for the death of a two-year-old child. There had been a gunfight in which I was involved, and innocence was caught in the crossfire. While facing trial and trying to figure out how to kill myself as painlessly as I could, I began to reflect on my life. Those reflections became jottings and things, poems and thoughts. The committing to paper helped me to see myself more clearly. It was as if I was on the outside looking in and could thus pass unbiased judgment. As evolution would have it, I am currently finishing up my autobiography, *The Passion of The Life: The Life, Death & Resurrection of Phillip A. Sample.* I believe it is my way to atonement; for although I was found not guilty for the death of the child by a jury of my peers, I was found profoundly guilty in the court of my conscience. I am four years and counting a free man after serving 15 years for lesser charges. Writing became and remains the way I breathe, express emotion, and pay for redemption.

Solo's Life Narrative

Freedom for Me Was an Evolution, Not a Revolution

Megan Sweeney

In the following narratives, you will encounter Solo, a fifty-six-year-old African American woman who has much to say about race, imprisonment, reading, and self-evolution.[1] I was privileged to meet Solo while conducting research for *Reading Is My Window: Books and the Art of Reading in Women's Prisons* (2010) and *The Story Within Us: Women Prisoners Reflect on Reading* (2012). Over the course of several years, I conducted extensive individual interviews and group discussions with ninety-four women imprisoned in North Carolina, Ohio, and Pennsylvania. Each woman participated in one life-narrative interview, one to two interviews about reading, and four to seven group discussions of books. As Solo and other women generously shared their stories and insights, they taught me that the act of reading helps many women prisoners to situate their experiences within broader contexts, experiment with new ways of being, and maintain a sense of dignity, hope, and human community. Dominant depictions of prisoners rarely emphasize their status as readers, let alone as thinkers; reading tends to be associated only with political prisoners or self-identified intellectuals. Solo's narratives thus offer a crucial reminder of the resourceful ways in which some prisoners seek to maintain vibrant intellectual lives in settings that radically limit their access to reading and education.

Since the prisoners' rights movement of the 1960s and 1970s gave way to the retributive justice framework of the 1980s, prisoners' opportunities for reading and education have sharply declined. Prisons radically reduced their library budgets, converted library space into prison cells, and deliberately installed televisions as a pacification tool. In the prisons where I have conducted research, the libraries are now funded entirely by revenue from the vending machines. Furthermore, due to security concerns, prisoners can only receive brand-new books sent directly from publishers, which means that buying books is far too expensive for most women. Even women's access to prison libraries is limited because some penal officials fear that libraries serve as a "gay bar"; women must sign up one week in advance to visit the library, and their visits are limited to thirty minutes. Many books are also banned, including Harry Potter because it depicts witchcraft, medical texts because they include images of women's breasts, and Toni Morrison's *Paradise* because it contains "information of a racial nature" that seems "designed to achieve a breakdown of prisons through inmate . . . strikes or riots."[2]

The extent to which penal officials limit prisoners' opportunities for intellectual engagement became painfully clear to me while I was conducting research in the prison where Solo was housed. As she indicates in her reading narrative, Solo and a few other women were participating in a reading group facilitated by a member of the prison staff. The group was discussing contemporary novels such as *The Lost Scrolls of King Solomon*, *The Wake of the Wind*, and *The Secret Life of Bees*; passages from Machiavelli's *The Prince* and Sun-Tzu's *The Art of War*; social issues such as community housing and the Israeli-Palestinian conflict; and concepts such as humility and freedom. Upon Solo's recommendation, I requested permission to interview the penal employee who started the group. Much to my chagrin, my request led the penal administration to disband the reading group because it was not operating under official approval.

Prisoners' opportunities for reading have been further curtailed by legal precedents. In its 2006 decision *Beard v. Banks*, the U.S. Supreme Court deemed it constitutional for a Pennsylvania prison to deny secular newspapers and magazines to prisoners in its long-term segregation unit, on the grounds that this denial of reading materials serves as an "incentiv[e] for inmate growth."[3] Because these prisoners have no access to television, radio, telephone, or visitors, they receive no current news. The dissenting justices in *Beard v. Banks* insist that access to the full range of ideas is crucial for preserving one's sense of humanity and citizenship, but the majority opinion deems such claims moot when "dealing with especially difficult prisoners."[4] Exacerbating these trends, Congress eliminated Pell Grants for prisoners in 1994, which sparked dramatic cuts in all levels of educational programming.

At a time when the Supreme Court has authorized the *denial* of reading materials as an "incentiv[e] for inmate growth," Solo's narratives draw much-needed attention to the roles that reading plays in many incarcerated women's vital and varied efforts to think, understand, grow, and remain connected to the world beyond the prison gates. Turning to reading as a means of self-education, self-discovery, and even self-transformation, some women use the limited reading materials available in prisons as tools that help them to develop their sense of agency and responsibility, change their ways of thinking, reoccupy the present, and craft their life stories as more open-ended tales of becoming, even if they may spend the rest of their days in prison.

Each time that I read Solo's narratives, I am reminded of her powerful presence, her keen intelligence and creativity, and her hard-earned wisdom. As she describes it, Solo's path toward freedom has been a long, gradual, often painful process of becoming. She has become a woman who knows her name and her purpose, feels at peace with her past, and refuses to allow prison or abuse to dictate the meaning of her life story. Solo recognizes, however, that she has not "reached the finish line." Drawing on her own poem as her "mantra," she remains deeply engaged in the ongoing work of authoring herself.

As you engage with Solo's narratives, I invite you to reflect on the ongoing work of freedom that we, as a community, must undertake if we want to stop the flow of our community members into prisons. "You just want to beat me, beat me, beat me, punish me, punish me, punish me," Solo says of current penal policy, noting that this approach leads prisoners to become the "monster[s]" that we expect them to be. Insisting that we must instead "nurture" our society to wellness, Solo illuminates our need to address the profound social problems that fuel crime rather than relying on prisons as sites for disappearing the human evidence of our social failures. We must perform a "balancing act," Angela Davis argues, of "passionately attending to the needs of prisoners" while at the same time "question[ing] the place of the prison in our future."[5] With eloquence and grace, Solo reminds us of all that we stand to lose by continuing our current penal practices, and of all that we stand to gain—in human terms—by developing more creative and collective efforts to achieve social justice.

Life Narrative: That's a Soul That You're Stepping On

I was born in Mississippi. My maternal grandparents raised me until I was six. And then they boarded me on a train. So at the age of six, I was on a train by myself. That's a very vivid memory. It's a good memory. And I arrived in Chicago, Illinois, with my great maternal aunt. I stayed there one year, so at the age of seven, I was boarded on the train again by myself to go to Cleveland where I remained ever since. . . . I stayed with my mother until she passed away.

When I was in Mississippi, I remember vaguely getting on a big yellow bus, going to school. School, of course, was segregated. I remember the bus picking me up and all the dust that would come up with the tires, and my grandmother would have me with these pretty little dresses. She had been a domestic for the same family until she passed, so I had grew up with a little girl, and her hand-me-downs were my clothes. Of course, I had really nice clothes. And I remember I didn't want my dresses—which my grandmother used to starch and iron like she did the family's daughter's dresses, and I had a lot of petticoats—I didn't want the dust getting under my petticoats. . . . And I was teased because I had nice clothes. I don't remember too much about school other than that there were no white kids. I only saw them when I went to the family where my grandmother worked. The girl and I, we played together. I remember her father had built this playhouse in the back, and we could go in and out of this playhouse. . . .

When I got to Cleveland, it was in the winter, and my grandmother who was sending me boxes of clothes didn't have any coats for me 'cause it wasn't snowing in Mississippi, and I remember she had ordered me something out of a catalogue and that was my first time getting a Sears & Roebuck catalogue 'cause she sent it to me for me to see the pictures. And she had sent me a little red coat with a red muffler that hung around and you could put your hands in. I thought it was the cutest thing. And I remember thinking if I wear these clothes to this new school in this new city, will I get picked on like I did on the big yellow bus?

Well there was no yellow bus. I had to walk to school, and I was living on [X and Y] streets, which was a very really poor area. And all up and down [X] street at that time, all the businesses were owned by Jewish people. And I remember going to school having to go past these stores. And it seemed like everybody knew everybody's kids. So whenever I would stop and linger around—because I really was afraid to go 'cause I was going to get picked on—this Jewish lady named Ms. [X] would always call me by my name and tell me, "You better get to school, [Solo], or I'm going to tell your mother." So there was a stark reality of white and black in my childhood, but I didn't feel it in the sense of racism because they all helped me. They were all sort of supporting me.

And my only issue really was that I was being called "country" because I was from the South. Maybe I talked different. I'm not sure what I did different, but I quickly knew that I wanted to fit in, really bad. . . . I was picked on. I'd be happy to get the clothes because they came from my grandmother and they were nice. But then when I would go outside, the kids who didn't have, they resented me, and they would pick on me so I didn't want that. But I wanted to be different at the same time. To this day I can't really explain it, but I know it was a root of my criminality. I just cannot articulate it. I wanted to be different, but I wanted to be accepted. The things that the kids that I grew up around did, I never could excel in that. I never could excel in sports. I never could cuss real good 'cause there's an art to calling your momma names and I couldn't never do it right. So I was teased for that, and then I always had some kind of different way of talking that they would make fun of. I physically developed later. So just a whole lot of stuff.

And then I had been watching my mother's humiliation too. At that time, the welfare system was not like it is now. They actually came and invaded your home. And you couldn't have things. Like the mother couldn't have a TV and you couldn't have toasters and wasn't supposed to have phones, and pretty much the state actually took care of you. And we had surplus food, and they pretty much controlled our lives. So if you ventured out of that, you had to hide stuff when they come over. . . . And again, they were white. And they always wore black. It felt like it was a stark world. It was a black world and a white world, seemed like. And my mother having had work and then couldn't work, she was in debt with Ms. [X] and it's like it never ended. . . . And it was almost like the people in the store knew everything about my mother, including when she had her period. And I was feeling some kind of shame for my mother, but I didn't know why. . . .

And I remember at the age of ten trying so hard to still fit in that I started lying. I started fabricating stories. Everybody was poor, but it was things going on in my head that were different than everybody else's head. The Sears & Roebuck's catalogue that my grandmother had sent me at the age of seven became my template for everything I thought was good. So I would get these catalogues, and at that time they used to mail them to people, and I would steal them off their porch [*laughter*]. I'm seeing it, and I would come home, and I would cut families out. Of course, all the families were white, and I would cut out furniture, and I would put it in sections, and I would play like that for hours and hours. By myself. And I would change it around. I would get the Kenmore washers. I would get a daddy 'cause there was no father figure in the house, and everything came out of this catalogue. My mother had four [children]. It was me, my two brothers, and then we had a little girl, little sister. And I was responsible for keeping my sister, but I would be so occupied with this fantasy world that sometimes I neglected to dry her, and she would get a diaper rash or I would hear her crying, but I would purposely ignore it. And I didn't really study the way I should have like for homework because I was in this fantasy. So I didn't excel well in elementary school. And they were always calling my mother to the school because of this. I didn't know the answers, and I was always having to write, "I will study" or something a hundred times. Then I would always go back to that catalogue and I would save my little families in this little shoebox and dare my brothers to touch it. This was sacred to me.

My grandmother was still sending me clothes but not as many and not as often, so pretty soon I did start to look like everybody else. The clothes didn't single me out anymore. So to compensate for not having the nicer things that I used to pretend was from my sister, I used to pretend I had a sister down South. My sister's going to send me clothes. So the little white girl that was really my age—and I can't remember her name now, really I can't. I remember the family's name, but I can't remember her name—I would pretend she was my sister.

So I guess around the sixth grade, it became apparent to me that we were really poor. And so my fantasy world then became a reality in terms of lying. I had already been lying about a sister I didn't have. I wasn't doing well in school. I wasn't reading. And there was a library over on [X] Street. [X] Street at that time was the same Jewish people who owned all the businesses. They lived there. Big beautiful homes. So what I started doing was venturing further into their area by myself, and I would go up and knock on their doors, and I would say I need some money to go to the YMCA. And they would give it to me. So this became my pastime. And whenever they would open their doors, I could take a peek in and it was always beautiful furniture and of course, color TVs and drapes and carpet, things that I had saw in the Sears catalogue, but we didn't have. So I wanted to get closer to this world.

So what I did, I went into the library, and they said, "Well you need a library card." And I said, "Okay." And I remember filling out the card, and I got the card because I just wanted to be in that environment, this little ol' black girl living in that library. I remember that. I was always aware of that, not in the sense of I'm black, but nobody looks like me. That's how I knew it. And I didn't feel uncomfortable because I'm a child, and obviously, I must have been likeable because no one ever hurt me or called me the "N" word. That never happened to me as a kid. Matter of fact, they were nice to me. And that made me want to stay closer. But the irony of it is this fantasy led me to reading because now I had something that would make me unique again when I went back to my poor environment 'cause I can read. . . .

It was so much happening to me at that age, and the only time I was able to escape was in books. . . . And I remember reading a story about a little prince who comes with his poor little twin and they switch places. Maybe it's *The Prince and the Pauper*.[6] Anyway, the little poor boy switches places, and this was a pretty big book for me to read 'cause there was a lot of pages. And I would read, and the more I would read, of course, I would come home and share with my brothers. My sister was still a baby. And I would get them caught up in my world 'cause they would sit and listen to me read, and that made me feel special 'cause I could read. Well, doing this helped me to get better in school. So when my graduation came, to my surprise my teacher had nice things to say about me.

So from there we moved, and of course, the riots had came about, and the climate was different. And they had burned down most of the Jewish establishments and then there was nothing there. So instead of this vibrant neighborhood where people were buying and selling, you had all these burnt down buildings, and you smelled the decay and the rats and burnt and charred, that's the environment I had for junior high. And at this time we were living on [X] and . . . they burned all of [X] Street down 'cause that was all Jewish. . . . The Black Nationalists were there, and I had to encounter them on my way to school. The first day my mother took me to school because they were recruiting young kids. . . .

And I'm feeling the difference in my mom now than when I was little. I'm sensing a pride in my mother. She watched the news every night because of Martin Luther King and the Civil Rights and things that were going on in the South, and she was conscious of it, and she wanted us to see it. So we were forced to watch it, and she would explain it to us. So I saw racial pride in my mother at that time and a defiance. She really resented that they had burnt down everything. The Nationalists, the riots, the angry people who had no plan. Just burn it up. They had no plan. Because what they did, they took away something and replaced it with nothing. And [X] Street to this day is still nothing, but instead of her saying, "I'm glad that you took away this oppressive Jewish business woman" who for real would keep my mother in debt—I know that now, 'cause they were forever overcharging her—she was angry that it was gone, because see, there were jobs with this. There was credit with this. There was unity, and they took that away, the Nationalists and the Panthers and that whole climate took that away and replaced it with nothing.

So here I am in junior high not really feeling different as I did as a kid. Nobody's really noticing me. My grandmother has long since stopped sending the clothes. . . . And all I have is the books. So now the books I'm reading are books about Marcus Garvey.[7] We had an African American teacher who first introduced us to black history, and that was not a given topic in the '60s, and he was always being called up to the principal's office because he was very radical. I mean, this man had an Afro before Afros was popular. And he had this big beard . . . and he was always spouting off about rights and slavery and stuff. And they was always calling him in telling him to talk it down.

In my school at that time, it was still all black [students]. Desegregation was happening, but I think they did the elementary schools first 'cause I didn't encounter interracial until I got to [X] High School, but there were white teachers. And that was becoming an issue for me. . . . The Nationalists would march up and down the street as though they were protecting something, but there's nothing to protect. It's burnt down. . . . They were this huge force, dressed in black and the berets and they had the flag, and they may have even had weapons. I don't know, but it was like this huge sea of them marching up and down the streets shouting out "Freedom from the fascists!" and "Freedom!" And I have to cross the street to get to school, and they're trying to tell me, "Don't get the white man's education," but you have nothing on me. So I was angry, and I wanted them gone. And my mother had already walked me to school the first day to let them know "this one you will not get." And she had told me, "If you even stop and listen to them," and I was terrified of my mother, far more so than them. So I never heard their indoctrinations. . . . See, I had read about Huey Newton, Eldridge Cleaver, Angela Davis, Jackson's *Soledad Brother*, the whole nine yards.[8] In my way of thinking—because I'm living where you're not, and I'm seeing the decay—I'm thinking you don't even have a plan. So I always knew to join that was nothing. You're not going anywhere.

So now I'm in school, and my whole world is consumed with black history. I want to know everything. I started reading books, very upsetting books. Have you ever read the books *Mandingo* and *Master of Falconhurst*?[9] They were about slave people. They were fictional. They were extremely popular. And it was always a illicit love affair in it and a whole bunch of abuse in it. . . . I started reading James Baldwin's books. I hadn't met Toni Morrison yet. Alice Walker was there. I think she must have been very young at that time because she was writing about her marriage and down in Mississippi. . . . And I was reading Langston Hughes. That's where my world went at that point. And I was just trying to get through junior high. And so I did. Nothing really traumatic happened, to be honest. No. We were still poor, but I think I had kinda accepted it, and I had little odd jobs to compensate for that. When I got to high school, that's where integration started, and white kids were being bused in. And I think my world at that point got fused with boys. Boys became paramount, and of course, I got pregnant and I didn't graduate.

And the seed that I had planted when I was ten, when I was going to those homes trying to make my home like Sears and Roebuck, led me to commit crimes later on the pretense that I have a baby now, and I got to take care of my baby. So at that time once you turned eighteen, you could get on welfare, and of course, you could get subsidized housing. So I got that. So I'm living in the projects. . . . I was a payroll clerk out at [X], and with my creative imagination, I thought, well, I'll just write myself two checks. Didn't play it out. Didn't know that the checks are going to come back and so I got caught, but not before I got about $500. And they didn't arrest me. They didn't make me pay it back. They fired me. But he sat me down and told me, he said, "If this is the life you're about to choose, you're going to end up in prison." I didn't believe that. I'm just nineteen. And I wasn't going to the library anymore, and I wasn't reading books. Pretty much didn't have time. And it's like the streets just sucked me up. Everything about the streets sucked me up. . . . It was around the '70s, and all you heard was "You can get money. You can get money. You can get money." It was all about illegal money. And my world had just spun out of control. I never gravitated toward the drugs, but I got deeper and deeper into crime. And I did go to prison. And pretty much that's how it went. . . .

When I very first went [to prison], my mother, of course, was alive, and it was humiliating 'cause I had hurt her so bad. And I felt every day of it. The second time I went, my mother had already passed away. My mother didn't even live to be fifty. And I had become so entrenched in it to where it was like a playtime. I continued my criminal activity in prison. As a result, I spent a lot of time in solitary confinement from violating the rules. My entire criminal record is financial stuff. And I just defied authority. I was going to do it my way no matter what, and of course, I had kids, but I still wasn't thinking about that. . . .

[Solitary confinement] is terrible. That is terrible. You're in a grave. You can't do anything. Everything's brought to you and you're in a room all day, except to come out of the showers. So when I would come out, I would entertain myself by singing, doing little mock concerts. And then when I was in the room, I would develop a routine. Like I have a lot of hair under here, so I would take my hair down and take all day to braid it on purpose. Stretch the hours out. Then I might write. And I would clean the floor. And I would look out the window. And then I'd devote a whole day to just reading. I was a Christian then, trying to be. So I would read the whole Bible. I would break it down into sections. You're in a grave and you're trying to live. That's how to best describe it: trying to live in a grave. You're trying to live 'cause you're not dead yet, but nobody hears you when you call out, "Hey, I'm alive!" . . .

I was in solitary confinement [when my brother was murdered], and I remember the chaplain coming back. And no one wanted to hear the chaplain call their name because you already know it's bad news. . . . I remember when I got in there, they said it was my brother. You're so restrained so I couldn't do nothing. So I cried when I got back in my cell. And I had two more months to do in the hole so I couldn't even call my family or anything. My sister sent me a news article and I remember praying—my brother was such a good, spirited guy—that whatever had happened to him that we would find out, that the good that he did in the world would bring back the good news of how it happened, and why it happened. . . . And maybe six months later, my sister wrote me and told me that the guy that did it surrendered. . . . My brother basically was a victim of his lifestyle, because he had gotten addicted to drugs. He was out there, and guns were part of his world. But I remember him always like he was. He just had such a vibrant personality even with nothing. "You want half of what I've got? I have nothing but you can have half of it though" [*laughter*]. That was my brother. . . . He loved me. I was his big sister. I had him for the time that I had him. That's about it. . . .

Nine months [was the longest stretch that I did in solitary]. I kept going back. I was angry. I was angry at all staff. That's when I first met Warden [X] and she was the first nurturer. She came back to see me and I thought she's going to let me out, and she didn't. She said, "No I'm not here to let you out. I'm here to let you know that you have too much potential to keep wasting it like this." That's when I started getting myself together. . . .

[This time,] I graduated from college while in prison. I got my GED while in prison. I now work as a law clerk in prison. I have been extremely successful in winning cases. I became Muslim in prison. I've learned Arabic in prison. I've learned to read the Qur'an in prison, and I have learned how to put things together where I have my own program here in prison. I have a program called Act Up, and it became a DRC[10] Reentry program so that means central office has approved it for this institution. They ultimately want to implement it for the male institution so it's a possibility I could get a job out of this thing if I do it right. . . . It's a character building program. It lasts eight weeks. We graduate, the whole nine yards. I just had a fundraiser . . . and I'm pretty much trusted, for lack of a better word. I'm in charge of twenty women every Saturday for eight weeks and the recidivism rate is only one [woman] has come back in two years. And they do change, and I'm pretty damn proud of that because I could have went other ways in prison, but I didn't. . . .

I know that we all play roles. I'm just tired of playing the role of a inmate. So how do I change that? I make a transition. Everything we do in Act Up is theatrical dialogue. I get center stage. I look around. I make a decision. Stage right, stage left, whatever. I decide to make a character embodiment. I transition from who I am to being what I want to be. How do I do that? I have to get rid of the negative character traits and incorporate positive character traits through whatever means possible, through conversations, reading, television, whatever. And then I work on it like I do a script. So I learn a new script, and it becomes memorized. And then I perform. And then as a result, I change.

I've been very fortunate that Mental Health is assisting me now [with Act Up]. I have some [local] professors that come in and assist me. I have evangelists who come in. And then me. I'm the main one. I do like a fifteen minute monologue basically. And I'm like in your face. I play the role of a very aggressive motivator. And I'm very dramatic with the women. And because I'm one of them, I know what they need. I know when to back up. I know when to proceed. And then I give them a small script, like six, seven, eight, nine sentences. And the first thing they do is get a piece of Shakespeare sonnet. . . . And they have to memorize this and create a way that's fun to present it. Because nobody wants to change when it's hard, but if you can show me where it's easy, I'll benefit. So they come back and that's their first time, and they present that. And they're so creative. . . .

I have a really good team. We call it our Act Up navigate team, is what we call it. I have a unit manager, she's on board. I have a doctor from Mental Health. We have a CO.[11] We have a professional from [a local university]. We have an evangelist from outside; she's a minister. And Dr. [X] from [another local university]. . . . They each come in for like a forty-five-minute guest speaker role. . . . Dr. [X] always talks on body language. And then we do little interactive drills. Like I'll say, "How am I feeling now?" and see if they can read it. Because body language is very important, and then I give them assignments like watch the news or watch some program and tell me how you perceive that person. The two anchors, do they like each other?

Can you feel that? You can see it in the body language. What's going on with them? And then they come back and they report, stuff like that.

Then around the fifth week, I'd give them the monologue, and I'd say now the first step, you've already conquered that. You know you can memorize 'cause you just did it with Shakespeare. Okay, so now you have these characters, and they're various characters. Some I've gotten out of a thespian book. Some I make up. And so they have to memorize these. And then they practice basically the remainder of the week on these scripts. And then they do what's called an audition, and we have outside guests come in, and we have several alumni sit in. And they come in by themselves. Because in real life, when you change, you're going to step out by yourself. So you have to be able to take constructive criticism, knowing that you gave it your best, and be critiqued. . . . So four inmates and two staff or two guests come in and evaluate the auditions.

And what has happened is that the women's self-esteem has been raised so high that they want to do it, and they are creative. . . . So it's a great thing. And from that group that went home, only one woman has returned to prison. . . . It's the group that changes the women. Nobody is the same afterwards. I've seen them go from being shy, insecure, scared, feeling like a failure, to getting your GED, enrolled in [college courses], completing the horticulture course, getting in the choir, becoming dancers, acting in my plays. And what it has done for my life, it has allowed me to see that even as tarnished as I am, people—even . . . professors—will deal with me or communicate with me if I have a focus. And I didn't think that before. . . .

[Before I came back to prison,] I was working for a woman who had her own leadership development firm. . . . The first time she sent me on assignment, it was at the headquarters for [a prominent company]. And my job was to do a three-day seminar at this resort. So everything is out of my league. And I get in there and this is chemical engineers, again out of my league. And I shrunk. I thought I could do it. She just kept saying, "They're just people." They're not just people. They're like super-smart people, and I'm playing these games with them that I know work, but they're like so smart until it's not working, and I'm trying to get them to understand that they have to allow the kid in them to come out in order to be creative because they were trying to develop a new [product for children]. . . . I lost control of the group. . . . So needless to say, that was a bad experience for me and when I came back, I just didn't feel like I fit in that world. So [my boss] gave me the [X] Schools assignment. My job was to meet with her and discuss what we could do to help the school kids' academic scores go up. And again, I felt overwhelmed because these people are very smart. And here I am an ex-felon. So it didn't take long before I reversed back to my criminal ways where I felt in control, where I felt I fit. . . .

Ironically, now my world has turned back to the experience I had gotten from working with her. . . . I learned a lot from her, a great deal more than I thought because when I step up in Act Up, really I'm imitating her. . . . She got results, you know, 'cause she allowed [clients to understand that] you can retain your intelligence, but you can also be a kid, and you can learn to create and play. . . .

I have been in relationships where I've had like black eyes. I've never been severely beaten. I don't think I would tolerate that, pretty sure I wouldn't. But I did tolerate some domestic violence with my children's father, who is now deceased. I was young. He was young. We were kind of like trying to work that out. I pretty much provoked a lot of it. He wasn't per se a violent man, but I would push buttons. . . . I was raped twice by strangers. . . . I was raped once on the street, taken behind a house. . . . The other time I was at someone's house, a friend of mine, and the insurance man came over and raped me. The insurance man was a friend of his. . . . I didn't even think to tell his job or anything. I don't know why I didn't think to do it. Maybe I thought no one would believe me because he kept saying that: "You're nobody. I'm everything." . . . And strangely enough, when I hear on television and I see in movies women who are so traumatized when they go through all of that, I wonder am I wrong or are they wrong? . . . I see all that they go through, and they don't ever want to have a relationship again, and I'm thinking, but it happened to me, and I didn't get stuck in it. I just don't get it. I don't know if maybe something's wrong with me. Why didn't you care enough about you, Solo, to report it and go through the process in court? . . .

The majority of [women] come [to prison] because they have allowed themselves to be victims. And then they got comfortable in that role. "I'm a victim of my environment. I'm a victim of my relationships. I'm a victim of my lack of education. I'm a victim of the skin that I was cased in. I'm a victim of my sex." I hear it, being their legal advocate. Like I'll say, "When were you incarcerated on this case?" "Oh I don't remember." [I say,] "This is too profound for you not to know the date the police came and arrested you. It's too traumatic. How could you not know? . . . The reason you don't know it is you want to stay a victim and you want me to enable you and I refuse to do that." Then they say, "Well, you know, I was on crack." I say, "Okay, so now you have to replenish your brain cells. Have a seat. Think about it. Do you want me to help you? Then you give me something to work with." . . . I'm not going to let them be a victim. Either you stand up and be a woman with me or you go to the next clerk. You're just not going to do it with me.

Because I think the majority of the women come in, and it's easier to say, "Well, my man this or my man that." When I do their judicials,[12] I tell them, "The judge only wants to hear three things. . . . The first thing I want to hear is admit responsibility. . . . The second thing, show some remorse. Who was hurt besides you?" And a lot of times they'll think because maybe they didn't actually physically hurt someone, that no one was hurt. Then I say, "Well, let's think about this. Who is taking care of you now?" "My mother." "She was hurt. If you took a check and you wrote it and you cashed it at a bank, you hurt customers. At some point somebody else had to pay for that bad check. So apologize to those customers. Apologize to that banking institution and apologize to your parents. Show some remorse. Let the judge know that you have sat in prison and thought about God, I did hurt people. The third thing, give me a plan. You want out of prison. What are you going to do if I let you out?" . . . Now when they come to me, they're prepared. Word gets out. "Go to her, and have your stuff together." . . .

[To keep women from coming to prison,] they have to be empowered, like I was. Someone like Warden [X] has to stop and say to them, "You have too much potential to just keep wasting it." Someone like my boss has to say to me, you know, "Use your natural talents." Someone like Dr. [X] from [the local university] has to come over and say to them like she said to me, "I believe in you." They have to be empowered. It has to start when they're kids. . . . It's too easy for parents to let their kids go. I call it the second form of slavery, you know, especially for African Americans. At some point in our history, our kids were snatched from us. They fought tooth and nail to try to get that which they have brought into the world back. It's too easy now to just let Children's Services have your kids. . . . You have to go to the schools. Maybe you go to the elementary schools, 'cause whether you want to face it or not, they have sex. And you got to let them know: don't just teach safe sex or abstinence. Teach nurturing. So that if you're going to have this baby, love this baby. Teach them to love themselves as little bitty kids. Don't let a little child like I was in the seventh grade with my hand up all the time, all the time trying to learn French 'cause I love the way it sounds, and the teacher instead ignoring me and then finally telling me I didn't look right. Don't let someone crush a child's self-esteem like that.

With my kids, because of my choices, I was away in prison, and I'm sure, no doubt in my mind, somebody crushed their self-esteem. Somebody stepped on my babies' life. I know they did because I can tell by the way they believe or don't believe in themselves, and I'm their only hero. That's why I got to get it right this time. But it has to start with nurturing. I don't know what it's like in a suburban family. I mean, I'm hearing more and more that there's not a lot of differences. It's just more affluence, but as a nation, I would just say that we just got to start going back to nurturing. . . . Fathers need to know what it is to nurture. That can't just be assigned to the female sex. Any human being needs to be nurtured, needs to know that they're cared about in every area. I care about you psychologically, emotionally, physically, spiritually. They need to know that, and then we'll have a more sensitive society 'cause we'll care more about each other because we have been talked to from a baby. You know, don't just take care of my needs, my physical needs. Take care of *me*! Let me know that I matter. And that's got to start . . . very, very young because it's hard to nurture someone when they get to my age if they've allowed themselves to become extremely hardened 'cause of their conditions. It's hard to get in there! Because there's a trust issue and so much damage.

Like look at me. I'm a wreck now, you know, from something that happened in the seventh grade. My God! You think it's gone and then as soon as you say it out loud, the words hit you again. I see her! I can hear her! [*pause*] And I didn't even know how to handle that as a kid. I didn't even know how to handle that insult. I didn't know where to go with that. And then I had to come back to her class, and I just shrunk. I didn't raise my hand again. I hoped that she wouldn't see me. I wanted to disappear. I just didn't know what to do. How am I going to tell my mother the teacher called me unattractive? . . . Who's going to reprimand her for what she said to me, and how is she going to know all the damage that she caused by just that one statement? [*crying*] Oh my god. I just can't get past it [*crying*]. . . . I know that there was some kind of reverse racism because she was biracial, you know, so she was bringing some of that in it, too. . . . I don't know what it's going to take for that hole to heal up. Maybe it's going to take me raising my hand somewhere where beautiful people are, and they call on me [*laughter*]. Maybe that's it. That one has got to go. It's vicious. My god, that's too old. . . .

I've never been able to write a book about my life 'cause I've been stuck in the seventh grade. . . . When I read about other women's lives, I usually [skip] to where I am right now. Like when I read *The Color Purple*[13] . . . I identify more with the adult Celie. . . . When I read Oprah's book about her life, I get past that part about being a little kid real quick. I jump over that and I get to the adult person and I marvel at what she's doing now. . . . Princess Diana's childhood, I jump over that and I get to the woman now. . . . I do that in autobiographies or just articles, where a person starts out telling you about how they were as a kid. So I know that's a block for me. . . .

I believe right now that that's the only thing that I'm not free from because I'm no longer enslaved or imprisoned by the changes, the physical abuse, the prison, the covering of my hair, the getting older, none of that stuff has locked me down. But there's a key that hasn't been opened yet to let that kid out who just wanted to be recognized. . . . [When something like that happens,] you go home, and you look in the mirror, and you tell yourself what you just heard, and then you just start letting other people beat up on you, and then that's what leads to the whole getting enslaved, becoming imprisoned to all this other stuff, the domestic violence, the whole nine yards. . . . When I have these emotional doubts, I'm not able to sit back and say, "You know what? I got to let the little kid heal. I've got to nurture her. I've got to love her." Because I want to move so far away from her and stand near the adult person 'cause the adult survived it. The adult is strong. . . . But the little kid gets in the way. If I'm in a room where I could make a contribution, the little kid'll get scared. If people are around me and they have a great command of the vocabulary, and I hear a word I don't know what it means, the little kid pops up. And if I'm asked something, and it's a little beyond my reach, the little kid is afraid to say, "I don't know." . . . So the little kid is a problem! And she won't go away until the woman frees her.

We have to nurture, and we have to say kinder things to people. We have to realize that that's a soul that you're stepping on, you know, and by me being Muslim, I understand more now that I need to protect the soul. The body, it's going to do what it's going to do, and it's going to decay. But the soul is too good for me to have lived as bad as I have and then condemn it to hell when all I have to do is ask for forgiveness because God is all merciful. And so with a God that's all merciful, I have to do my part to preserve my soul. And then *you* have a soul. So I can't just damage your soul just because I'm in the world and I've got a mouth to say stuff. Because when I damage your soul, it blackens my soul, and then that's more cleaning that God has to do to clean me up because of things I said to an innocent soul. And if we look at people like that instead of looking at she's white, she's Spanish, she's fat, she's this, if we look at them as souls the way God looks at us, I think we'd be able to nurture more. . . .

The staff that work with me in this program, they nurture me, you know. They tell me things that inspire me. They tell me things that I don't see about myself. They tell me, "Good job." They tell me, "You're good at that." . . . Yeah, I've been nurtured here. And maybe that's why I'm done because I got it, you know. I kept coming back until I got it. . . . [The prison staff] used to be the enemies, you know, it was always a battle. But now I've received quite a bit of nurturing here. . . .

In five months, God willing, I have to step outside these gates, and I'm stepping into a Islamic world 'cause I wasn't Muslim before, so I've got to find that community and be accepted. And then I have to reenter my adult children's lives with their children. And I have to try to develop this entrepreneur mind that's busting out of my head. And I also have to work [*laughter*]. . . . So what's next is how am I going to balance all these things that I do while I'm in here as opposed to what I have to do out there, 'cause I'm not going to have that kind of time. . . . So basically what I am going to do is try to manage my time. Continue to meet inspiring people. . . . I'm going to have to adhere to all the tenets of Islam, you know. How am I going to be perceived, even my family? How are they going to feel about me, you know, all covered up? And how are people in the workplace going to perceive me with all this going on in the media?

So mainly I'm going to have to manage my time and work on staying focused and staying in character. Like I tell them in Act Up, stay in character. No matter what people say outside, stay in character. No matter if somebody calls your name, stay in character. . . . What is my character right now? That's a good question. 'Cause I'm in this transition. I want to say so bad "entrepreneur," but I know that's not real. About the only one that's really real is "woman" 'cause I can be that even without being "mother." 'Cause my kids are adults now. . . . I can play the role of woman really well now 'cause I know that's what I am.

Reading Narrative: Freedom for Me Was an Evolution, Not a Revolution

[Here in prison,] we can get a lot of fiction, but we can't get anything that they deem would incite us to rise up against them . . . or become conscious of the fact that you may be infringing on my rights. Any type of book that would give us a sense of knowing that they're wrong, they won't let us read that. They'll censor magazines if it gives that indication. But they lull us to sleep with romance! I'm telling you, four shelves of romance! Danielle Steel has a whole big huge section, and then they give us science fiction. And they'll give us a few *Newsweek*s or whatever, but you're not going to get any type of, like, *The Nation*. They won't let us have that. And no revolutionary-type biographies of say Castro or stuff like that, or anything that will cause you to get passionate and want to rise up. That's not happening.

It's books mainly to entertain. You get a lot of African American stuff dealing with fictional stuff. So you'll see women, they'll be over in the corner reading that, and they're not going to leave that corner. They don't have to worry about them [saying], "Come on, let's riot." . . . Basically, they give us books or will allow us to even order books that will either give the play to our fantasy of creating a business, or being a entrepreneur, or falling in love, or solving some kind of mystery, or knitting, stuff like that. We have a whole section of books over there on starting your own business.

The reason I say that they play to the fantasy is because it's not a realistic approach. These books are designed for people who have the capital and the wherewithal to go do it. We're in here. We're a whole 'nother segment. Then they got books that tell you how to write a cover letter and a resumé, but in reality, it's never going to be that. It's gonna be who you know that knows somebody, because as soon as you walk in with your beautiful little resumé and cover letter, there's the image of you being an ex-offender. I've tried it, and that's not how I got my job. . . . Those girls will get those books, and they'll sit in there, and they'll draft out business plans and all that stuff, and they'll be really, really excited about it. And you go home, and it's not gonna happen. No one's gonna loan you money. You haven't even worked for the last seven, eight, nine years. What kind of credibility do you have? . . .

[Useful books would be] the books that are designed to tell ex-offenders or people leaving where to go to these county, state, and federally funded places that are getting incentives for hiring us. Don't tell me I can go down here to the Marriott, 'cause I already know all they're going to hire me to do is clean a room. Send me to a place that's getting a tax abatement for hiring me. Tell me that part. Don't keep me asleep to that part. But they keep that out of here because they don't want you to know this company gets a tax break. So tell the truth and put in there the realistic positions you can really get. It doesn't matter if you come out of school with a master's. You're gonna have to first get rid of that, wash that ex-offender stuff off. Tell the truth, and tell me that what I need to learn is social interaction skills. Because I'm going to have to meet someone who knows someone to get me somewhere. So they need to have more books on that, on how to communicate with people, how to make good impressions. They need to have more books on how to survive the first six months 'cause that's the hardest. . . . How to let your pride down. I mean, I sleep in a little two by four, but when I go home I don't want to sleep in a shelter!

. . . Well, you can't afford more, so just go from one little shelter to another shelter until you're able to get you an apartment.

They need to have a book on what to expect when you get out for real, and that's what I want to do with Act Up. . . . [I need to know] what I say to the person when I meet them. How to walk into a place and impress somebody that "hey I've got some baggage, but I know I'm a good employee and I'm willing to do it. Bottom line, you want productivity. I'm gonna make that happen. You give me a chance. You don't have nothing to lose. I'm gonna show up and no, my crime didn't have anything to do with what you do. . . . Give me a chance. And you can get a little money from it, and if you don't know how, I'll tell you. They got abatements for you. Hire me, and let me be the first token. Doesn't nobody have to know."

And they need to have realistic books on that because . . . I've seen the turnover. And I'm one of the ones who they didn't expect to come back but I did, because I've gone to college, got a degree, can articulate in some situations. But I had other issues. So we need to have books dealing with those issues. 'Cause you pack all these people into this compound and you don't have the staff nor the time nor the resources, including money, to really deal with why are you an inmate? . . . And it's just like if you have a drug offense, you can't get a Pell Grant. Well, don't you think I need it? Let me get it! Can I go to college please? But if you have any drug offense, whether it's drug abuse, or it's drug trafficking, or trafficking and paraphernalia, you cannot get a federal Pell Grant. . . . You leave me no choice but to start drugs again and hope I don't get caught. 'Cause you won't let me go to school. It's crazy! And in ten years, they're going to regret these decisions. . . . You gotta nurture a society. You can't continue to punish it and punish it and punish it 'cause you cannot beat the sin out. You have to nurture the sin out. . . . You just want to beat me, beat me, beat me, punish me, punish me, punish me. And then expect me to come out of prison reformed. At some point I'm just going to become what you expect me to. I'm gonna become that monster. . . .

For me, reading is not to escape. It's more to understand me, like I read a lot of philosophy, a lot of psychology. Right now I'm reading Islamic philosophies and a book called *The 48 Laws of Power*.[14] I just got finished reading *The Prince* by Machiavelli.[15] I didn't read it because I wanted to know any military strategy. I read it because here was a man who influenced Italy, who pretty much turned the whole system around because he felt that he could change it. And he did, and he wasn't this great somebody. But the irony is that what Machiavelli did, we're doing now. We've adopted the same principles. Because President [George W.] Bush, there's no doubt in my mind he has a Machiavellian attitude because he really believes that he is the commander in chief of everything, of the universe, you know. . . . And he doesn't care if he has to lie. He doesn't care and doesn't respect anything. I am the American president! . . . And that's what Machiavelli was. Machiavelli said pretty much by any means necessary.

And then I read Dante's *Inferno*, to have an imagination of what Hell would be like and all these different levels, you know.[16] I find that interesting. And then I also find books on self-help. I'll pick them up, like a little psychology. I'll read that. I'm not too big on romance books. . . . It's always the woman waiting on some man to come and rescue her, and she run off in the sunset. I don't care how you dress it up. That's how it is. And it's too fairytale, you know. I don't care how intriguing Danielle Steel try to make it; in the end result the woman is waiting on the man to come and save her. . . . I'm not too big on fiction, but if I do read it, it's got to be mystery. It's got to be something to hold my attention. I have to be trying to figure out the end result because I will always—my DNA—I need to be in control of something. I'm a controller. So I need to have some idea of how this is going to end. . . . And I like autobiographies if you catch my attention. Like I read Oprah's book, and I read some stuff about Princess Diana. . . .

I read the book about the Delany sisters.[17] They were interesting to read. . . . [Their father] was accepted as the minister in this school, which afforded the Delany sisters—there were the two sisters and their brother—afforded them an opportunity for a very good education. . . . And the mother taught the Delany sisters independence. They can make their own soap. They could sew their own clothes, and they never got married because neither of them ever met a man that equaled their father. And one was the first black dentist in New York, and one was a teacher. . . . I just found them to be interesting because they didn't really speak of racism in the sense that you would think it would have been. They kind of like used it to their benefit. Like their father told them, "You are who you are. But it shouldn't stop you," you know. And then they had the example of their father who was very dark complected, but it didn't seem to bother him. And he was able to get a lot done, and then their mom was very fair, and she knew a lot of stuff: how to make hats and dresses, and she knew how to do teas, and so they had those cultures mixed together. . . .

But mainly, [I read] philosophy. I like the Greek philosophers. . . . I had taken a course on women's philosophy. And there was a female professor teaching it, and she was feminist. And of course, she was bringing in her own personal biases. And so she just destroyed Descartes and Socrates and Aristotle and some more that I can't pronounce their names. And she said, "Do you understand that there were no women in this group?" She said, "Why do you think that is? . . . You know why? Because the women were considered nothing. And it was all about the earth and the church and the men. And why do you think in the Bible in Timothy it says that women should not preach?" She was like, "Because they believe that we are too emotional, and we're not rational and we're not logical." . . . So she was teaching us from that perspective how women were never considered important enough, but what's more important than bringing you into the world? And she was like, "How do you think it got so twisted that men who had to be raised up from a baby couldn't respect women once they became men? Why do you think that is?" And we were trying to figure it out. And she said, "Because men are stupid! [*laughter*] 'Cause how else could you turn your back on what brought you here?" It made a lot of sense. That was a really good course that I took with her. . . .

Islam, I've been studying five years now. I get the books from the chaplain. She'll go to the Cleveland Public Library and get it. Like the philosophy of the hijab, which is what this [head wrap] is called. It's in the Qur'an as a commandment. It says that the Muslim woman should be covered so that she'll be known and respected. . . . Now it's a shariah; a shariah is the law that Muslim women should adhere to the commandments, but they don't always do it. It's still a personal choice. Like you have some Muslim women will wear it only when they make their prayers. . . . I always have to wear white in here. That's the rule. But I can't wait to wear bright, vibrant colors. . . . It's going to be fashionable. And I'm not gonna have that shrouded look like that barbarous stuff they were doing in Afghan[istan].

With this [head] covering comes a big responsibility. People see me coming, so I can't be on the yard cursing. I can't get in homosexual relationships. I can't disrespect staff. . . . This is a discipline that makes me know I'm serving God. . . . If I have a concern about something in Islam, [the imam][18] will get a book and bring it in, and I'll read it. And one of my concerns right now is that there are not many Muslim women teaching. Because the term for teacher is imam, and traditionally that's men. It's a man that comes in here. If a woman comes in, she's just coming in as a advisor. Because in Islam, the man prays in the front and the woman prays behind. . . . And I question stuff. Well why is this? But I understand why because we bend over and you know, your shape is revealed. And men . . . are not as logical as we think, and they'll be distracted quick. . . . God knows it 'cause he created us, so to avoid that temptation, don't have the women bending over.

Then I'm supposed to pray five times a day at certain times of the day. I questioned that. But now I understand it. That's done to regulate your day, to keep your mind on the right things. Because if I can stop in the middle of the day around 3:00, no matter how much money I'm making at a business, and I say no, I got to go and pray, that's going to keep me balanced. . . . [In the spiritual library,] there's an entire volume of Hadifs. The Hadifs are sayings of Prophet Mohammed written down. And some of them, I question them. Some of them, I *really* question them. Like the makeup for the Muslim women. But you have to put it in the context of where they were. Like they were really only allowed to use like henna and some sort of pomegranate. So that tells me I can still wear makeup. You just can't have it made from pork base. So it's not as constraining as people think. It's all in how you perceive it, you know. And during the course of these years of me studying it, I think it's more of a liberation to me. . . . If you adhere to all the tenets of the religion, it pretty much guides your life. And I think I needed this as opposed to Christianity. . . . It's just an orderly way to live your life. . . . Everything's supposed to be in balance. . . .

I wanted to read the Qur'an in Arabic . . . so now I know how to read Arabic. I can pronounce it and I can read it, and I know what I'm reading. . . . I read the Qur'an every day. You're supposed to read it every morning. . . . Ramadan is coming up this month. That's when we fast for thirty days, and you have to read a section called the juz. There are thirty juz in the Qur'an and you're supposed to read one every single day. And some of them are like fifteen, twenty pages. So you get up early in the morning and you read. It's sort of like a meditation. . . . And it pretty much covers everything. They have a section on nothing except women's issues. . . .

For instance, if a man has a daughter and son, and he dies, the son gets two-thirds and the daughter gets one-third. And the reason being the son is going to marry someone, and he's going to need more. The daughter's going to get married, and the husband is to provide for her. Of course, in some Islamic countries, they've abused that. . . . But if they follow it the right way God intended, then it's very equitable for the woman. And it even goes into how long you should nurse. You should nurse a baby for two years, and it's really explicit. And just like Deuteronomy talks about the woman's menstrual and all that, well it's very detailed in the Qur'an as well. . . . Basically, it's a time to leave the woman alone. . . . So it pretty much tells men how to treat you all the way around, you know.

And there's even a section in there on chastising, which I questioned that. It says that if a husband has a disobedient wife, that he should first admonish her and then refuse to sleep with her, and then third, strike her lightly. So I asked the imam about this, and I said, "Well, this here is real close to domestic violence. If somebody gets this, they might read it wrong." He said, "Well, if you get to this third stage, you should really consider not being there." And so I said, "What constitutes disobedience?" And he said, "Well, that was made in the Qur'an because of the fact that men and women argue. They don't always agree, but if you're in a relationship where every time your husband tells you something, you want to question it or argue about it, then there's a problem there. And so if you don't respect him, and he admonish you or sort of chastise you verbally and you continue to do it, then it's a problem. But if it gets to the point to where you think he's going to hit you, then that problem has escalated too far." So that's really how it's meant. It's not meant to be, "Look, didn't I tell you to stop?" Pow! . . .

A lot of my reading is for my job as a law clerk. That was one of my assigned jobs. I knew nothing about it. And when I started reading the [law] books, I was angered at first because I could have gotten out of prison that last time a lot sooner had I known the law. And then I was impressed with the male inmates who do become jailhouse lawyers. . . . And then I started winning cases, so then I felt powerful a little bit. And then you get a reputation. So the women now when they see me, "That's the lady that helps you with law," you know, so it feeds my ego. It feeds that instant gratification thing that I still have. And it also helps me do right by other souls. And then I'm able to empower them when they sit in my chair. . . . I do my best, so I just read every single law book that comes through there. . . . I read something legal every day. . . .

The way I like to read law cases, I'll get a law book, and I'll just read down the table of contents, and whenever I see cases that say "*State v.*," I already know those are inmate cases. So I read them just to see what type of cases there are. And I find it very interesting what male inmates particularly get back into the courts with. And sometimes they're successful because I guess they go to prison with a different mindset than a woman. It's always a battle with them, where we [women] become complacent and we form these little communities, you know. Men, they're constantly in a fight. . . . The more astute ones battle in the courtroom rather than out in the yard. . . .

I don't even have access to an internet. I do all my research just by reading. And every single book in that library that pertains to law, I've gotten a sense of what it means. . . . It's my job to do all the inventory, and every week we get something on the Supreme Court, federal, and state. . . . What interests me is anything pertaining to jail credit. Reduction in sentences, 'cause that's what the women need. . . . I do a lot of domestic stuff as far as getting your kids back. Divorces, custody, child support issues. . . . Mainly what I do is criminal stuff, trying to get out of prison, trying to win an appeal, trying to get jail credit or judicial hearings. . . .

What I think about the law, I understand now why lawyers start out doing it. I think they really sincerely believe in the system. Because if it's right, it works. That's what I have learned. And it's constructed beautifully, because there's a pro and a con to every single law. And you're protected by the Constitution and your right to due process. Those are beautiful rights. . . . But now that I know the law, I know that it's corrupt. It's racist. . . . I know that they play with it, and they use so many words 'til you really do get dizzy. . . . I know that the attorneys I had didn't work as hard for me. They couldn't have, because it's too accessible to me. If you were to put forth some effort, you could have found it, too. . . . I know that there's issues of racism, and when a judge knows the penalty and he leans more this way because of his personal biases, because I've read cases where I was biased. When I read those cases of those guys raping kids and they have the nerve to be in court again, I'm biased. So I know a judge sitting on a bench hearing this stuff and seeing the graphics, he's got to be biased.

But if they were to take it on face value, law is beautiful, and that's what I've learned. Had I had the knowledge of law that I have now, I would not have become a criminal. I probably would have become a lawyer because it still satisfies that drive, and that instant gratification, and that sense of controlling something. And also, predicting the outcome like I do [with] my clients. . . . I believe I could pass the bar now. I really believe that because I apply myself. . . .

One thing they do a lot, they say "pursuant to, pursuant to, pursuant to." You're the judge and I say "pursuant to Sections 777." I'm letting you know that I have gone through this book. And those cases they take more serious. If I don't put that in there and I say "pro se," they're just, "She's just an inmate. She don't know what she's doing." So I make sure I say what they say. I use their language. I look at cases in the law books and I use what I see real attorneys use. I just straight out plagiarize their language. . . . If you don't use their language, they know you're not from their club. So I use their language "pursuant to" and some of the Latin. We have a *Black's Law Dictionary*. I look up the Latin, and I put it in there. Their little codes. I've learned how to put them in there with the computer, the little legal squiggly. I put that in there, and the term "defendant humbly prays." I use that because that shows humility rather than "defendant requests," "defendant demands." That doesn't get it. But if you say "humbly prays," or if I say "wherefore defendant respectfully requests," I've learned how to embellish it to where when this judge reads it, he'll feel good inside, you know [*laughter*]. . . .

I have written things, and some things have been published. I've written what it was like to be a Muslim on 9/11 in a maximum state prison. That got published in a Muslim magazine. That got me a scholarship for a year through a Islamic university. But you had to maintain a C average, and I got a D on one paper 'cause I didn't have the resources to do a thorough job. So I lost that scholarship after two semesters. And I've written things in magazines like *VIBE*. . . . Will Smith, the actor, was criticizing his father who had been a maintenance man when he was growing up, and he was saying how he used to go with his father to fix people's refrigerators, and there would be dead rats on the floor. So I got angry, and I wrote back. And I said, "You've blown up so much that now your father's beneath you, dah, dah, dah." Whatever I said, they liked it. They put that in there. And I've written to *Ebony*, mostly letters to the editor. And when the fanatical Muslims blew up a train, I wrote a piece to the [newspaper] and I called it "Islam: The Good, the Bad and the Ugly." . . . I was saying the good of it. The bad of it is the media depicting all Muslims as those idiots were.

I wrote one piece that was published in a prison magazine, and it was a tribute to a friend of mine who is deceased now. She was an inmate, and she died of AIDS. But before she passed away, she educated all of us to her disease. And she started the first AIDS awareness program in [the prison], and she was very honest. This was at a time when we didn't know a lot about it, and a lot of people ostracized her, but I thought she was so courageous. . . . We watched her just waste away because her sentence was longer than her condition. . . . She was always telling me, "My cell count, if I can just get my cell count up." . . . And she was like really rushing to get her program together 'cause she wanted something to last, and she was like, "[Solo], promise me that you'll write to the Red Cross, and promise me that you'll write to the Disease Center in Atlanta, and promise me," and all these promises. . . . There's a team of girls now who do come around and educate you about AIDS. And they do write to the Disease Center, and they do write to the American Red Cross, all the things I promised but didn't do. So I felt kind of guilty. So I wrote an article, and it's called "Cell Count." It starts out describing her and her vibrant personality and everything, and how her life ended up just being a count. 'Cause in prison we get counted, and it's in our cells. So I thought it was really ironic that we stand up for count, cell count, and then her life ended up just being nothing except a cell count. . . . I sent it to *Angola Speaks*. The men produce it in the prison in Louisiana. And one of the editors, he wrote me back, and he's been in solitary confinement for thirty years. . . . So I wrote him back, and we corresponded for about a year. And he made sure that it got published in its entirety. . . .

I'm thankful for [a reading group led by the unit manager] 'cause that keeps me healthy intellectually because that's all we deal with is the intellect.[19] It's not a group where you go and cry or get built up. It's just a group where you go and you logically talk about something. He sets it out, and then we research, and we come back. And he allows us an opportunity to write short stories. He'll give us the vocabulary words that we have to learn, like one of the words we had was "nocturnal," which I did know what that meant. "Incident," I didn't know what that meant. Had to look it up. "Macrocosm," I didn't know what that meant. I had to look it up. And then you had to put it in a short story. . . . When I'm going to his room, I know that I'm going to have to be sharp, and I know that he expects me to bring my best. He won't accept papers with misspelled words or scratchy outs. You know, if you're going to present it, present it right. . . . If he gives you an A, that means he was really impressed with it. And then you want to see an A on your paper. . . . Then he gives us these titles of books to read, and it's an assignment so you have to read it and then you have to give a summary on it. And then you have group discussions, and you have to articulate, and you have to explain yourself. So you stay sharp, you know. You don't get dull. . . .

In a lot of groups, you start digging in, and when you dig in, stuff comes out and you cry. So it's good to have a group where I know I'm not going to be dug into. He's not even trying to get there. He's only here [pointing to her head]. We don't talk about my childhood or my past or my crime or addictions or men or relationships or my self-esteem. None of that comes up. So I don't have to deal with it. All he's dealing with is my intellect. . . . Everybody in the room is here [pointing to her head] . . . and I'm not passing tissues, you know. . . . Even in the law library I have started crying with people. Just sheer knowledge of what they're telling me sometimes just tears me up. And I end up crying and they're crying, too. Even when I go to my Islamic services, I cry at some of the things the imam will say about the prophet or the mercy of God and how he loves me so much. . . . In this group, the posture is totally different. Everybody's sitting there with a folder. They're sitting up erect. And he's at his desk. And we're like surrounding him, and he plays real soft jazz in the background. And he just throws stuff out there. He'll say, "What do you think about that?" And he'll wait a moment and he'll say, "You do have an opinion?" And we say "of course." He says, "Well then, what do you think about it?" . . . And before it's over everybody has said something, and you feel like Wow! . . .

I believe tears have their place. It's just I don't want to cry all the time 'cause it bogs me down. I can't see the end when I'm stuck in that emotion. And I couldn't proceed. It's like inertia. You cannot move, and I don't like that. But it's okay sometimes because it's a slowing down. Sometimes I hear spiritual music, and I'll slow down and I'll cry. I keep my family pictures [hidden] on purpose so that when I pull them out, I can be like whoa. You know, I don't want to see them all the time . . . so I can bring them out and feel the whole emotion rather than pass them every day and they become blurs. So yeah, those groups are good, you know, because a lot of pain gets out. But you have to be careful when you're exposing pain because we become vindictive here. And I'm okay with you today but do something to me next week, and I'm gonna mention what happened to you in group, and I'm gonna hurt you with it. . . .

I want to be impacted when I read. Like for instance, the one book that he had us read [in the group], *Wake of the Wind*,[20] that book impacted me, and I was also able to carry something with me because . . . it wasn't just a slave story. It was a love story, and then it was a story of survival. . . . And the woman in the book, her name was Lifey, and she was biracial and she knew it because of her lighter complexion. The real wife didn't want her in the house because she knew that [her husband] was Lifey's father. . . . That story impacted me, and I was able to feel the hurt of the slave, but then I was also able to rejoice with Lifey when at the end [she and another former slave] had settled in Georgia. She had saved up enough money, and here's this man she loved. He couldn't read, he couldn't write, he couldn't do nothing, but he was a hard worker, and he was able to build them a home. . . . So I rejoiced with her, and then I was able to move forward knowing wow, I can do it. Lifey did it. I mean, I loved it so much I made a crossword puzzle about it. That's how much that impacted me.

[For one assignment,] the group leader said, "Okay, I want you to write a poem about freedom," and everybody else was writing all this historical stuff and all that. I just sat down, and I just started thinking about myself. And I wrote this poem called "Freedom," and after I reread it to myself, then I went to the class and I had to read it out loud. You have to stand up and you have to present yourself. And he listened and everybody else listened. Then he asked them what they thought about it. So after I heard all their opinions of it, I really liked it a lot more. And now it's like my mantra. I love that poem. . . . And when I had to read it outside at the poetry fest, I read it, and I just was feeling it, and I had put on a black—I was defiant that day; I wouldn't wear white—I had a black headpiece on, and I was standing out there in that hot sun, and I read it like this:

> The essence of the word freedom is a state free of restraints, liberated, independence, exempt from unpleasant or onerous conditions, free will, unrestricted access and the ability to pursue unalienable rights.
>
> I, [Solo], exemplify freedom in its totality of this description. From the covering of my splendidly natural hair, to my brown eyes which no longer endure the pain of blue and blackened eyes swollen from abuse, to my mouth unclosed and expressive, to my ears now open to receive instruction, advice, and acknowledgment, to my neck, elegant, loosed from shackles of ignorance, to my shoulders erect and bold, not bent from shame, to my heart filled with optimism and expectancy, to my stomach less flat yet more satisfying, to my broader hips, which still retain the rhythm of the drum beats, clear down to the very soles of my Black feet, calloused from all the years of walking towards freedom.
>
> I am Free!
>
> For me, freedom has been an *evolution* not a *revolution*. See, my freedom was gained through years of self-inflicted struggle, through increments of embraced ignorance, which was demonstrated in collective acts of pure foolishness. Freedom for me was elusive. I could not purchase it; consequently, I saw no way to ever own it. I could not believe in this reality because I had no faith. Freedom for me was always close, like my baby sister and like my child. I had birthed it but I would not name it; consequently, I could not claim it. Remember, freedom for me was an evolution and not a revolution. For me, freedom crept in slowly on cat's paws, quietly and unassuming.
>
> It happened like this. One day I opened my mouth and said exactly what I meant to say and I liked it. Then, I stood up refusing to dine on entrees of morbid lies and delicacies of hypocrisy and petite deception, and I liked it. I walked away from plentiful dependence to limited independence, and I liked it too! Freedom for me was an evolution and not a revolution.
>
> There were no star-spangled banners, no rockets' red glare. Instead, it was dark and I was naked, just standing there. Standing for my faith, standing for unalienable right to exist, standing for my children's children to have a voice, and standing for my choices, which today define who I am.

Freedom for me was an evolution and not a revolution. Yes, I have run the longest race, but I have not reached the finish line. Indeed, I have developed, but only God can create. Surprisingly, I have harbored, but few have I actually helped to freedom and for this, I apologize.

Each day, I evolve the woman you perceive me to be, yet tomorrow, I will rise a new creature conceived in love and renewed hope. Freedom for me was an evolution and not a revolution. America, America, God shed his grace on thee, and crown thy good with brotherhood from sea to shining sea! Not so, sista! Freedom for me meant shaking off the dust from the Mississippi slave cabins hot and stifling like the heavy air hanging over unpicked cotton fields to a cold and barren, empty grave with the letter X as its marker.

Freedom for me crept in around my edges and around my corners, in places so unprotected that I became helpless to stop its advancement, hallelujah! Freedom landed on my shore, set up camp, declared victory, and pledged allegiance to my soul!

For me, freedom came and slept with me, it held me close during the midnight of my existence, and baptized me with my own tears until I was thoroughly thoroughly cleansed of inferiority, low esteem, and self-loathing.

Then I awoke in the beautiful morning of my middle age, early before the sun came up, then I *stood* up a woman who knew her name, knew her purpose, knew her past was that and nothing more than that, knew her life was meaningful, worthy of saving from both prison and abuse, and knew that her spirit was a merciful and most precious gift from God Almighty.

Freedom for me was an evolution, not a revolution.

Then I ended it like that. I just love it. I was proud of that. And I wouldn't have gotten that had it not been for that class. . . . I've never written anything that has impacted me back, you know what I'm saying? And I like it. Because when I read it, see, I'm all of what I'm saying. I evolved into who I am. I didn't just like break out and be, like some sort of revolution. It was slow, and everything that's been done to me, I did it. I mean, nobody made me do anything. . . . I know now that I was just foolish. There was absolutely no reason for me to come back and forth to prison, but I chose the lifestyle that could only result in prison. . . . I chose to limit my potential. So it wasn't like my environment. It wasn't because of my poverty. It wasn't any of that, or lack of education. It was a conscious choice to live on the edge and do illegal activities. So there's no man to blame or drugs or any of that. None of that. It was just a conscious decision.

And I didn't know that freedom was this easy because had I known it, I would have had it a long time ago. I birthed it, but I couldn't claim it. I couldn't name it 'cause I didn't know what it was. I thought being with a man maybe was freedom, or having a lot of money was freedom. But really it's none of that. It's just knowing who I am, the woman that I am, and knowing my history. Not per se black history; just knowing my part of it. Where did I come from? And who am I? And just taking a real good look at me. And like when I say, "It was no star spangled banner," it was no big celebration. Didn't nobody say, "Oh Solo, you've arrived." That's not how it was. I was just by myself in this prison cell. Naked, not literally, but void of all the material wrapping and trappings, you know. . . .

I have already missed my children's little voices. They're adult voices now, but they have kids. So I gotta make a stand now for them. Stand for something, and my choice to stay free. And you know, I'm an American, and I love that. I wouldn't trade it, but I know what I am in America, too. And I know on any given day depending on where I am, I won't be accepted. . . . I don't have the same freedom in America. 'Cause there's not no brotherhood from sea to shining sea, now. That's not it. 'Cause see, that Mississippi slave cabin still goes with me, and somebody without a name, like X, still goes with me. . . . But I can honestly say that my mother, I think she'd be proud of me because I didn't turn out a racist. . . . I understand that it's not just a person waking up hating me. That it's a lot of stuff going into that. . . . And I understand the fear that feeds that hate because I saw a lot of that stuff. . . .

When I say, "I evolve the woman you perceive me to be," they see me one way here, but really I'm different every day. I mean, they're very quick to tell me who I am here. . . . 'Cause they watch me, you know, and they tell me who I am, or who they perceive me to be at least. But what they don't know is that every day I wake up, I'm different. Some of what I was yesterday comes with me . . . but each day brings a new challenge. . . .

And I keep repeating the refrain "Freedom for me was an evolution and not a revolution" more so for me to hear it. That where I've come so far; just remember girl, you didn't always have this. You have evolved and evolution is continuous. Revolutions come and go. . . . It wasn't like a violent change for me that would require me to always be on the ready. It's gradual. . . . Things change with me, and I don't see them. . . . So it's like an evolution. Things happen in your sleep, you know. . . . I repeat it for me, to know that I'm steadily evolving, and then I end it with "freedom crept in around my edges" 'cause I didn't see it coming [*laughter*]. I didn't see that, you know. It must have landed on my shore and just set up camp 'cause I didn't even know it. It must have got down and said, "Hey, I'm here to stay." I did not know it, and it must have slept with me and just held me close or something because I just didn't know it, and I know I cried a lot, but I didn't know that crying was cleansing me. . . . And then I woke up in my middle age. I'm not sad about that because I got up early enough before the sun came up, and I saw me first before the world saw me, and by the time you met me about eight or nine [o'clock], I was a middle-aged woman. And I'm okay with it. And now I know my purpose.

NOTES

1. The interviewee chose the pseudonym "Solo" to protect her privacy. Solo's narratives are composed entirely from spoken, audiotaped interviews. I am nonetheless aware that my interviewees inevitably filtered and shaped their stories for me, telling me only what they chose to tell and how they chose to tell it, and our interactions were inevitably inflected by my position as a white, middle-class literature professor. Furthermore, I recognize women's descriptions of their reading practices as constructed accounts rather than literal reports of what takes place when they read. I gave participants an additional opportunity to shape their narratives by asking them to review and redact a complete transcript of their interviews. In editing Solo's interviews, I removed my own questions, omitted some portions to reduce length and repetition, and excised details that would compromise confidentiality. I also rearranged some paragraphs to enhance the narrative flow and make Solo's contributions as clear as possible; doing so was particularly important in editing her reading narratives, which stem from two separate interviews. I include ellipses to indicate places where I removed words, and I have taken care not to erase contradictions or alter the meaning of Solo's statements.

2. Toni Morrison, Letter to Wahneema Lubiano, September 1998.

3. Quoted in Stephen Breyer, Majority opinion, *Beard, Secretary, Pennsylvania Department of Corrections v. Banks*, No. 04–1739, Supreme Court of the United States, June 28, 2006, 2.

4. Ibid., 11.

5. Angela Davis, *Are Prisons Obsolete?* (New York: Seven Stories, 2003), 103.

6. Mark Twain, *The Prince and the Pauper* (Boston: James R. Osgood and Co., 1881).

7. Marcus Garvey was a Jamaican intellectual, publisher, journalist, and entrepreneur who was a staunch proponent of Black Nationalism and Pan-Africanism.

8. Huey Newton, Eldridge Cleaver, Angela Davis, and George Jackson were all involved in the Black Power movement. George Jackson, *Soledad Brother: The Prison Letters of George*

Jackson (New York: Coward-McCann, 1970).

9. Kyle Onstott, *Mandingo* (Richmond, VA: Denlinger, 1957), *Master of Falconhurst* (New York: Dial Press, 1964).

10. Department of Rehabilitation and Corrections.

11. Corrections officer.

12. A "judicial" is a petition for early release.

13. Alice Walker, *The Color Purple* (New York: Harcourt Brace Jovanovich, 1982).

14. Robert Greene, *The 48 Laws of Power* (New York: Viking, 1998).

15. Niccolò Machiavelli, *The Prince* (1532).

16. Dante Alighieri, *Inferno* (c. 1317).

17. Sarah L. Delany, A. Elizabeth Delany, and Amy Hill Hearth, *Having Our Say: The Delaney Sisters' First 100 Years* (Thorndike, ME: G.K. Hall, 1993).

18. An imam is a Muslim religious teacher or leader.

19. Upon the recommendation of a few women participating in this group, I requested permission from penal officials to interview the group's organizer. Unbeknownst to me, the administration was not aware of the group until I brought it to their attention, and they promptly shut it down because it was not operating under official approval.

20. J. California Cooper, *The Wake of the Wind: A Novel* (New York: Doubleday, 1998).

Outside the Fences

The Rewilding of the Motor City Viewed from a Prison

Rand Gould

O utside the fences, the tom turkey jumped up on the rock, stump, or some piece of junk he was using as his stage, spread his feathers, and gobbled away, noisy and impressive. All the more so as it was happening just a few feet away from the fences of Mound Correctional Facility, a state prison in the city of Detroit.

It was 2010 and I'd just been returned to Mound after being transferred out in '05 and taking a five-year tour of the Michigan prison system, pulling chain from Kincheloe in the Upper Peninsula to Ionia, St. Louis, and back to Detroit. During which, I managed to see my fair share of wildlife, as expected when you're plunked down next to a woods or fields in an isolated rural area.

Born and raised in Detroit, the Motor City, I was familiar with this neighborhood, as I worked several blocks away prior to being framed by the police on this case in '98. At the time, the local wildlife consisted of various small birds, such as sparrows, starlings, robins, and pigeons; rabbits living in the nearby cemeteries; and a pair each of red-tailed hawks and snow owls that stopped by every spring and autumn to feast on rats—the denizens of the Coney Island next door to where I worked. After it was condemned and torn down in '97, the rats left and the hawks and owls disappeared.

I had first arrived at Mound prison in 2003 and was pleasantly surprised to see it was part of the hawks' travel itinerary, where they preyed on a large population of pigeons, fattened up on the bread thrown to them by prisoners leaving the chow hall. A pair of Canada geese and some seagulls also benefited from prisoners' generosity. There wasn't much else in the way of wildlife, except a couple of pheasants, mourning doves, and rabbits living in the saplings and brush alongside the railroad tracks just outside the fences.

Upon my return, I was happy to find a veritable cornucopia of local wildlife. Outside the fences, along the railroad tracks, the saplings had become trees and the brush denser, creating a greatly improved habitat for over a half dozen pheasants, a dozen or so mourning doves, and numerous rabbits. A flock of turkeys roamed up and down the tracks, a red fox could be glimpsed making a quick foray out of the brush, red-winged blackbirds sang in the reeds, swallows flitted back and forth, and goldfinches fed on thistles growing in between the fences—none of which I had ever seen in the city before.

The hawks were still boldly slaughtering pigeons, and I once saw a peregrine falcon join in the fray, willing to abandon its downtown skyscrapers to dine on our pigeons. The guards informed me they've seen skunks (I've smelled 'em), possums, raccoons, wild dogs, and what they think are coyotes inhabiting the abandoned properties outside the fences.

No doubt the animals are using the all-but-abandoned railroad tracks as a corridor to move into and around the ruins of Detroit—a veritable sea of abandoned properties, where block upon block of homes sit vacant and derelict. The only businesses that seem to thrive are nearby junkyards and scrap yards, aside from Mound and its sister prison, Ryan Correctional Facility, with Mound scheduled to close and become one of those abandoned properties in 2012.

It's only a matter of time before the remaining people in Detroit will be able to hear coyotes howling in the night and feed deer in their backyards—making the traditional family trip to the Detroit River's Belle Isle to feed the wild herd of little Formosan deer unnecessary. All of which gives me some hope for the future of the planet. If the animals can survive and thrive here, in the toxic ruins of the former industrial powerhouse known as the Motor City, they can survive anywhere, and that goes for us Motor City humans too!

Criminal Justice, Disconnected Youth, and Latino Males in the United States and in Michigan

Rubén O. Martinez, Bette Avila, and Barry Lewis

The turn toward penalty and mass incarceration through mandatory sentencing policies in American society has placed the United States as the leading incarceral society in the world.[1] Between 1980 and 2016, the number of persons under the control of the American criminal justice system increased by 259 percent, from 1,842,100 to 6,613,500.[2] Dramatic increases in the number of incarcerated men of color raise serious questions about the criminal justice system in this country and their detachment from labor markets.[3] While incarceration rates and the number of prisoners have declined slightly in recent years, Latinos and African Americans are still overrepresented in America's prisons.[4] Moreover, we can expect that the extreme punitive policies of the Trump regime against immigrants will continue increasing the number of Latinos in the nation's jails, prisons, and detention centers.[5] For example, of the 66,873 sentencing cases reported to the U.S. Sentencing Commission for federal offenses for the period October 1, 2016, through September 30, 2017, there were 35,198 Latinos, and 19,445 of the cases involved immigration offenses. Today, immigrants are the fastest growing segment of the federal prison population, making up approximately 22 percent of the total, many of whom are in private facilities.

The State of Michigan, with approximately 0.5 million Latinos, has the second largest Latino population in the Midwest. Although Michigan had historically been regarded as a leading social democratic state in the nation, in which capital and labor had reached a compromise in sharing profits in pursuit of a higher social order, it took a punitive turn in 1984, when incarceration rates began to climb rapidly.[6] The disproportionate incarceration of Latinos and other minority group members demonstrates the influence of the state's punitive approach under the combined ideologies of social conservatism and neoliberalism.

We emphasize both neoliberal policies and racism in relation to the large numbers of Latinos incarcerated across the nation and in Michigan, and call on policymakers to consider the disparate impact of mass incarceration, coupled with increasing racist rhetoric, on racial/ethnic minorities. Passel and Cohn at the Pew Hispanic Center estimate that as early as 2050, whites will constitute a numeric minority of the population (47 percent) at the national level due to low growth rates, while Latinos and other racial/ethnic population groups will experience higher rates.[7] Latinos are projected to increase to about 29 percent of the population by 2050, which looms on the horizon, and policymakers should consider the fact that "managing" minority populations through mass incarceration will be politically difficult as the population landscape continues to change, especially in the context of broad public concern about racial issues in incarceration and sentencing rates. Furthermore, full incorporation of Latinos and other racial/ethnic minorities into the nation's mainstream institutions is vital to national progress and requires abandoning the repressive measures that are part of neoliberalism.

The number of incarcerated Latino males has risen in recent decades.[8] Between 2000 and 2010, the number of Latino males in state and federal prisons increased by 118,800 prisoners, reflecting an increase of 57 percent, while white male prisoners increased by 12,900, or 3.0 percent. The number of black male prisoners decreased during the same time period by 14,200, or by 2.5 percent.[9] A report from the U.S. Department of Justice set the number of state and federal prison inmates at the end of 2010 at 1,612,395, representing the first decline since 1972, and possibly signaling a shift away from the trend toward increased mass incarceration.[10] There were 9,228 fewer prisoners at the end of 2010 than there were at the end of 2009, reflecting a decrease of 0.6 percent. Still, according to the *Statistical Abstract of the United States, 2017*, an estimated 9.5 million persons were under some type of correctional supervision (community supervision, probation, and parole) in 2014.[11] Of these, 4.7 million were under community supervision, 3.9 million were on probation, and 0.8 million were on parole.[12] Those in jail numbered 0.76 million, and another 1.5 million were in state and federal prisons that same year.[13]

A breakdown by race/ethnicity shows that 320,000 Latino males were incarcerated in state or federal prisons at the end of 2016, up from 308,700 in 2014.[14] In 2016, some 466,600 African American males and 390,900 white males were incarcerated in state or federal prisons, down from 516,900 and 453,500, respectively, in 2014. The incarceration rate for Latino males sentenced to at least a year in prison was 1,092 per 100,000 Latino male residents, compared to 2,415 for African Americans, and 400 for white males.[15] Latino males were approximately 2.7 times more likely to be held in custody compared to white males at the end of 2016. Overall, if current trends continue, one out of every six Latino males can expect to go to prison in their lifetime compared to one out of every seventeen white men.[16] However, a word of caution is warranted with regard to the number of Latinos within the criminal justice system given that standard categories of race/ethnicity are not used uniformly across the states, with several classifying Latinos as "white" without providing for the recording of ethnicity.[17] Mass incarceration patterns in Michigan are similar to those at the national level.

In Michigan, where incarceration rates increased sharply from 1985 through 2007 despite decreases in homicide rates,[18] the number of Latinos in the prison system is unclear due to the lack of transparency in the state's criminal justice system and the absence of readily available official statistics on its prison population by standard categories of race/ethnicity. Some sources suggest an incarceration rate of 397 per 100,000 Latinos in the population in Michigan.[19] This figure places Michigan near the bottom of state rankings relative to Latino inmates, although this figure should be interpreted with caution because of the historical inaccuracy of data collection on Latino inmates. The state prison system does not report data on Latinos, citing insufficient resources and time, or the absence of a requirement to do so. The result is that the Michigan Department of Corrections does not use standard "race" and "ethnicity" categories to report on prison populations. The latest report available uses "White" and "Non-White" categories.[20] Twenty years ago, annual reports used the standard categories, but that is not the case today. One study found that when given a choice of White, African American, or Asian, 95 percent of Latinos selected "White" or "Other," resulting in severely skewed data that undercounts the number of Latinos in the prison system.[21] Further, Michigan is one of a handful of states that still automatically prosecutes seventeen-year-olds as adults, with the option to remand to the juvenile justice system.

A study by Villarruel et al. showed disproportional numbers at the national level of Latino youth under the age of eighteen in prison systems.[22] After surveying fourteen states and the District of Columbia (sites chosen for their large Latino populations or significant growth in the Latino population), researchers found that Latino and Latina youth were disproportionately within the grasp of the criminal justice system. For example, in the year 2000, Latino/a youth were seven times more likely to be institutionalized or held in juvenile detention facilities in Michigan compared to white youth. Additionally, Latino/a youth in Michigan were twice as likely to be incarcerated than white youth, and of the fifty states, Michigan was the sixth worst in its overrepresentation of Latino/a youth in the criminal justice system in 1999.[23] These statistics reveal the harsh reality that Latinos tend to become involved with prison systems at a young age, and many experience cycles of imprisonment throughout their adult lives.

Consequently, it is not a surprise that a 2006 U.S. Census Bureau report showed that nearly three times as many Latinos were living in prison cells than in college dorms—that is, 2.7 Latinos in prison for every Latino in college housing.[24] These numbers were driven primarily by men, illustrating the growing number of racial/ethnic minority men who have become part of a mass incarceration epidemic. The Latino population in general increased by 495 percent between 1970 and 2016, and now represents the largest ethnic minority group in the United States.[25] It is of critical importance to move beyond the historical dichotomization of incarcerated populations into white and black categories.[26] This should be done in Michigan as well, despite the fact that the Latino population is relatively small (5.0 percent of the state's population), and where it is difficult to locate official data on prisoners by standard categories of race/ethnicity. Given the relatively high numbers of Latino youth within the criminal justice system, it is important that official statistics in Michigan include Latinos as a specific population group.

The failure to report Latinos in official statistics in Michigan not only neglects the nation's largest ethnic minority group, but also fails to provide transparency and limits investigator capacity to examine factors that impact Latino incarceration and the resulting consequences on future life chances and the impact on families.[27] An abundance of literature documents that young Latino males lack connections to mainstream social institutions, such as formal employment and education,[28] and that these disconnections are associated with participation in gangs and illegal activities, and other behaviors that may lead to arrest and subsequent incarceration.[29] Although Latinas also are disproportionately represented in state and federal prisons compared to white women, Latino men are more likely to occupy state and federal prisons than their female counterparts and white men.

The Drive to Incarcerate, Neoliberalism, and Racist Rhetoric

The drive to incarcerate was set in motion by the rise to power of the New Right (best represented by the election of Ronald Reagan to the presidency in 1980), which has disparately impacted communities of color through its anti-drug and zero-tolerance policies.[30] In particular, racial/ethnic minority men have suffered as a result of policies aimed at incarceration, as evidenced by their large and disproportionate numbers in the criminal justice system. We argue that neoliberal or free-market fundamentalist policies based on the principles of radical individualism, a small state, deregulation, privatization of government functions, and flexible labor have contributed to the increased marginalization of communities of color.[31] Specifically, the most vulnerable have been left behind as legislators cut funding to schools, health care, and social services, and outsourced basic services for human well-being.[32] Overall, it is poor people in disadvantaged communities that suffer the consequences of neoliberal policies, as they languish in underfunded schools and confront barriers to formal training and employment. In 2016, for instance, 36 percent of Latinos and 38 percent of African Americans ages twenty to twenty-four years who were living in poverty were neither in school nor employed, compared to 27 percent of their white counterparts.[33] Ultimately, neoliberal policies result in cyclical patterns of disconnectedness from society's mainstream institutions among poor persons.[34] As Latinos have become the largest ethnic minority group in the country, indicators of their status have begun to converge with those of African Americans, who historically were the largest, most disadvantaged minority population in the country.

Latino populations today are segregated in disadvantaged communities, thereby bearing the brunt of neoliberal policies while corporations reap the benefits both here and abroad.[35] To manage the problems of those living in disenfranchised communities without adequate social supports, education, and employable skills, and who may be forced to turn to illegal activities to survive, neoliberal politicians have offered up a morbid solution: a prison system to lock up the "surplus population" even if it works against the financial interests of the state.[36] However, this approach provides a double benefit to the most powerful in society as politicians are able to tout a message of "cleaning up the streets" while corporations incarcerate prisoners in their privatized prison systems, where every prisoner contributes to profits.[37] Thus, it is to be expected that the New Right has not only emphasized neoliberal ideas, but also punitive measures against criminals, rather than their rehabilitation.[38] This includes longer sentences that contribute to the profit margins of private prison corporations, such as CoreCivic (formerly Corrections Corporation of America, or CCA) and the GEO Group, Inc., and their investors, despite evidence to suggest that the promised cost savings have not materialized and the general public prefers rehabilitation measures over punishment.[39]

However, it isn't just neoliberal policies that sustain the mass imprisonment of racial/ethnic minorities. Criminal justice policies are often formulated around the fear of crime, and criminal justice is inherently racialized.[40] For example, while African Americans (particularly males) have historically served as dangerous "superpredators" in the psyches of white Americans, Latino males, "the bandidos," have begun to fill this role as rapid Latino population increases have engendered powerful nativistic movements among white Americans who are threatened by the unfolding, rapid demographic shift that has been underway since the 1980s. Interestingly, the rise of the Latino population to the largest ethnic minority group in the country has been attended by increases in their numbers in prisons across the country as fear about a violent and imagined "other" in need of containment coalesces with the New Right's emphasis on using punitive measures against those deemed criminal.[41] As Jose Luis Morín points out: "Latino/as, like African Americans, are perceived as a poor class of people of color that pose a threat to the social order, and thus must be controlled and dominated."[42] This message is often exacerbated by mass-media portrayals of Latinos as criminals in the daily news where law-enforcement officials convey stereotypes of violent crimes committed by Latino gangs.[43] More recently, President Trump has described Latino immigrants as drug-dealing criminals and rapists, frequently including native-born Latinos in his public diatribes.

Theories of Racial/Ethnic Minority Crime and Incarceration

Several theories have been presented that specify the causes of criminal activity among racial/ethnic minorities. Specifically, structural theories, cultural theories, and theories of police and criminal-justice system bias have been used to explain the higher rates of crime in minority communities relative to white communities.[44] However, other theories emphasize ecological explanations, such as residential inequalities that isolate the truly disadvantaged within particular neighborhoods, leading to structural barriers and negative cultural adaptations in these communities.[45]

Structural Theories

Relative deprivation theory suggests that low educational attainment, joblessness, and employment in low-paying jobs are linked to higher crime rates.[46] For example, the absence of suitable employment opportunities that offer stability and livable wages is likely to promote higher levels of crime and violence as increased idle time due to unemployment or unstable employment places individuals in contexts that contribute to criminal activities.[47] Additionally, lack of adequate employment and high rates of unemployment contribute to the likelihood that individuals will participate in the black market or illegal economy to survive.[48]

These theoretical perspectives have some pertinence to Latino men, who have higher rates of both poverty and unemployment than their white counterparts. Poverty rates among Latinos (19.4 percent in 2016) have remained consistently higher than the national rate (12.7 percent) and that of non-Hispanic whites (8.8 percent).[49] And those who are employed tend to be concentrated in three industries: production and transportation, construction and maintenance, and services. Latino males have consistently had the second highest unemployment rate among the largest population groups. In the third quarter of 2016, for example, 5.2 percent of Latino males in the civilian labor force were unemployed, compared to 4.3 percent of white males and 8.9 percent of African American males.[50] Moreover, the rates for males sixteen to nineteen years of age were 19.0 percent for Latinos, 13.9 percent for whites, and 33.3 percent for African Americans.[51] As Latinos in general are integrated into the nation's racial division of labor, with Latino males occupying mostly "blue-collar" jobs that no longer offer the pay rates or fringe benefits of a few decades ago, the current education crisis in today's neoliberal policy environment ensures that they will become the majority of the low-wage workforce.[52]

Studies that have examined school dropout and delinquency among Latino adolescents have shown that one of the main factors linked to delinquent behavior is poor academic status. That is, consistent attendance and academic success in school coincided with a lower incidence of delinquent behavior. Those youth who attend school but are not educationally successful have a greater propensity to engage in delinquent behavior, and those who drop out (or who are pushed out) of school completely are more likely to become involved in delinquent activities.[53] A large percentage of Latino males never complete high school, as research suggests that only one in every two (49 percent) graduates from high school.[54] The 2009 Current Population Survey of 16 million Latino males age eighteen or older found that only about 30 percent were high school graduates and less than 10 percent graduated from college.[55] Furthermore, in 2015, only 3.3 percent of Latino males eighteen to twenty-four years of age had a bachelor's degree compared to 11.1 percent of non-Hispanic whites and 5.7 percent of African Americans.[56]

The importance of school in keeping youth connected to mainstream society begins at an early age. For example, studies have found that early childhood education (beginning in preschool) helps to keep youth engaged in school and out of the criminal justice system in the long run.[57] Conversely, the results of a study of inner-city high school students in Chicago suggest that contact with the juvenile justice system is associated with increased school dropout, leading to poorer employment opportunities in the future.[58] Similar to the figures for high school completion and college graduation rates, Latino children are also disproportionately impacted by lower early-childhood education compared to other racial/ethnic groups.[59] Data from the U.S. Department of Education show that white, Asian, and African American children three to five years of age are more likely to be enrolled in preschool programs compared to their Latino counterparts.[60]

Overall, for children and younger teens, attachment to school takes on a greater significance, while the workplace begins to take on a more critical role in later adolescence.[61] This pattern of findings for Latinos suggests the need for an increased focus on school participation for Latino youth throughout the early life course, thereby increasing the likelihood of better opportunities for employment in the future. This assumes, of course, that the social order provides resources for effective secondary socialization of Latino and all other youths.

Research suggests that even within schools, racial/ethnic minority youth often are ensnared in a school-to-prison pipeline wherein schools marginalize and push them out into the streets, where they become involved in activities that ultimately result in prison sentences.[62] As Meiners argues, schools have begun to function more like juvenile detention centers where poor persons of color are tracked into lives behind bars.[63] Equipped with armed security guards and metal detectors, some urban schools operate in ways similar to the prison system, where students are treated like would-be criminals, making it difficult for them to focus on schoolwork. Meiners holds that while school districts spend increasing amounts of money on security measures relative to instruction and ancillary programs per pupil, students are more likely to become victims of violent crime away from, than at, school.[64]

While schools must provide safe environments for students, it is equally important that the structural dimensions of the problems facing Latino and other minority youth also be addressed. For example, structural factors such as racism prevent Latino boys (and girls) from fully participating and succeeding in school. Between 2000 and 2006, a larger percentage of Latino than white boys were likely to be suspended or placed within special education programs, while the percentage of white boys in gifted and talented programs was nearly double that of Latino boys in similar programs.[65] In general, while gifted and talented programs provide access to high-caliber curricula and college-track courses, Latinos are provided with limited opportunities that, if accessed, not only would enhance their future employment possibilities, but also their roles in community and societal institutions.

Subcultural Theories

Despite the abundance of evidence suggesting that racial/ethnic minorities are disadvantaged in terms of school enrollment, educational attainment, and employment opportunities, some theorists take a culturally based approach to explain violence in minority communities. Cultural-based theorists argue that a "subculture of violence" pervades lower-class populations of youth who seek status but are unable to achieve it within the structure of society, which uses middle-class values to judge them.[66] Unable to achieve status within that context, frustrated youth react by developing expressive cultures of criminal behavior in which they can gain status. This includes values, norms, and other cultural dimensions conducive to violence, vandalism, and other criminal behaviors. From this perspective, the disproportionate representation of racial/ethnic minorities arrested and charged with crimes has *commonly* been reduced to "innate" qualities ascribed to them ("superpredators").[67] Wilson, for example, denies that the root causes of crime can be found in the structural features of society.[68]

Subcultural theories recognize the structural strain that gives rise to "status frustration," but they tend to emphasize the nonutilitarian aspects of antisocial expressive behavior rather than the utilitarian features associated with material wealth. This perspective ignores the institutionalized racial/ethnic bias within the criminal justice system and the larger society, and the failure of neoliberal values and policies to provide the educational and job opportunities needed to rise above persistent poverty.[69] That is, institutionalized racial bias of the dominant group generally prevents racial/ethnic minorities from rising above their impoverished status.[70] For example, stereotypes surrounding African American male offenders are linked to a mindset that African American men tend to be irresponsible, disrespectful toward authority figures, and ultimately, dangerous.[71]

Similar stereotypes have also been applied to Latinos, as studies have found that common prejudicial attitudes toward Latinos tend to characterize them as "lazy, irresponsible and dangerously criminal," as well as "hot-headed" or "Latin tempered."[72] These stereotypes are historical and extend to police perceptions of young Latinos and Latinas, but particularly to young men, and prompt law-enforcement officials to unfairly target certain neighborhoods and groups of people living in those neighborhoods. For example, Durán found that police stereotype predominantly Mexican American communities as "gang infested" and equate gangs with criminal activities.[73] These perceptions tend to result in the racial/ethnic profiling of young minority males by police. Rather than policing criminal acts, police target those individuals perceived as perpetually criminal people. In the same vein, particular crimes are attributed to certain racial/ethnic groups because of stereotypes, such as drug traffickers and other drug-related criminals, that are often linked to young Latinos. For instance, Demuth found in his national study of pretrial decisions that Latino defendants are more often charged with drug-related offenses (42 percent) than with property (31.6 percent) and violent (21.6 percent) offenses.[74] Despite relatively high poverty levels, Latinos, including immigrants, have lower rates of violence than whites and African Americans, and this is especially the case with regard to homicide.[75]

Instead of arguing for a subcultural propensity to engage in criminal behavior, Demuth echoes the arguments of relative deprivation theorists and concludes that Latinos commonly share the same social problems as African Americans, such as high unemployment and high levels of poverty.[76] In addition, some Latinos also experience a lack of English language fluency, citizenship status issues, and anti-immigrant hatred that affect their abilities to take advantage of educational opportunities and secure, stable, well-paying jobs.[77] When they face criminal sanctions, unfamiliarity with the criminal justice system and criminal procedures leaves them vulnerable to individuals willing to use institutional power to promote their own ideological or career interests.

Evidence from several sources demonstrates that Latinos are confronted with discriminatory procedures within the criminal justice system that result in higher rates of imprisonment and tougher sentences compared to their white counterparts.[78] Several studies have found that Latinos receive the harshest sentences compared to whites and African Americans because of their perceived cultural dissimilarity to "U.S. culture," and this is particularly the case for drug-related charges.[79] Additionally, in the pretrial phase, Latinos are more likely to be detained, more likely to be required to pay bail to be released, and least likely to be able to afford bail compared to whites and African Americans.[80] Similar results were found for Latino, African American, and Native American youth compared to white youth, as minority youth were more likely to be detained during pretrial phases and receive more severe juvenile-court outcomes.[81]

Ecological Theories

The ecological perspective combines structural and psychological theories of minority crime and incarceration, and advocates for a community-level approach to the study of crime. Specifically, borrowing from William Julius Wilson's notion of the "truly disadvantaged," Sampson and Wilson argue that the ecological context is the strongest predictor of violence, rather than the cultural characteristics of minority groups.[82] They find that the "concentration effects" of neighborhoods—or the effects of living in a neighborhood that is overwhelmingly impoverished—are a result of the limited opportunities and barriers that residents in these neighborhoods face relative to accessing high-quality schools, adequate employment and employment networks, and good role models. While they do not dismiss the impact of culture on violence, they argue that culture varies systematically with the ecological context or neighborhood impoverishment level, and that this explains intragroup variation in crime within racial/ethnic populations. Historically, the majority of prior research that has utilized this theoretical perspective has focused on African Americans, but scholars have begun to focus on Latinos to test for similar results.[83]

The Fallacy of the American Dream and the Neoliberal Panacea

Despite evidence to the contrary, Americans are socialized to believe that hard work, perseverance, and sacrifice will ultimately result in success, regardless of the factors described in the previous section (i.e., racism, relative disadvantage, and community impoverishment). This belief system is intricately woven into the political and ideological messages received in schools, in the media, and from politicians. Americans are socialized to believe that, as individuals, they are largely in control of their own destinies, and that whatever happens to them is a result of their own actions and, thus, their responsibility. However, the fundamental institutions of the United States have not operated—and do not operate—in a neutral and egalitarian manner to ensure fair treatment and equal access to opportunities for all people, and this situation is exacerbated by the inequalities brought about by neoliberalism (high rates of poverty and concentrations of wealth).[84]

Increased market liberalization and the rise of private prisons, connected through a political philosophy and attendant policies that emphasize the privatization of government functions, have created and promoted a school-to-prison pipeline.[85] Global market expansion has displaced millions of workers in this country, especially those with lower levels of education, who once found reasonably good employment in the manufacturing sector without having to have a college education. As Wilson explains, manufacturing corporations that once employed large numbers of workers moved their plants outside of large cities, and as other scholars argue, outside of the United States altogether.[86] Since the early 1980s, multinational enterprises engaged in production have moved, and continue to move, their factories to other countries in search of cheaper labor than is available domestically.[87] Consequently, low-paying service positions have replaced the manufacturing jobs that required little educational attainment but offered livable wages due to the agreements between capital and labor. That is, blue-collar work was the only option for many workers who lacked the necessary skills or education for other types of jobs to earn a "living wage."[88] Today, the occupational structure is skewed toward jobs that pay minimum wage and do not provide fringe benefits, such as health insurance.

Disconnected Youth

The large numbers of minority and Latino youth who are either "disconnected" from mainstream social institutions or incarcerated are reminders that America's structural inequalities persist, and have been exacerbated by neoliberal policies for some groups. Not only is the mass incarceration of young minority men costly to

TABLE 1. Disconnected Youth (Ages 16–24 years) by Race/Ethnicity in the United States and Michigan, 2000–2004, 2005–2009, and 2010–2014.

YEARS/GEO UNIT	RACE/ETHNICITY					
	WHITES	LATINOS	AFRICAN AMERICANS	ASIANS	OTHERS	TOTAL
2000–2004						
United States	11.0%	19.5%	20.9%	9.6%	20.8%	13.9%
Michigan	10.3%	19.6%	23.8%	8.9%	14.0%	12.8%
2005–2009						
United States	10.1%	17.9%	21.0%	8.1%	20.4%	13.2%
Michigan	10.6%	19.4%	23.7%	7.4%	20.8%	13.2%
2010–2014						
United States	11.3%	17.0%	21.9%	8.1%	19.5%	14.1%
Michigan	11.6%	16.6%	25.8%	8.7%	20.1%	14.4%

Source: U.S. Census 2000. American Community Survey, 2001–2004; 2005–2009; 2010–2014.

states, but the loss of their talents is a loss to society that is problematic; worse yet is the poor quality of life experienced by these youths. This is a critical problem in Michigan, especially in Detroit, compared to the United States. For example, at the turn of the twenty-first century, an estimated 27,500 young adults between the ages of sixteen and nineteen were disconnected from education and employment and did not have a high school diploma.[89] Further, between 1998 and 2008, the budget of the Michigan Department of Corrections rose from $1.2 billion to $1.9 billion.[90]

Disconnected youth rates are presented in table 1 by race/ethnicity for the United States and Michigan using rate averages for five-year time periods based on 2010 Census data and American Community Survey estimates. The time periods are 2000–2004 (period one), 2005–2009 (period two), and 2010–2014 (period three). Disconnected youth are from sixteen to twenty-four years of age and are neither in school nor formally employed. As shown in table 1, the rates for Latinos, African Americans, and Others are consistently higher than those for (Non-Hispanic) Whites and Asians at both the national level and in Michigan. The category of Others consists of Native Americans, Other Race, and Two or More Races. African Americans have the highest rates, followed by Others and Latinos. This pattern is similar to that cited by Fernandes-Alcantara, who concluded that rates of

TABLE 2. Disconnected Youth (Ages 16–24 Years) by Race/Ethnicity and Sex in the United States and Michigan, 2000–2004, 2005–2009, and 2010–2014.

YEARS/GEO UNIT	RACE/ETHNICITY												
	WHITES		LATINOS		AFRICAN AMERICANS		ASIANS		OTHERS		TOTAL	
	MALE	FEMALE	MALE	FEMALE	MALE	FEMALE	MALE	FEMALE	MALE	FEMALE	MALE	FEMALE
2000–2004												
United States	9.4%	12.6%	14.0%	25.8%	21.3%	20.6%	8.0%	11.2%	18.5%	23.1%	11.9%	16.0%
Michigan	9.8%	10.8%	16.0%	24.1%	23.7%	24.0%	1.4%	15.9%	15.2%	12.5%	12.0%	13.5%
2005–2009												
United States	9.8%	10.4%	14.5%	21.7%	23.9%	18.1%	7.5%	8.7%	21.4%	21.2%	12.8%	13.6%
Michigan	10.9%	10.3%	15.9%	23.3%	27.5%	23.3%	4.3%	10.7%	23.5%	18.0%	13.8%	12.6%
2010–2014												
United States	11.6%	11.0%	15.6%	18.6%	25.2%	18.6%	7.6%	8.6%	20.8%	18.1%	14.4%	13.7%
Michigan	12.1%	11.1%	16.0%	17.2%	30.1%	21.4%	5.8%	11.7%	24.7%	15.8%	15.4%	13.4%

Source: U.S. Census 2000. American Community Survey, 2001–2004; 2007–2009; 2010–2014.

TABLE 3. Disconnected Youth (Ages 16–24 Years) in Detroit by Race/Ethnicity and Sex, 2005–2009 and 2010–2014.

YEAR	RACE/ETHNICITY												
	WHITES		LATINOS		AFRICAN AMERICANS		ASIANS		OTHERS		TOTAL	
	MALE	FEMALE	MALE	FEMALE	MALE	FEMALE	MALE	FEMALE	MALE	FEMALE	MALE	FEMALE
2005–2009	9.0%	12.7%	18.2%	22.3%	25.9%	23.1%	7.3%	11.1%	16.9%	15.6%	16.1%	19.2%
2010–2014	10.6%	11.6%	20.0%	19.4%	27.1%	21.7%	10.4%	7.0%	18.6%	17.6%	18.7%	17.4%

Source: American Community Survey, 2005–2009; 2010–2014.

disconnected youth are highest among African Americans and Latinos.[91] In table 1 the rate of disconnection among Latinos was higher in Michigan in time periods one and two, but in the most recent time period, their rate is slightly higher at the national level than in Michigan. While the disconnection rate has decreased for Latinos and Asians over time, it has increased for African Americans and slightly for Whites at both the national level and in Michigan, and for Others in Michigan. Although the rate gap between Latinos and Whites closed slightly over time, the rate for Latinos remained from 5 to 6 points higher than those for Whites in time period three.

For African Americans, the rates are consistently higher in Michigan than in the United States across all time periods, while those for Latinos were similar for the two geographical units in time period one, but higher in Michigan for time period two (during the period of the Great Recession, 2007–2009), and again similar in time period three. Overall, there were some slight decreases in the rates from time period one to time period two among Latinos, Asians, and Others, but they seem to be increasing or holding steady for all groups except Latinos in the post–Great Recession period. Overall, the total disconnection rate has increased slightly since the beginning of the century.

Table 2 presents five-year average rates for disconnected youth by race/ethnicity and sex for the time periods 2000–2004, 2005–2009, and 2010–2014. Overall, the patterns between men and women varied across the groups across time. Generally, at the start of the century, for all groups except African Americans, women had higher disconnected youth rates than men. This pattern held across the time periods for Latinos and Asians, with women having higher rates than men at both the national level and in Michigan. This pattern was reversed for Whites in Michigan, with men having higher rates than women, beginning in time period two, while for Others it was consistently higher for men in Michigan across the time periods. In time period three, Whites, African Americans, and Others all had higher disconnected youth rates among men. Latinas and African American women had the highest disconnected rates among women. They had similar rates in time periods one and two, but in time period three in Michigan the rate for Latinas dropped 4.2 percentage points below the rate for African American women. Across time, the rates have tended to increase for men while decreasing for women.

Table 3 provides five-year average, disconnected youth rates in Detroit by race/ethnicity and sex for the time periods 2005–2009 and 2010–2014. Data were not available through the American Community Survey for Detroit for time period one

(2000–2004), so that time period is not included here. Overall, the total rates for Detroit are higher for both men and women across time than at both the national level and Michigan. In general, the rates for all groups except White and Other men in Detroit are higher than their respective rates at the national level, while they tend to vary at the level of Michigan (table 2). African American men have the highest rates in Detroit, followed by African American women, Latinas, Latinos, and Other men. Overall, the rates for men increased across time, while they decreased for women (except for Other women). Across groups the rates increased across the time periods among African American men, Latinos, Asian men, White men, and Other men and women.

Clearly, Latino and Latina youth in the United States, Michigan, and Detroit face particular difficulties in accessing society's mainstream institutions. This is especially true for these youth in Detroit, where the decline of the automobile manufacturing sector and the local economy has had a marked negative impact on racial/ethnic minorities, as evidenced by the high rates of disconnected youth. Granted, Detroit is a unique context given its continuous economic decline and dramatic exodus of population since the middle of the last century. Indeed, in 1960, on a per capita basis, Detroit was the wealthiest major city in the country, and in 2013 it set a historic precedent by being the first major city to file bankruptcy.

The percentage of Latinas disconnected from mainstream social institutions across the nation, in Michigan, and in Detroit is in some instances twice the rate of their white counterparts. Further, despite the higher rate of disconnection among Latinas than Latinos, there is a disproportionate number of Latino males in the criminal justice system. This suggests that there is something operating beyond just school attachment or formal employment that yields the differences in incarceration rates between Latinas and Latinos. We refer to this difference between men and women in the effects of school or employment attachment on criminal activity as "differential disconnectedness." We suggest that differential disconnectedness is linked to, among other factors, family and the different levels of social control that it exerts upon females and males. That is, the family is more likely to protect the young woman than the young man, and this difference contributes to different relationships with the criminal justice system.

The criminological literature has historically recognized the gender gap in criminal activity, and has offered several explanations for men's greater participation in crime. For example, Steffensmeier and Allan cite gender norms as powerful forces shaping women's and men's involvements in criminal activity.[92]

Black Top Mourning
©2001 by Martin
Vargas. Pastel on
sanded paper, 16" ×
20". Painted at the
Ionia Correctional
Facility. Used
courtesy of the
artist.

Veritas—The Lifer ©2017 by Martin Vargas. Charcoal on illustration board 16" × 20".
Presented to Supreme Court Justice Sonia Sotomayor. Painted at the Ionia Correctional
Facility. Used courtesy of the artist.

The Puddle Jumper ©2006 by Martin Vargas. Pastel on sanded paper, 18" × 24". Painted at the Ionia Correctional Facility. Used courtesy of the artist.

My Life My Wife
©2006 by Martin
Vargas. Water soluble
oil on canvas, 30" ×
40". Painted at the
Ionia Correctional
Facility. Used
courtesy of the artist.

Painting His Way Home ©2018 by Martin Vargas. Oil on canvas, 30" × 40". Painted at the Ionia Correctional Facility. Used courtesy of the artist.

Elevacion Del Espirito aka *Detroit Rising* ©2012 by Reuben Kenyatta. Acrylic medium on stretched canvas, 24" × 30". Painted at the Carson City Correctional Facility, Carson City, Michigan. Depicts the "Spirit of Detroit" rising gloriously under the creative power of the people, shining brightly upon the world once again in an effort to help move our great nation forward with innovation, facilitation, and social transformation. Used courtesy of the artist.

Don't look down. Look up ... to the best in yourself and your city.

Sun Setting ©2017 by Reuben Kenyatta. Acrylic medium on canvas panel, 16" × 20". Painted at the Carson City Correctional Facility, Carson City, Michigan. It is that dazed moment of reflection we often find when basking in the warmth of the sun. The stillness of thought sometimes leads us to ponder the simple beauty of life and our true purpose of being born in it. Used courtesy of the artist.

Specifically, a societal taboo exists against women's participation in crime, and gender norms provide scripts for women's behavior, such as nurturant role obligations as a wife or mother. Women are generally rewarded for their ability to maintain familial relationships and to accept family obligations such as child-rearing. Additionally, expectations for femininity may include submission, weakness, or domestication, which are largely incompatible with criminal behavior. By contrast, masculine stereotypes are less at odds with criminality, serving as reference points that make crime more stigmatizing for women when they do participate in illegal activities.

These gender norms may be even more pronounced in Latino families, with research suggesting that Latinas are socialized into more "traditional" gender-based roles through messages surrounding femininity, household responsibilities, and unacceptability of "tomboy" behaviors. By contrast, Latino boys are allowed more freedom to participate in various activities and are not expected to engage in as many household chores.[93] Overall, the socialization of Latinas to preserve their femininity may be at odds with criminality, so that despite their lower levels of participation in school or the labor force, they are more protected than males from engaging in criminal behaviors. This is an area in need of further empirical studies aimed at disentangling the effects of gendered expectations for behavior in Latino families and the relationship between disconnection from mainstream social institutions and criminality.

Nativistic Movements and Racism

Coupled with their disconnectedness from schools and formal employment, racism plays a large role in maintaining a prison pipeline among Latino males because they tend to face a persistent array of negative stereotypes. For example, as cultural theorists of crime argue,[94] stereotypes surrounding Latino males portray them as predisposed to violent behaviors because of their natural "hot-headedness" or "Latin-temperedness."[95] This often leads to racial/ethnic profiling by police and unfair pretrial and trial outcomes.[96] Furthermore, imagined fears perpetuated by negative media images of the poor and racial/ethnic minorities sustain American society's need to patrol the neighborhoods of people already stomped down by neoliberal policies and the subsequent slashing of social programs that help the poor survive and maintain a minimum level of resources.

Generally, this need to patrol minority communities reflects the racial ideology of the dominant group that includes racialized images of Latinos threatening to destroy the institutional and cultural fabric of American (dominant group) society. That is, an American society that is white. The dangers presented by the race/ ethnic minority "other" are highlighted by popular stereotypes that historically have surrounded African Americans and now surround Latinos.[97] In an editorial in *Latino Studies*, Oboler describes the fears surrounding immigrant Latinos. She discusses how it is difficult to imagine that immigration was one of the "key foundational pillars of this nation's self-image and development" given that there exists today a "widespread hysteria about the presence of immigrants."[98] Oboler rightly attributes this to the racialization of immigrants, particularly those of Latin American origin. While nativistic movements occurred in response to waves of European immigrants, the relative absence of racial dynamics and the structural upgrading and expansion of the economy at the expense of Mexican Americans and other minority groups provided for their ultimate incorporation. Today, Latinos are primarily perceived by dominant group members as undocumented immigrants who leech from the nation's public resources, thereby "requiring" the development of repressive laws and policies aimed at protecting whites ("us") from Latino immigrants ("them") and Latinos generally. The separation of families at the border in 2018, for example, represents the social hatred of Latino immigrants and refugees that has been perpetrated by the Trump regime.

The Paradox of Prison Systems in the Age of Neoliberalism

The growth in incarceration of racial/ethnic minority populations is also linked to the boom in the construction of private prisons in the 1980s and 1990s, although a relatively small proportion of prisoners today are in private prisons (5.6 percent of state prisoners and 18.1 percent of federal prisoners).[99] The more racial/ethnic minorities have been incarcerated, the more neoliberal policymakers and investors sought to capitalize on the need for increased prison space. For example, investigative journalist Eric Schlosser outlined the movement from government-run to private-run prisons in New York and how the notion of private prisons gained tremendous popularity in the 1970s and 1980s, especially with the Reagan and Bush administrations, as it reflected their neoliberal beliefs in small government and privatization of public services.[100]

Private prisons were presented as inherently less wasteful and inefficient in comparison to state-run prisons, and able to provide better services at a much lower cost, although studies have not borne this out.[101] The privatized prison system has commonly been referred to as the "prison industrial complex," one of the industries that experienced substantial growth in the final quarter of the last century, with many stakeholders (including large investors such as Merrill Lynch, Allstate, and American Express) helping to sustain private prison booms in states like Texas.[102] Politicians capitalized on the fear of crime to gain votes and offered up private prisons as a means to contain "violent offenders," with African Americans and Latinos portrayed as inherently dangerous and criminal. The construction of private prisons also appeased individuals living in rural areas, where the construction of more prisons meant more stable jobs. As Hartnett explains, at the same time that some segments of society became part of the unwanted "surplus population" as a result of neoliberalism, others benefited, as some workers, especially those in more impoverished rural areas, were guaranteed "virtually permanent jobs on prison construction, prison staffing, and increased police forces."[103] Indeed, during the 1990s, the building of prisons in rural areas was seen as economic development.

Yet, while private prisons do provide employment opportunities for local communities, they are also an invitation for prisoner abuse, including longer incarceration terms, victimization through lack of adequate health care, poor food quality, and mental and physical violence. These conditions exist even as private prisons are portrayed as superior to state-run prisons, with new prison buildings often highlighted. Because private prisons are run by corporations interested in maximizing profits, they seek to reduce operating costs as much as they can and are prone to incarcerate people for as long as possible since each prisoner contributes to the profit margin.

In addition to longer sentences, prisoners are also subjected to abusive physical treatment at private prisons, as corporations are able to act relatively freely in the absence of adequate government oversight. One such example occurred at a private prison facility in Willacy County, Texas, run by GEO Group Inc. There, prison staff allowed inmates to use socks stuffed with padlocks to beat to death a fellow prisoner, Gregorio De La Rosa Jr., shortly before his release date. The GEO Group was also engaged with the American Legislative Exchange Council (ALEC, a national neoliberal policy organization), which, with the involvement of the Corrections Corporation of America (today CoreCivic), helped draft Arizona's notorious SB 1070 anti-immigrant bill.[104] A 2010 National Public Radio report also uncovered a shareholder conference call in which the GEO Group's CEO admitted that bills like SB 1070 would result in greater profits for the company and joked about the company's involvement with the bill's passage.[105]

In 1999, Wackenhut Corrections Corp., a subsidiary of Wackenhut Corporation, which ultimately became GS4 Secure Solutions (a British-owned international security firm), opened North Lake Correctional Facility, a maximum security facility in Baldwin, Michigan, to house violent youth offenders on behalf of the state. In 2005, following an exposé by the *Grand Rapids Press* and a critical study by the Citizens Alliance on Prisons and Public Spending, the State of Michigan terminated its contract with Wackenhut, which by then had become part of the GEO Group. These studies pointed to excessive costs and chronic understaffing, high personnel turnover, and corporate violations of the contract with the state, which included failure to provide counseling programs and to maintain the required staffing levels. Similar to the Willacy County prison, the Baldwin facility also tended to operate with little government oversight.[106] Following the termination of the contract, the GEO Group sued the State of Michigan but lost the case.

Ironically, the GEO Group attempted to reopen the Baldwin facility in 2011 to house "imported" prisoners from the California Department of Corrections and Rehabilitation. The facility in Baldwin was slated to begin accepting prisoners in April 2011; however, a change in California's approach from "exporting" its prisoners to keeping them in the state resulted only in a temporary reopening of the facility, which was forced to shut down later in the year. According to U.S. Census Bureau estimates, Baldwin, Michigan, is extremely rural, with 963 residents over the age of eighteen.[107] Additionally, the median household income was $15,550 in 2010, and almost 35.9 percent of families living in the area fell below the federal poverty line. These factors made Baldwin appealing to a corporation like GEO in search of both land on which to build a private prison and cheap labor in a rural town desperate for work.

Interestingly, the North Lake Correctional Facility was originally developed as a solution to Michigan's prison dilemma, illustrating the paradox of its prison system in the age of neoliberalism. The paradox in Michigan involved increasing incarceration rates as the violent crime rate declined. This occurred in a context in which politicians promoted the use of private prison facilities while reducing the size of state government through tax cuts (mostly to the wealthy). Michigan's violent crime rate had been consistently higher than the national rate, reached a peak in the early 1990s, and has been in decline since then, going down from 803 per 100,000 population in 1991 to 416 in 2015.[108]

Over the past three decades, Michigan policymakers have repeatedly emphasized the need to reform the state corrections system due to rising costs and declines in violent crime rates. At the request of former governor Jennifer Granholm and legislative leaders, the Council of State Governments Justice Center provided an overview of the status of Michigan's corrections system.[109] Despite a difficult economic climate, including high unemployment rates and declining state revenues, state spending on corrections rose considerably between fiscal years 1998 and 2008. Estimates by the Council of State Governments Justice Center suggest that state general-fund spending on corrections rose from $1.26 billion to $1.99 billion between 1998 and 2007, accounting for 22.6 percent of the state general-fund expenditures.[110] Overall, spending on corrections represents such a large percentage of state spending that one in three state employees works for the Michigan Department of Corrections. In 2016, the Michigan Department of Corrections budget was $1.96 billion, down slightly from a high of $2.04 billion in 2008, and constituting 19.2 percent of the state's budget.[111] In 2017, the figures were just over $2.0 billion.[112]

The fiscal austerity approach of shared sacrifice and privatization touted by the ideology of neoliberalism is attended by reduced government regulation in the economy (deregulation) and reduced taxation (especially among corporations and the wealthy). Prisons, of course, require funding obtained through taxes, whether run or outsourced by the government, and this provides a structural contradiction within neoliberalism—stricter sentencing leads to increased incarceration rates as the revenues to government are decreased. Still, taxpayers continue to foot the bill. As a result, in order for politicians to uphold the messages of fiscal austerity, reduced government, and fewer taxes, which legitimated the use of private prisons, they must now convince the public that reductions in the prison population do not present threats to public safety.[113]

Recidivism

A problem stemming from incarceration is helping former inmates adjust to life outside of prison walls. Overall, the neoliberal agenda and the boom of the private prison industry have inhibited the rehabilitation of prisoners, as the emphasis is on keeping offenders locked up for as long as possible while reducing costs (and rehabilitation programs cost money) to maximize profits, even if this logic works against the financial interests and well-being of the state. However, Michigan has made some strides in this area with the implementation of the Michigan Prisoner Reentry Initiative (MPRI), which was implemented in 2005. Prompted by a prison system literally bursting at the seams with inmates, Michigan lawmakers realized that the state's high incarceration rate was because many prisoners were serving more than the minimum sentence imposed for crimes committed. Furthermore, when prisoners were released, they reverted to committing crimes, ultimately returning to incarceration. Without adequate programming support while in prison, they were left largely to fend for themselves after release—they were burdened by the stigma of "ex-convict," lacked work skills, could not find stable housing, struggled with adjusting to life back at home with their families, and were burdened by other factors such as addictions. These problems pushed many back into a life of crime.[114]

The MPRI program has three steps to help inmates adjust back to life outside of prison:

1. GETTING READY: Prisoners are processed through a reception center on the day that they enter prison, where a comprehensive assessment is taken to determine each prisoner's individual risks, needs, and strengths. A Transition Accountability Plan (TAP) is then developed to determine the services a prisoner will need in order to adjust back to civilian life after prison.
2. GOING HOME: About two months before their expected release date, prisoners identified as needing more intensive preparation and support are transferred to a lockup facility closer to home where they receive help developing a plan to find work and housing, as well as substance abuse counseling, sex offender therapy, and/or other mental health services if they require these additional supports.
3. STAYING HOME: Prisoners are sent home during the middle of the week so as to enable them to promptly meet with their parole agents and other service providers. This phase includes a mix of services (e.g., parolee supervision, services, discharge, and aftercare) that promote integration into society and prevent recidivism. The Michigan Department of Corrections (MDOC) cites that the recidivism rate has declined from one-in-two to approximately one-in-three individuals following the implementation of MPRI in 2005.[115]

Despite such success in reducing the recidivism rate, a 2012 program evaluation by Michigan's Office of the Auditor General found that there were still significant gaps in terms of internal control within the MDOC to effectively implement MPRI.[116] In general, at each phase of the program there were significant problems. For example, in the first phase, the program evaluation found that the MDOC did not ensure that the TAPs identified the available programming to meet prisoners' needs, did not ensure that prisoners were ranked by release date and program priority, and did not efficiently schedule prisoners for MPRI programming. In the second and third phases, MDOC did not ensure that the reentry TAPs were completely prepared. In fact, 22 percent of reentry TAPs were incomplete, and some did not include pertinent information such as provider services, service tasks, service start dates, or referral dates for services. There were also problems with accurate filings, and the MDOC did not record the parolees' discharge status, making it difficult to know the actual effectiveness of MPRI. Finally, the audit uncovered the fact that double-billing and overpayment of contractors was a problem, resulting in canceled contracts and thousands of dollars in returned payments to the state. The major audit finding was that MDOC provided only moderately effective oversight of MPRI services provided by contractors.[117] Renamed "Offender Success" in 2018, the program today costs $67.8 million per year, and it is critically important that problems such as these be remedied for the long term.[118] MDOC officials claim to have remedied many of these problems despite the extensive evidence to the contrary.

Compared to parole supervision costs, which are estimated at $3,740 per year, the cost of keeping a prisoner locked up, which is approximately $36,000 per year, far exceeds this amount. However, these cost-savings programs do not mesh well with the neoliberal ideology of increased spending on prisons to enhance conservative agendas, which brings into question the viability of long-term approaches to integrate prisoners back into mainstream society. This was evidenced by Michigan Governor Rick Snyder's 2012–2013 budget, which included a recommendation that Michigan privatize more of its prisons as a viable cost-savings measure, in addition to an increased focus on the MPRI.[119] This suggests that major ideological changes must also occur in the way that the American public views government's role in protecting and promoting the public good. While the MPRI has the potential to significantly cut prison costs and help inmates adjust to life outside of prison walls, it has clearly suffered from poor management and provides yet more evidence that the outsourcing of government functions not only does not necessarily lead to greater efficiency or effectiveness, but may actually result in their opposite. Still,

MPRI provides individuals with the potential to pursue productive careers outside of crime.

Moving Back toward the Center

The future of the United States is bound up with the well-being of Latinos and other racial/ethnic minority groups. Their lot can be improved by moving public opinion back to the center, where ideas about government serving the public good through social programs again become acceptable and corporations pay their fair share of taxes. Contrary to President Reagan's pronouncement that government is the problem rather than the solution, government is indeed the solution when it comes to promoting equality and the public good in a capitalist society, as the market order is the source of inequality, and neoliberal policies exacerbate that inequality. Good government programs are not only able to address the structural dynamics that marginalize Latinos, they are also able to promote their incorporation into the nation's institutions and ensure that the nation's democratic future remains as vibrant and full of promise as it was for European immigrants of the nineteenth and twentieth centuries.

The current political climate is highly polarized between neoliberal and reactionary nationalists and social democratic liberals, with the former groups currently entrenched in the federal government and the latter pursuing collectivist policies over radical individualist policies. In addition to needed changes in neoliberal policies, in order to reduce racial/ethnic minority crime and incarceration, change must come at several other levels, including in education, employment, and the criminal justice system.

Education

It is important to radically reduce the numbers of disconnected youth in Michigan and across the country. The white–Latino achievement (academic performance) gap has not changed significantly since 1992, even as the proportion of Latinos has increased significantly throughout the nation's educational systems.[120] Latinos and other racial/ethnic minority youth need greater support in school, including access to a safe environment where they feel part of an educational community. Treating schools as would-be prisons inhibits the educational process and deters students from engaging with teachers and their classmates during instructional time. Furthermore, Latinos also need incorporation into mainstream classrooms and less punitive punishments for misbehavior that lead to their needless placement in special education classrooms or suspension from school. To Michigan's credit, lawmakers in 2016 passed a law that moves school discipline policies away from "zero tolerance" in order to reduce the suspension and expulsion of Michigan's public school students, the implication being that the policy will lead to higher graduation and success rates among students. Still, Latinos need increased access to high-caliber programs such as gifted and talented courses that would place them on the path to college. With better educational opportunities, Latinos will have enhanced future prospects in terms of employment and their contributions to society. Finally, in turning to the effects of neoliberal policies on educational outcomes, policymakers must begin restoring funding to public schools and take the poor performance of charter schools seriously. Not everyone can afford private educational services when public education declines, and this disproportionately affects minority communities. This is a reality that the nation can no longer ignore or justify, as the population landscape continues to change and people of color will outnumber the white majority within a few decades.

Employment

In Michigan, employment in the manufacturing sector is no longer a guaranteed route to livable wages. If the neoliberal agenda continues unabated, jobs within the auto industry will continue to disappear as manufacturing continues to move abroad and production becomes more and more mechanized. Such jobs will be replaced by low-paying service positions. While we may not be able to stop this from happening, we can prepare today's youth for better job prospects by ensuring that they have the skills and education necessary to create and excel in other jobs that do provide livable wages. Indeed, a shortage of skilled labor has already been identified in Michigan and across the nation, and the challenge now is to effectively educate young adults from all ethnic groups—something the American education system has been unable (or unwilling) to do for the past century.

Criminal Justice System

Several changes must be made in the criminal justice system. First, in order to begin to solve the problem of mass racial/ethnic minority incarceration, we must have accurate accounts of the populations in prison by standard categories of race/ethnicity. This is especially important for Latinos, as research clearly shows that Latinos are often undercounted in prison populations because of the failure of prison systems to adequately collect this information. Official data-collection tools must utilize standard categories that include an appropriate ethnicity box on forms so that Latino inmates have the opportunity to identify as Latino. These simple steps will go a long way toward producing an accurate estimate of Latinos in the state's prison population.

Second, the problem of racism remains prevalent and seems to be getting worse, from police bias to failure to incorporate culturally competent prison personnel. As Villarruel et al. demonstrate in their analysis, Latinos engaged with criminal justice systems are confronted with language barriers and prison personnel who lack cultural competence.[121] Additionally, prisons are institutions where racism festers at all levels, both among prisoners and personnel. Unfortunately, it seems that the nation and Michigan have regressed rather than moved forward in these areas since the civil rights movement. Although Michigan has led the nation in reducing the number of correctional facilities and the number of incarcerated persons, it continues to maintain high levels of incarcerated populations without providing the public with transparency in official statistics using standard categories of race/ethnicity. In 2012 and again in 2015, the Center for Public Integrity gave the State of Michigan an "F" on its "state integrity" scorecard for, among other things, lack of transparency and lack of public access to information.

NOTES

1. R. Martinez, "The Turn toward Incarceration in the U.S. and Michigan," *NEXO* 15, no. 2 (2012): 1, 17–23; M. Mauer, *Race to Incarcerate*, rev. ed. (New York: The New Press, 2006); C. Parenti, *Lockdown America: Police and Prisons in the Age of Crisis* (New York: Verso Books, 2008); L. Wacquant, *Punishing the Poor: The Neoliberal Government of Social Insecurity* (Durham, NC: Duke University Press, 2009); B. Western, *Punishment and Inequality in America* (New York: Russell Sage Foundation, 2006).

2. The Sentencing Project, *Trends in U.S. Corrections*, June 22, 2018, https://

sentencingproject.org.

3. Paige M. Harrison and Allen J. Beck, Bureau of Justice Statistics, "Prisoners in 2004," NCJ 210677 (Washington, DC: U.S. Department of Justice, Bureau of Justice Statistics, 2005); "New Court Commitments to State Prison, 2009: Offense, by Sex, Race, and Hispanic Origin," 2009, http://bjs.ojp.usdoj.gov/index.cfm?ty=pbdetail&iid=2065/; S. D. Bushway, "Labor Markets and Crime," in *Crime and Public Policy*, ed. J. Q. Wilson and J. Petersilia (New York: Oxford University Press, 2011), 183–209; J. McFarland, B. Hussar, X. Wang et al., *The Condition of Education 2018* (NCES 2018–144), U.S. Department of Education (Washington, DC: National Center for Education Statistics, 2018), https://nces.ed.gov.

4. Pew Research Center, "Blacks and Hispanics Are Overrepresented in U.S. Prisons" (2018), http://www.pewresearch.org/fact-tank/2018/01/12/shrinking-gap-between-number-of-blacks-and-whites-in-prison/ft_18-01-10_prisonracegaps_2.

5. U.S. Sentencing Commission, "Sourcebook of Federal Sentencing Statistics" (2017), https://www.ussc.gov/research/sourcebook-2017.

6. Prison Policy Initiative, *Breaking Down Mass Incarceration in the 2010 Census: State-by-State Incarceration Rates by Race/Ethnicity: Michigan Profile* (2017), https://www.prisonpolicy.org/reports/rates.html.

7. J. S. Passel and D. V. Cohn, "U.S. Population Projections: 2005–2050," Pew Hispanic Center (2008), http://www.pewhispanic.org/2008/02/11/us-population-projections-2005-2050.

8. P. M. Harrison and A. J. Beck, *Prisoners in 2005*, NCJ 215092 (Washington, DC: U.S. Department of Justice, Bureau of Justice Statistics, 2006).

9. P. Guerino, P. M. Harrison, and W. J. Sabol, *Prisoners in 2010*, NCJ 236096 (Washington, DC: U.S. Department of Justice, Bureau of Justice Statistics, 2011).

10. Ibid.

11. ProQuest, *ProQuest Statistical Abstract of the U.S. 2017 Online Edition*, https://www.proquest.com/products-services/statabstract.html.

12. Ibid.

13. Ibid.

14. E. A. Carson, *Prisoners in 2018*, NCJ 251149 (Washington, DC: U.S. Department of Justice, Bureau of Justice Statistics, 2018).

15. Ibid.

16. M. Mauer, "Addressing Racial Disparities in Incarceration," *Prison Journal* 9 (2011): 875–1015.

17. Urban Institute, "The Alarming Lack of Data on Latinos in the Criminal Justice System," 2016, http://apps.urban.org/features/latino-criminal-justice-data.

18. Michigan Department of Community Health, *Michigan 2010 Critical Health Indicators:*

Violent Crime Rate, Social, Economic, and Environmental Factors Report 24 (2010), http://www.michigan.gov/documents/mdch/CHI2010_WebFinal-24_340418_7.pdf. See also J. Aiken, *Era of Mass Expansion: Why State Officials Should Fight Jail Growth* (Northampton, MA: Public Policy Initiative, 2017), https://www.prisonpolicy.org.

19. M. Mauer and R. S. King, "Uneven Justice: State Rates of Incarceration by Race and Ethnicity," July 2007, https://www.sentencingproject.org.

20. Michigan Department of Corrections, *Michigan Department of Corrections 2016 Statistical Report* (Lansing, MI: Michigan Department of Corrections, 2017), https://www.michigan.gov/documents.

21. F. A. Villarruel, N. E. Walker, P. Minifree et al., *¿Dónde está la justicia? A Call to Action on Behalf of Latino and Latina Youth in the U.S. Justice System* (Washington, DC: Michigan State University/Building Blocks for Youth, 2002).

22. Ibid.

23. Ibid.

24. S. Ohlemacher, "More Blacks and Hispanics Live in Prison Cells Than College Dorms," *Associated Press*, September 26, 2007.

25. A. Flores, "How the U.S. Hispanic Population Is Changing," Pew Research Center, 2017, http://www.pewresearch.org/fact-tank/2017/09/18/how-the-u-s-hispanic-population-is-changing/; J. L. Lauritsen and N. A. White, "Putting Violence in Its Place: The Effects of Race, Ethnicity, Gender, and Place on the Risk for Violence," *Criminology & Public Policy* 1 (2001): 37–60; M. T. Lee, R. Martinez, and R. Rosenfield, "Does Immigration Increase Homicide? Negative Evidence from Three Border Cities," *Sociological Quarterly* 42 (2001): 559–80; R. Martinez, *Latino Homicide: Immigration, Violence, and Community* (New York: Routledge Press, 2002).

26. A. Aguirre and D. V. Baker, "Latinos and the United States Criminal Justice System: Introduction," *Justice Professional* 13 (2000): 3–6.

27. A. L. Nielsen, M. T. Lee, and R. Martinez, "Integrating Race, Place, and Motive in Social Disorganization Theory: Lessons from a Comparison of Black and Latino Homicide Types in Two Immigrant Destination Cities," *Criminology* 43 (2005): 837–72; T. Schlesinger, "The Cumulative Effects of Racial Disparities in Criminal Processing," *Journal of the Institute of Justice & International Studies* 7 (2007): 261–78; S. deVuono-powell, C. Schweidler, A. Walters, and A. Zohrabi, *Who Pays? The True Cost of Incarceration on Families* (Oakland, CA: Ella Baker Center, Forward Together, Research Action Design, 2015).

28. M. Torres and E. Fergus, "Social Mobility and the Complex Status of Latino Males: Education, Employment, and Incarceration Patterns from 2000–2009, in *Invisible No More: Understanding the Disenfranchisement of Latino Men and Boys*, ed. P. Noguera, A.

Hurtado, and E. Fergus (New York: Routledge Publishers, 2011), 19–40; M. A. Winters and J. P. Greene, "Leaving Boys Behind: Public High School Graduation Rates," Civic Report no. 48, Center for Civic Innovation at the Manhattan Institute, April 2006.

29. F. A. Esbensen, *Preventing Adolescent Gang Involvement*, Youth Gang Series (Washington, DC: U.S. Department of Justice, Office of Juvenile Justice and Delinquency Prevention, 2000), https://www.ncjrs.gov/pdffiles1/ojjdp/182210.pdf; Karl G. Hill, Christina Lui, and J. David Hawkins, *Early Precursors of Gang Membership: A Study of Seattle Youth* (Washington, DC: U.S. Department of Justice, Office of Juvenile Justice and Delinquency Prevention, 2001); J. C. Howell and A. Egley Jr., "Moving Risk Factors into Developmental Theories of Gang Membership," *Youth Violence and Juvenile Justice* 3, no. 4 (2005): 334–54; P. A. Wyrick and J. C. Howell, "Strategic Risk-Based Response to Youth Gangs," *Juvenile Justice* 9, no. 1 (2004): 20–29.

30. K. Beckett, *Making Crime Pay: Law and Order in Contemporary American Politics* (New York: Oxford University Press, 1997); E. R. Meiners and K. B. Reyes, "Re-making the Incarceration Nation: Naming the Participation of Our Schools in Our Prison Industrial Complex," *Penn GSE Perspectives on Urban Education* 5 (2008): 1–13, http://www.urbanedjournal.org/archive/volume-5-issue-2-spring-2008.

31. R. O. Martinez, "The Impact of Neoliberalism on Latinos," *Latino Studies* 14, no. 1 (2016): 11–32.

32. S. J. Hartnett, "The Annihilating Public Policies of the Prison-Industrial Complex; or Crime, Violence, and Punishment in an Age of Neoliberalism," *Rhetoric & Public Affairs* 11, no. 3 (2008): 491–515.

33. McFarland, Hussar, Wang et al., *The Condition of Education 2018*.

34. L. Wacquant, "The New 'Peculiar Institution': On the Prison as Surrogate Ghetto," *Theoretical Criminology* 4, no. 3 (2000): 377–89; Wacquant, *Punishing the Poor*.

35. J. L. Morín, "Latino/as and US Prisons: Trends and Challenges," *Latino Studies* 6, nos. 1–2 (2008): 11–34; R. A. McCormack, "America's Biggest Companies Continue to Move Factories Offshore and Eliminate Thousands of American Jobs," *Manufacturing and Technology News* 10, no. 1 (2013).

36. R. G. Shelden and W. B. Brown, "The Crime Control Industry and the Management of the Surplus Population," *Critical Criminology* 9, no. 1/2 (2000): 39–62.

37. Hartnett, "The Annihilating Public Policies."

38. S. A. Beale, "The News Media's Influence on Criminal Justice Policy: How Market-Driven News Promotes Punitiveness," *William & Mary Law Review* 48 (2006): 397–481.

39. A. R. Piquero and L. Steinberg, "Public Preferences for Rehabilitation versus Incarceration of Juvenile Offenders," *Journal of Criminal Justice* 38 (2009): 1–6.

40. J. L. Morín, "Latino/as and US Prisons."

41. S. Demuth, "Racial and Ethnic Differences in Pretrial Release Decisions and Outcomes: A Comparison of Hispanic, Black and White Felony Arrestees," *Criminology* 41 (2003): 873–907; M. Romero, "State Violence, and the Social and Legal Construction of Latino Criminality: From El Bandido to Gang Member," *Denver University Law Review* 78, no. 4 (2000–2001): 1081–118.

42. J. L. Morín, "Latino/as and US Prisons," 15.

43. T. Chiricos and S. Eschholz, "The Racial and Ethnic Typification of Crime and the Criminal Typification of Race and Ethnicity in Local Television News," *Journal of Research in Crime and Delinquency* 39 (2002): 400–420; R. J. Durán, "Legitimated Oppression: Inner-City Mexican American Experiences with Police Gang Enforcement," *Journal of Contemporary Ethnography* 38 (2009): 143–68.

44. J. R. Blau and P. M. Blau, "The Cost of Inequality: Metropolitan Structure and Violent Crime," *American Sociological Review* 47 (1982): 114–29; M. E. Wolfgang and F. Ferracuti, *Subculture of Violence: Towards an Integrated Theory in Criminology* (Thousand Oaks, CA: Sage Publications, 1967); I. Piliavin and S. Briar, "Police Encounters with Juveniles," *American Journal of Sociology* 70 (1964): 206–14.

45. R. J. Sampson and W. J. Wilson, "Toward a Theory of Race, Crime, and Urban Inequality," in *Race, Crime and Justice: A Reader*, ed. S. L. Gabbidon and H. T. Greene (New York: Routledge, 2005), 177–89; R. Sampson, J. Morenoff, and S. Raudenbush, "Social Anatomy of Racial and Ethnic Disparities in Violence," *American Journal of Public Health* 95 (2005): 224–32.

46. P. E. Bellair, V. J. Roscigno, and T. L. McNulty, "Linking Local Labor Market Opportunity to Violent Adolescent Delinquency," *Journal of Research in Crime and Delinquency* 40 (2003): 6–33; Blau and Blau, "The Cost of Inequality"; M. T. Lee, *Crime on the Border: Immigration and Homicide in Urban Communities* (New York: LFB Scholarly Publishing LLC, 2003).

47. L. Krivo and R. Peterson, "Labor Market Conditions and Violent Crime among Youth and Adults," *Sociological Perspectives* 47 (2004): 485–505; S. Raphael and R. Winter-Ebmer, "Identifying the Effect of Unemployment on Crime," *Journal of Law and Economics* 44 (2001): 259–83.

48. C. Uggen and M. Thompson, "The Socioeconomic Determinants of Ill-Gotten Gains: Within-Person Changes in Drug Use and Illegal Earnings," *American Journal of Sociology* 109 (2003): 146–85.

49. R. B. Freeman and H. J. Holzer, "The Black Youth Employment Crisis: Summary of Findings," in *The Black Youth Employment Crisis: National Bureau of Economic Research*

Project Report, ed. R. B. Freeman and H. J. Holzer (Chicago: University of Chicago Press, 1986), 3–20; J. L. Semega, K. R. Fontenot, and M. A. Kollar, *Income and Poverty in the United States: 2016*, P60-259 (Washington, DC: U.S. Census Bureau, Current Population Reports, 2017), https://www.census.gov.

50. Bureau of Labor Statistics, *Table E-16: Employment Rates by Age, Sex, Race, and Hispanic or Latino Ethnicity* (Labor Force Statistics from the Current Population Survey, 2016), https://www.bls.gov/web/empsit/cpsee_e16.htm.

51. Ibid.

52. M. Torres and E. Fergus, "Social Mobility and the Complex Status of Latino Males: Education, Employment, and Incarceration Patterns from 2000–2009," in *Invisible No More: Understanding the Disenfranchisement of Latino Men and Boys*, ed. P. Noguera, A. Hurtado, and E. Fergus (New York: Routledge, 2011), 19–40.

53. E. Chavez, E. Oetting, and R. Swaim, "Dropout and Delinquency: Mexican American and Caucasian Non-Hispanic Youth," *Journal of Clinical Child Psychology* 23 (1994): 47–55.

54. R. O. Martinez and A. Aguirre Jr., "Resource Shares and Educational Attainment: The U.S. Latino Population in the Twenty-First Century, in *Latinos in Higher Education*, ed. D. J. Leon, (Greenwich, CT: JAI, 2003), 37–55; M. A. Winters and J. P. Greene, "Leaving Boys Behind: Public High School Graduation Rates," Civic Report no. 48, Center for Civic Innovation at the Manhattan Institute, April 2006.

55. Torres and Fergus, "Social Mobility and the Complex Status of Latino Males."

56. U.S. Census Bureau, "Table 1. Educational Attainment of the Population 18 Years and Over, by Age, Sex, Race, and Hispanic Origin: 2015," *Educational Attainment in the United States: 2015—Detailed Tables*, 2016, https://www.census.gov.

57. L. J. Schweinhart, J. Montie, Z. Xiang, W. S. Barnett, C. R. Belfield, and M. Nores, *Lifetime Effects: The High/Scope Perry Preschool Study through Age 40* (Ypsilanti, MI: High/Scope Press, 2005).

58. P. Hirschfield, "Another Way Out: The Impact of Juvenile Arrests on High School Dropout," *Sociology of Education* 82 (2009): 368–93.

59. R. O. Martinez, "Demographic Overview of Latino Children," in *Latina and Latino Children's Mental Health*, vol. 1, ed. N. J. Cabrera, F. A. Villarruel, and H. E. Fitzgerald (Santa Barbara, CA: Praeger, 2011); Martinez and Aguirre, "Resource Shares and Educational Attainment."

60. Martinez, "Demographic Overview of Latino Children"; A. KewalRamani, L. Gilbertson, M. A. Fox, and S. Provasnik, *Status and Trends in the Education of Racial and Ethnic Minorities* (Washington, DC: U.S. Department of Education, 2007), http://nces.ed.gov/pubs2007/2007039.pdf.

61. Krivo and Peterson, "Labor Market Conditions and Violent Crime among Youth and Adults."

62. C. G. Robbins, *Expelling Hope: The Assault on Youth and the Militarization of Schooling* (Albany, NY: SUNY Press, 2008); C. C. Spohn, "Thirty Years of Sentencing Reform: The Quest for a Racially Neutral Sentencing Process," *Policies, Processes, and Decisions of the Criminal Justice System* 4 (2000): 427–501.

63. E. R. Meiners, *Right to Be Hostile* (New York: Taylor & Francis, 2007).

64. Ibid.

65. Torres and Fergus, "Social Mobility and the Complex Status of Latino Males."

66. A. K. Cohen, *Delinquent Boys: The Culture of the Gang* (Glencoe, IL: Free Press, 1955); D. M. Downes, *The Delinquent Solution: A Study in Subcultural Theory* (New York: Free Press, 1966); Wolfgang and Ferracuti, *Subculture of Violence.*

67. J. Q. Wilson and R. J. Herrnstein, *Crime and Human Nature: The Definitive Study of the Causes of Crime* (New York: Simon and Schuster, 1985); R. J. Herrnstein and C. Murray, *The Bell Curve: Intelligence and Class Structure in American Life* (New York: Simon and Schuster, 1994).

68. J. Q. Wilson, *Thinking about Crime*, rev. ed. (New York: Basic Books, 2013).

69. R. J. Durán, "Legitimated Oppression: Inner-City Mexican American Experiences with Police Gang Enforcement," *Journal of Contemporary Ethnography* 38 (2009): 143–68; L. S. Salinas, *U.S. Latinos and Criminal Injustice* (East Lansing: Michigan State University Press, 2015); Chavez, Oetting, and Swaim, "Dropout and Delinquency," 47–55; Krivo and Peterson, "Labor Market Conditions and Violent Crime among Youth and Adults"; Torres and Fergus, "Social Mobility and the Complex Status of Latino Males."

70. R. Blauner, *Racial Oppression in America* (New York: Harper and Row, 1972); Salinas, *U.S. Latinos and Criminal Injustice.*

71. Chiricos and Eschholz, "The Racial and Ethnic Typification of Crime."

72. Demuth, "Racial and Ethnic Differences in Pretrial Release Decisions and Outcomes," 882; Salinas, *U.S. Latinos and Criminal Injustice.*

73. Durán, "Legitimated Oppression."

74. Demuth, "Racial and Ethnic Differences in Pretrial Release Decisions and Outcomes."

75. Ibid.; Sampson and Wilson, "Toward a Theory of Race, Crime, and Urban Inequality"; Lee, Martinez, and Rosenfeld, "Does Immigration Increase Homicide?"; Lee, *Crime on the Border*; R. Martinez, *Latino Homicide: Immigration, Violence, and Community* (New York: Routledge, 2002).

76. Demuth, "Racial and Ethnic Differences in Pretrial Release."

77. Torres and Fergus, "Social Mobility and the Complex Status of Latino Males."

78. P. K. Brennan and C. Spohn, "Race/Ethnicity and Sentencing Outcomes among Drug Offenders in North Carolina," *Journal of Contemporary Criminal Justice* 24 (2008): 371–98; T. R. Curry and G. Corral-Camacho, "Sentencing Young Minority Males for Drug Offenses: Testing for Conditional Effects between Race/Ethnicity, Gender and Age during the US War on Drugs," *Punishment & Society* 10 (2008): 253–76; Demuth, "Racial and Ethnic Differences in Pretrial Release"; N. Rodriguez, "The Cumulative Effect of Race and Ethnicity in Juvenile Court Outcomes and Why Preadjudication Detention Matters," *Journal of Research in Crime and Delinquency* 47 (2010): 391–413; T. Schlesinger, "Racial and Ethnic Disparity in Pretrial Criminal Processing," *Justice Quarterly* 22 (2005): 170–92; D. Steffensmeier and S. Demuth, "Ethnicity and Sentencing Outcomes in the U.S. Federal Courts: Who Is Punished More Harshly?," *American Sociological Review* 65 (2000): 705–29; D. Steffensmeier and S. Demuth, "Ethnicity and Judges' Sentencing Decisions: Hispanic-Black-White Comparisons," *Criminology* 39 (2001): 145–78.

79. Steffensmeier and Demuth, "Ethnicity and Sentencing Outcomes"; Steffensmeier and Demuth, "Ethnicity and Judges' Sentencing Decisions"; Brennan and Spohn, "Race/Ethnicity and Sentencing Outcomes."

80. Demuth, "Racial and Ethnic Differences in Pretrial Release"; Schlesinger, "Racial and Ethnic Disparity in Pretrial Criminal Processing."

81. Rodriguez, "The Cumulative Effect of Race and Ethnicity in Juvenile Court Outcomes."

82. W. J. Wilson, *The Truly Disadvantaged: The Inner City, the Underclass, and Public Policy* (Chicago: University of Chicago Press, 1987); Sampson and Wilson, "Toward a Theory of Race, Crime, and Urban Inequality," 177–89.

83. M. L. Small and K. Newman, "Urban Poverty after *The Truly Disadvantaged*: The Rediscovery of the Family, the Neighborhood, and Culture," *Annual Review of Sociology* 27 (2001): 23–45.

84. M. Marable, "Incarceration vs. Education: Reproducing Racism and Poverty in America," *Race, Poverty & the Environment* (Fall 2008): 59–61; C. Parenti, *Lockdown America: Police and Prisons in the Age of Crisis* (New York: Verso Books, 2008).

85. K. Beckett, *Making Crime Pay: Law and Order in Contemporary American Politics* (New York: Oxford University Press, 1997); E. Bell, *Criminal Justice and Neoliberalism* (New York: Palgrave Macmillan, 2011).

86. Wilson, *The Truly Disadvantaged*; A. S. Alderson and F. Nielsen, "Globalization and the Great U-Turn: Income Inequality Trends in 16 OECD Countries," *American Journal of Sociology* 107 (2002): 1244–99; Ted Mouw, "Job Relocation and the Racial Gap in Unemployment in Detroit and Chicago, 1980 to 1990," *American Sociological Review* 65 (2000): 730–53.

87. Alderson and Nielson, "Globalization and the Great U-Turn."

88. Mouw, "Job Relocation and the Racial Gap."

89. Council of State Governments Justice Center, *Justice Reinvestment in Michigan: Analyses of Crime, Community Corrections, and Sentencing Policies*, 2009, https://csgjusticecenter. org/wp-content/uploads/2012/12/Analyses.pdf.

90. Citizens Research Council of Michigan, *Growth in Michigan's Corrections System: Historical and Comparative Perspectives*, Report 350, 2008, https://crcmich.org/ growth_corrections_system_historical_comparative_perspective-2008.

91. A. L. Fernandes-Alcantara, *Disconnected Youth: A Look at 16 to 24 Year Olds Who Are Not Working or in School* (Washington, DC: Congressional Research Service, 2015).

92. D. Steffensmeier and E. Allan, "Gender and Crime: Toward a Gendered Theory of Female Offending," *Annual Review of Sociology* 22 (1996): 459–87.

93. M. Rafaelli and L. L. Ontai, "Gender Socialization in Latino/a Families: Results from Two Retrospective Studies," *Sex Roles* 50 (2004): 287–99.

94. M. E. Wolfgang and F. Ferracuti, *Subculture of Violence: Towards an Integrated Theory in Criminology* (Thousand Oaks, CA: Sage Publications, 1967).

95. Demuth, "Racial and Ethnic Differences in Pretrial Release."

96. Durán, "Legitimated Oppression"; Rodriguez, "The Cumulative Effect of Race and Ethnicity in Juvenile Court Outcomes."

97. Chiricos and Eschholz, "The Racial and Ethnic Typification of Crime"; M. DeJesus-Torres, "Microaggressions in the Criminal Justice System at Discretionary Stages and Its Impact on Latino(a)/Hispanics," *Justice Professional* 13 (2000): 69–89; D. E. Mastro and E. Behm-Morawitz, "Latino Representation on Prime Time Television," *Journalism & Mass Communication Quarterly* 82 (2005): 110–30; Romero, "State Violence, and the Social and Legal Construction of Latino Criminality, 1081–118.

98. S. Oboler, "'Vivendo en el Olvido': Behind Bars, Latinos and Prison," *Latino Studies* 6 (2008): 1–10.

99. E. A. Carson, *Prisoners in 2016*, NCJ 251149 (Washington, DC: U.S. Department of Justice, 2018).

100. E. Schlosser, "The Prison Industrial Complex," *The Atlantic*, December 1998, http://www. theatlantic.com.

101. J. D. Donahue, *Prisons for Profit: Public Justice, Private Interests* (Economic Policy Institute, 1988), https://www.epi.org/publication/epi_virlib_studies_1988_prisonsf/; Government Accounting Office, *Private and Public Prisons: Comparing Operational Costs and/or Quality of Service*, GAO/GGD-96-198 (Washington, DC: U.S. Accounting Office, 1996).

102. Schlosser, "The Prison Industrial Complex."

103. Hartnett, "The Annihilating Public Policies," 497.

104. Alliance for Immigrant Rights and Reforms Michigan, "Deportation Profiteers Stand to Benefit from Proposed Private Prison," March 9, 2012, https://griid.org/2012/03/18/deportation-profiteers-stand-to-benefit-from-proposed-private-prison-in-michigan/.

105. National Public Radio, "Prison Economics Help Drive Ariz. Immigration Law," 2012, http://www.npr.org.

106. E. J. Melzer, "Private Prison Corporation Charged with Murder," *Michigan Messenger*, November 12, 2008.

107. Suburban Stats, *Population Demographics for Baldwin Village, Michigan in 2016 and 2015*, 2016, https://suburbanstats.org/population/michigan/how-many-people-live-in-baldwin-village.

108. FBI Uniform Crime Reporting Program, 1976–2013, www.disastercenter.com/crime.

109. Council of State Governments Justice Center, *Justice Reinvestment in Michigan: Analyses of Crime, Community Corrections, and Sentencing Policies* (2009), https://csgjusticecenter.org/wp-content/uploads/2012/12/Analyses.pdf.

110. Ibid.

111. R. R. Risko, *Background Briefing: Corrections* (Lansing: Michigan House of Representatives, 2015), http://www.house.mi.gov/hfa/PDF/Briefings/Corrections_BudgetBriefing_fy15-16.pdf. Also see R. R. Risko, *Budget Briefing: Corrections* (Lansing: Michigan House Fiscal Agency, 2019), https://www.house.mi.gov/hfa/PDF/Briefings/Corrections_BudgetBriefing_fy18-19.pdf.

112. R. R. Risko, *Line Item and Boilerplate Summary: Corrections* (Lansing: Michigan House of Representatives, 2016), http://www.house.mi.gov/hfa/PDF/LineItemSummaries/line17_MDOC.pdf.

113. Schlosser, "The Prison Industrial Complex."

114. Michigan Department of Corrections, "2010 Progress Report: Making Strides in Public Safety" (Michigan Prisoner Reentry Initiative, 2010), http://www.michigan.gov/documents/corrections/MPRI_2010_Progress_Report_343664_7.pdf.

115. Michigan Office of the Auditor General, "Performance Audit of the Michigan Prisoner Reentry Initiative (MPRI) Department of Corrections," 2012, https://audgen.michigan.gov/finalpdfs/11_12/r471040011.pdf.

116. Michigan Office of the Auditor General, "Performance Audit of the Michigan Prisoner Reentry Initiative (MPRI) Department of Corrections."

117. Ibid.

118. Department of Corrections, "Offender Success," State of Michigan, 2016, https://www.michigan.gov/corrections/0,4551,7-119-33218--,00.html.

119. C. Kirkham, "Michigan Private Prisons Law Could Reopen Facility With Checkered Past," Huffpost, January 12, 2013, https://www.huffingtonpost.com/2013/01/12/michigan-private-prisons-_n_2453117.html.

120. L. Musu-Gillette, J. Robinson, J. McFarland et al., *Status and Trends in the Education of Racial and Ethnic Groups 2016* (NCES 2016-007) (Washington, DC: U.S. Department of Education, National Center for Education Statistics, 2016), http://nces.ed.gov/pubsearch.

121. Villarruel, Walker, Minifree et al., *¿Dónde está la justicia?*

Lox (The Wolverine)

The Struggle to Express a Native American Identity in the Carceral State

Aaron Kinzel

T his chapter is a critical self-narrative and will be appropriately woven throughout the following pages with peer-reviewed literature to discuss some of the phenomenological occurrences of Native American prisoners in the carceral state. This style has been shown in scholarly works such as autoethnography, which is an example of blending personal experience with academic research and writing.[1] Autoethnography is used as a mechanism to discover unique ways of understanding perspectives between authors, audiences, and texts. This methodology is used to develop literature and understand personal experience.[2] It is my intent to present a short memoir of my life while incarcerated that is connected to various scholarly works.

I grew up surrounded by a life of crime with family members who were in and out of the criminal justice system. I have spent several months in different juvenile detention facilities before the age of eighteen. Shortly after legally becoming an adult at the age of eighteen, I was locked up in a county jail awaiting trial, and then at nineteen years old, was sentenced to 19 years in prison and then served nearly 10 of those years, in several different adult correctional facilities, before I was granted a mandatory parole. These incarceration experiences give me a profound insight into the inner workings of the criminal justice system and the correctional process.

There is literature that surrounds the emic point of view from a formerly incarcerated perspective as well. Newbold et al. describe the importance of autoethnography from a convict perspective, which can provide a unique viewpoint in connection to prison life that cannot be found in conventional research or interviews.[3] This chapter will describe what is experienced by a formerly incarcerated individual who was deeply immersed within various aspects of prison culture, convict identity, and civic engagement within the carceral state.

Living the Life of Delinquency/Criminality

I am a directly affected individual who was born and raised in a life of crime. My earliest memories and a great deal of my existence has exposed me to all levels of the juvenile and criminal justice system. As a child, my social network was filled with family members and friends who were in and out of jail and prison. I grew up in poverty and was homeless on several occasions and was often subjected to abuse from different men, involved in criminal activity, that my mother was living with over the years. I learned about the darker side of life in the beginning of my childhood development.

A formerly incarcerated individual who later became a tenured academic, John Irwin shared a unique perspective on the development of criminality.[4] According to Irwin, a criminal is often initiated through some type of direct contact with other criminals who are involved in criminal or deviant behavior. This personal environmental exposure begins the track of criminal identity formation, which is a set of beliefs, values, understandings, meanings, and self-definitions that are relative to one or more criminal lifestyles. Irwin described identity in connection to subgroup typologies such as thieves, dope fiends, and hustlers.[5]

I saw family members, including my mother and various men that she had relationships with, abuse drugs and commit crimes in the community. Family and friend gatherings brought many individuals together with criminal records who often spoke about life in prison around me, and I learned how to identify the formerly incarcerated through black and gray tattoo styles with occasional gang-specific markings. By the time I was eight years old, I probably already knew more about crime and prison than most college students studying criminal justice. My first math lessons as a child were learning how to break down an ounce into 28 grams and convert fractions for narcotics between ¼ and ½ amounts of various illegal products. These early educational lessons also included the preparation and loading of firearms and my observance of violent acts against random people.

Irwin found in one of his studies that many convicted felons have had significant exposure to criminal systems prior to their initial arrest.[6] However, there are some individuals who have not yet had these criminal exposures and could be defined as first-time offenders. Not all convicted felons have an established criminal identity before their entrance into a correctional facility. Past poignant and disorienting experiences of a convicted felon can certainly assist in the shaping of future criminal behavioral patterns.[7]

I am a multiracial male with a Caucasian, Hispanic, and Native American background who knew very little about my Native ancestry. As a child, I never met my real father, which caused me to not know about my rich cultural heritage until I became trapped in the carceral state. My negative upbringing allowed me to observe extreme acts of violence in my youth, and I was subjected to neglect, beatings, and even torture by violent adult criminals, who were often drunk or under the influence of multiple narcotics or suffering from severe mental health issues. There were other individuals that suffered violent attacks through stabbings or shootings in my community and were sometimes left for dead or made to disappear, never to be found. I was traumatized at a very early age and developed behavioral issues from the chaos I observed at home. I struggled in school and was given detention, suspensions, and expulsions, which eventually led me to drop out of high school at the age of sixteen.

For short periods of time, I was on probation and incarcerated in several different juvenile detention facilities, in both Michigan and Ohio, at the age of fifteen and sixteen for both moderate and serious offenses. These experiences hardened me and only made me more aggressive and criminally sophisticated. I learned how to destroy my community by becoming hypermasculine from the violence I was subjected to as a child, and I in turn committed violent offenses against anyone who challenged my authority on the streets, whether they were community members or law-enforcement officials. Through the illicit activities of my family and my involvement in the black market (illegal) economy, selling firearms and narcotics, I profited from the exploitation of drug addicts and weak gang members. I am sure that my actions directly caused great bodily harm and devastated various communities, and it is also possible that these negative actions indirectly caused death to some individuals. In 1997, as an eighteen-year-old teenager, I was arrested for a serious confrontation with law enforcement during a traffic stop in which I started a shootout with two officers. I fired one shot from my gun at one of the officers and they returned fire with a hailstorm intended to kill me, by blasting sixteen rounds into my vehicle at point-blank range. Miraculously, no one was killed or injured during this tragic event, which I foolishly and arrogantly started. A manhunt ensued in Northern Maine on the border of Canada, and I was eventually captured the following day. I was taken to a local county jail and charged with the attempted murder of a police officer. During my initial arraignment in court, I was told that I was facing life in prison, and I spent almost a year and a half awaiting trial. As I look back upon my actions now, my heart is heavy from regret, but unfortunately I cannot change my past, although I have certainly learned from my transgressions.

Insider Perspective of the Carceral State

Nationally there is an outcry to end mass incarceration within the United States. According to the American Civil Liberties Union, the U.S. has approximately 5 percent of the entire world's population and has more than 25 percent of the world's prison population.[8] This makes the United States the world's largest jailer. From 1978 to 2014, the U.S. prison population has risen 408 percent. Approximately one in every 110 adults are incarcerated in a local jail or state/federal prison. One in every 35 adults are under some type of correctional control, which includes jail, prison, probation, and parole populations.[9] It is also important to note that there is evidence that most of the formerly incarcerated will not become successful upon their release. According to the Bureau of Justice Statistics, many returning citizens fall into a cycle of recidivism, which is the return rate to prison for a technical violation or a new criminal charge; this peaked at 67.8 percent (roughly two out of three return to prison) within three years of release and 76.6 percent (roughly three out of four return to prison) within five years of release.[10] Correctional systems are experiencing many hardships that may impact the administration of justice. Of these hardships, recidivism seems to be the most significant issue that needs to be addressed. Enacted federal public policy such as HR3355, "The Violent Crime Control and Law Enforcement Act of 1994," has taken an oppositional stance against giving prisoners access to educational opportunities and created numerous barriers to reentry.[11]

While in the county jail, I observed a strong racial dynamic in which most of the inmates were white and seemed to have power, through their strength in numbers, over racial minorities. Many staff and other inmates assumed that I was just another white teenager, but I quickly became associated with a minority group of Native American inmates and built strong bonds with them. The Natives were a small group and subjected to racist comments by other inmates on occasion and by some of the jail correctional staff.

I took on a leadership role in the jail that was very negative in nature and remember getting into fights with young white inmates about their racist comments towards Native Americans and a couple of African American inmates. Asserting control over others was not a challenging task as when I was on the streets, I was a leader in my community despite never becoming part of a formal gang like the Bloods, Crips, or Latin Kings. However, I did build small gang-like groups of youth who were loyal to me and helped with illegal activities. What I did different than traditional larger gang structures was to be all-inclusive with diverse groups of racial and ethnic backgrounds. I also did not have formal codes of conduct or have members display identifying tattoos and symbols. My members were in the shadows, which gave them more autonomy while secretly being part of a collective. In all honesty, I exploited other youth and utilized power dynamics to establish control over other individuals. This was done using psychological techniques of intimidation over others through fear and developing a hierarchal structure. I would give others a false sense of power by giving them control over certain resources, and reward or punish them accordingly for their efforts. Extending this street mentality into the county jail was a rather easy and seamless process, which allowed me to influence other inmates and even some correctional officers for my benefit.

I began to recruit young white inmates to join me and the other racial minorities as I felt that this diversity gave us strength. Within several months, I had a large following of about twenty members in my group, of a population of approximately one hundred inmates. My crew became the majority, as others did not gather in groups of more than two or three people. I began to wreak havoc on the jail and had my crew robbing weak inmates and started a small drug-smuggling operation. I also fought with several correctional officers who put their hands on me during different heated confrontations. I probably spent close to half of my time in and out of solitary confinement in the county jail, and these experiences made my mental health deteriorate and enhanced my aggression and violence. As I reflect upon the trauma of these times, it reminds me of the Kalief Browder story from a couple of years ago. For three years, Browder often fought and spent more than half of his time in solitary confinement, as a pretrial detainee on Riker's Island, when he was only sixteen years old. I understand Browder, because I too fell apart from these experiences inside and contemplated suicide as well. Shortly after his release, Browder struggled with community acclimation and mental health issues, and unfortunately, he eventually committed suicide due to the trauma that he faced while incarcerated.[12]

The solitary confinement of youth and adults can cause serious pain and suffering and can violate international human rights and United States constitutional law.[13] Youth are psychologically unable to handle solitary confinement with the resilience of an adult. Youth are still developing, and traumatic experiences like solitary confinement may have a profound effect on their chance to rehabilitate and grow. Solitary confinement can exacerbate, or make more likely short- and long-term mental health problems. The most common deprivation that accompanies solitary confinement, denial of physical exercise, is physically harmful to the health and well-being of an adolescent.[14]

Many Native American cultures utilize oral histories to share wisdom and teach lessons about life. My personal story included no fear of physical confrontations, initiating random acts of violence, and my resilience of being shot at sixteen times by law-enforcement officers at point-blank range and cheating death, which earned me the Native name in jail "Lox" or "The Wolverine." I learned that in Wabanaki Native American tradition, the Lox was a malevolent wolverine spirit of the northern tribes. The Lox had an aggressive, impatient soul who was quick to fight much larger opponents and was feared throughout the land and was known to quickly heal from injuries and rise from the dead. These Native stories were likely the basis for the Marvel comic book mutant character Logan the Wolverine from the X-Men. The irony is that the incarcerated Native elder named (Sleeping Wolf) who gave me this name was not aware I was from Michigan, or that the common animal associated with that state is a wolverine. Sleeping Wolf would observe me interact with the young Native inmates and often tried to warn me about the wrongfulness of my actions. This elder spoke of the power of dreams and described the importance of seeking balance throughout our journey in life. He told me that there was a darkness in my spirit, and that if I continued to take from this world without giving back that I would become consumed by my anger and suffer eternally. He was certainly right, as I had faced trauma my entire life and it was beginning to consume me, but I was not about to tell him that he was correct. I remember telling Sleeping Wolf in a very sarcastic tone that it was quite hypocritical of him to judge me when he too was sitting in jail. He then told me that it was his choice to come to jail for him to uplift the spirit of his people. I thought that his story was bullshit, but I later learned that he had a nephew in the jail and other members of his tribe who had confirmed that Sleeping Wolf would get drunk and disorderly on purpose in public on rare occasions so he could spend time with his people. I was quite perplexed that a senior citizen would purposefully come to jail and that his purpose was to try and instill hope in others.

I started to warm up to Sleeping Wolf and listen to his stories that describe how sometimes we must break things in this world, but it is necessary to restore that which has been broken. My favorite story was about a selfish young Native boy who stole a bunch of beans and corn that was meant for his entire tribe. He secretly stored the food in a nearby cave and became very fat over the next several weeks as his entire tribe was confused by the missing crops and began starving as the winter weather approached. One day the fat young Native boy went to his secret cave to enjoy his food while letting his tribe starve, and was slashed across his chest by the claws of a large brown bear who emerged from the shadows above his hidden, stolen treasure. Frightened and seriously injured from the brown bear, the fat young Native boy fell down a cliff and hit his head upon some large rocks. He awoke the next day dizzy and covered in blood and falling snow from a massive blizzard that had begun the night before. The fat young Native boy returned to his tribe and they were gone. The tribe had left to find more food and avoid the snowstorm that would have trapped them in the valley near the mountains. The snow had fallen so quickly and heavily that the fat Native boy did not know in which direction they had traveled. He walked for several days, freezing in the cold without any food or shelter, and eventually died from starvation. His tribe had reached a new area safely away from the blizzard of the mountains and had found plentiful wild game, but many other tribal members died during the journey as well because the fat Native boy's self-interest was stronger than his love of the tribe.

Sleeping Wolf described the ignorance of the fat Native boy and the importance of sharing in the tribe and the interconnectedness of life in general. Sometimes the damage we cause will not only harm ourselves but can bring suffering or death indirectly to others, as in the story where others from the fat Native boy's tribe died from starvation for his selfishness as they fled the blizzard in the mountains seeking shelter and food. Sleeping Wolf also told a short story about harvesting crops from the land and how you must destroy the life of a plant and burn the remains to enrich the surrounding soil. This destruction can be viewed as a violent act, but sometimes it is necessary to survive. He described how the intent of an action can have a profoundly important impact on the outcome of any given situation. Restoration comes through planting new seeds the following spring in the fertile ground to harvest a new crop and continue the life cycle. In retrospect, I see that this was a powerful narrative that contained many ethical guidelines for behavior, and lessons regarding community and selflessness and the cycles of life and death. However, at the time, I was not ready to value the wisdom of this elder and I continued down a destructive and downward spiral. This was the beginning of my connection with Wabanaki Natives, but it would not be my last, as during my incarceration journey, I would reunite with tribal members who would visit me in prison.

Prison Culture

The environment of prison has been socially constructed in a way to oppress prisoners above and beyond their criminal sentence delivered by a court of law. To understand prison culture, it is necessary to intently observe various phenomena within a correctional setting. This begins with the exposure to the physical structure of the prison environment, which is often made of solid concrete and steel bars to reduce or eliminate the possibility of escape from the institution. A prison is a paramilitary complex that controls everything that a prisoner does throughout the day.[15] From the first day an individual enters a correctional facility, the state is supposed to be responsible for ensuring safe treatment and supervision of every person, holding individuals accountable for their actions, and promoting rehabilitation for a safe return to the community. But in many instances, the experience of getting locked up can pose serious risks to a person's safety and mental health and often can increase a person's risk of harming themselves or committing further crime. Under the Eighth Amendment of the U.S. Constitution, individuals convicted of a crime have the right to be free of "cruel and unusual" punishment while confined within jail or prison. This includes any punishment that is clearly inhumane or that violates basic human dignity. Prisons basically limit your civil rights and liberties and subject you to an array of violent acts. The concept of qualified immunity makes it nearly impossible to sue government officials and protects them from liability for civil damages "insofar as their conduct does not violate clearly established statutory or constitutional rights of which a reasonable person would have known."[16]

As I reflected upon my incarceration as a young teenager, I thought about some aspects of why I became successful and did not recidivate upon my release from prison despite the difficult circumstances inside the system. I believe that the secret sauce of my success has been strongly influenced by mentorship and the pursuit of higher education. My preliminary thoughts directed me back to how I initially entered prison without an education and had limited rehabilitative opportunities inside different correctional facilities. Other than earning my GED during my first year locked up in a county jail, as a pretrial detainee, I did not really have a formal education or legitimate work history. While in prison, I slowly began to become less violent and involved in illegal activities as I physically and mentally matured in my early twenties. I began to educate myself through self-help books, with a focus upon public policy and law.

I have observed over the years that most of the people who enter the criminal justice system have numerous socioeconomic deficits. I am not alone in this perspective, as many youth and adults held within correctional facilities lack basic educational attainment and have faced traumatic events throughout their lives. Gottschalk has found that correctional populations often come from chronically marginalized communities that lack formal education, adequate employment, and mental health treatment.[17] One in three prisoners were unemployed during their initial arrest and entry into the criminal justice system. Approximately 78 percent of these prisoners did not graduate from high school, and approximately 25 percent have a recent history of mental health issues.[18]

Tregea has supportive documentation from prisoner essays, which were utilized to capture real-life connections to criminological theory, that discuss some of the mechanisms that capture individuals in a life of crime.[19] He highlights the implications of theory for prevention, and incites readers to become active in dealing with social problems. In addition to the usual assortment of theories, he raises issues of prison education, the incarceration binge, politics, media, and the criminal-justice industrial complex. All criminals are basically given the equivalent of a life sentence as they are locked up and then locked out of conventional inclusion in society upon their release. They often cannot vote and are denied jobs and public assistance because of having a felony conviction.[20]

Correctional environments utilize oral histories, which are similar in nature to how Native American tribal elders share knowledge among a broad range of diverse individuals. I was mentored by these elders that visited me in prison, and "lifers" (convicts who are sentenced to a term of life in prison) and "long-timers" (convicts that are sentenced to a long sentence, generally 10 or more years). Fortunately for me, I stayed connected to a small subpopulation within prison that was composed of mostly Native prisoners, who taught me positive values inside the darkness of prison and helped me to evolve from extremely negative activity that I participated in during my stay in the county jail. However, I still had strong bonds and connections to other prisoners from different racial or gang affiliations. I found that I was discriminated against more by correctional staff due to my self-identification as a Native American prisoner than as a perceived white prisoner who was convicted of trying to murder a police officer. This is a notable example of white privilege in action at a correctional facility.

In my experience, correctional institutions have their own unique culture, and it is important to learn how to navigate that system successfully as a prisoner to benefit the most from the limited rehabilitative programs. I found that prisons are also extremely political environments that have their own unwritten rules and codes that provide the framework of their subculture, which often has very different norms than conventional society. Donald Clemmer is one of the first to develop a strong prison-culture narrative, in a well-known study conducted in the 1930s entitled *The Prison Community*.[21] Clemmer collected data for several years during his employment as a sociologist on the mental health staff at a prison. He developed a theory during this study called prisonization, which is essentially the process of incarcerated individuals becoming accustomed to prison culture. They adopt the social structure of a correctional environment by following informal prisoner codes of conduct, which inevitably makes reintegration back into society extremely difficult. According to Clemmer, a great deal of this process was negative in nature.[22] Ross and Richards describe the importance of the so-called "convict code" as a necessity for survival within a correctional environment.[23] Prisoners who do not abide by the established unwritten rules will often face adversity, which ranges from disrespectful glances to a swift and violent death. Most convicts will be quite respectful of each other unless someone is from the lower end of the hierarchical scale, such as an informant or child molester. The convict code is nuanced at different correctional facilities and is learned through social interactions and passed down through the oral histories of more established convicts. The convict code establishes acceptable behavior, such as you should mind your own business, pay your debts, and be loyal to the convict group. It also establishes unacceptable behavior, such as snitching on another convict or getting too friendly with correctional officers.[24]

Clemmer also discussed the convict code, but referred to it as the prisoner's code that is learned by word of mouth.[25] He mentions that this code is not new and was previously called a "phenomenon of communication" that can be traced back at least forty years before his study, which would be in the late 1800s.[26] Every prisoner learns this code quickly, as the consequences for violations of these rules can be more severe than breaking formal correctional policies.[27] In my experience, the convict code is a learned behavior that many prisoners follow without questioning the origin. Each facility may have more nuanced versions of the code depending on the convict hierarchy of that place.

Our Native American group also had more specific rules, some of which were conflicting with the mainstream convict code. Tribal elders would visit us in prison, and we were able to smudge with them and share tobacco in a traditional manner. They would teach us through telling stories that often had positive and negative elements, very similar to the stories I heard while in jail. One elder always talked about how we are born with equal parts of light and darkness in our souls, and that with time we become out of balance, like a scale. How we stack up our actions on each side will determine who we are when we pass on back into the spirit realm. In Native culture, it is important to live a life of peace and always respect those around you and the environment. It is a challenging task to live by a peaceful code inside an institution that is predominantly volatile and violent in nature.

Prisons often have a separation of racial groups, and conflicts arise amongst these groups over territory or illegal trades. Our group collectively followed traditional Native peacemaking as a practice, especially when large groups would have issues that could have led to unnecessary violence. However, there were members of this group, myself included, who did not always abide by the peacemaking paradigm and on occasion resorted to violent activity out of personal necessity. I committed acts of violence with and without dangerous weapons when I felt threatened or disrespected by other young prisoners. I also conspired with other prisoners to cover up acts of violence that were perpetrated by close friends, particularly in my Native circle. While I was certainly no angel while incarcerated, it is important to note that our Native group, including me ("Lox") and my best friend inside the system, known as "Little Hawk," prevented several riots and organized acts of violence, which could have easily turned into murders, through the utilization of restorative practices. Native elders from the streets taught us about these restorative practices during religious visits that they made while we were incarcerated. The theory of restorative justice, which was developed from knowledge given by Native Americans, incorporates the repairing of the harm that is caused by an offender and attempting to make all parties involved in an incident whole again.[28] Conventional restorative practices usually involve a three-step model, which includes (1) identification of harm and implementation of a repair process, (2) involvement of all stakeholders (offender, victim, and community), and (3) the transformation of communities or schools responding to crime as opposed to the government. Under the restorative justice model, questions are framed differently, such as asking: What is the nature of the harm resulting from the behavior or the crime that was committed? What do we need to repair the harm? When we bring together victims, offenders, families, schools, and other key stakeholders in a variety of settings, restorative justice helps offenders understand the implications of their actions and provides an opportunity for them to become reconnected to the community.[29] If we respond in a restorative manner, we do things with them and involve them directly in the process. A critical element of the restorative approach is that, whenever possible, we also include victims, family, friends, and community—that is, those who have been affected by the offender's behavior.[30] We utilized these theoretical concepts in a very practical way by bringing together different racial groups who felt harmed in some way by the other group. Allowing prisoners from diverse groups to come together and give voice to their problems in a nonviolent way was an incredible experience. Many issues were solved through mediation and just talking through problems and involving influential leaders from each racial group to agree upon terms that would benefit the entire prison community.

Convict Identity

While incarcerated, I developed what I call a convict identity, which was also strongly aligned with Native American culture and the convict code. I learned through various forms of self-help educational materials and from other prisoners who had spent decades behind bars. Prisoners shared their oral histories and became my first real positive male role models; inspired me to further develop an advocacy agenda; and assisted me with learning about public policy and civil/criminal law. Much of what I learned from listening to diverse prisoners while incarcerated assisted me in solidifying my convict identity. Environmental factors, such as prison culture, and social interactions with Native prisoners and tribal elders who visited us from the community also had profound impact on my development as well. I feel that this convict identity was built upon my interactions while in prison and the acceptance of many aspects of the convict code. I also feel that this convict identity still influences my perspective, career, and academic studies to the present day.

Erikson discusses the origins of one's life cycle, and that constructed identity can be traced back to pivotal moments during the developmental stages.[31] There are two key areas that are intertwined throughout this process, called group identity and ego identity. Group identity refers to individuals' perceived status within a specific group of individuals and includes the ability to make or break social bonds—where ego identity is a notion of the conscious sense of self that is developed through distinct types of social interactions. Both group and ego are constantly being changed due to new experiences and information collected throughout the life cycle. Who we become regarding our character and personality in adult life therefore is intricately connected to the initial stages of development, which creates the core of our humanity or the lack thereof.[32]

Convict identity formation could also be attributed to various interactions between prisoners in which they observe illegal acts, gambling, violence, advocacy, and legal procedures. Bandura's Social Learning Theory (SLT) demonstrates how both children and adults can identify with a specific model who has certain values, beliefs, and attitudes.[33] These individuals may then internalize and adopt the qualities of the individuals that they observe within an environment. SLT focuses on the interactions of mental factors in the process of learning. Bandura believed that individuals are active information processors and they establish links between cognitive processes that allow observational learning to occur. Therefore, it is necessary to understand that individuals do not automatically imitate behavior that is observed without some type of cognitive processing of that behavior. Identification is considered different than the imitation of a model, as it is the adoption of numerous types of behaviors as opposed to copying a single behavior, as was observed within the Bobo doll experiments in which children copied the violent acts of adults.[34]

Civic Engagement

My observation of prison culture and acceptance of a convict identity has transformed me into an engaged citizen who fought for the civil rights of myself and other prisoners. The question then becomes: are people born with a moral compass, or is there a process of differentiating the notions of right and wrong within society?

While working in prison, I received several life-altering physical disabilities from work-related injuries. I filed hundreds of grievances for myself and other prisoners who believed that they were being treated unfairly or unjustly. I initiated numerous policy changes to protect the civil rights of myself and my peers within prison. My areas of focus were due-process-related grievances, Equal Employment Opportunity Commissions cases, equal religious rights, and access to legal materials. While locked up, I learned a great deal about other cultures and the necessity of diversity when my Native group advocated for our ability to practice our religious beliefs and become a formal religious organization, which later helped other prisoners form new religious groups as well. I helped set a precedent and assisted organizations such as Ancient Egyptian, Asatru, Buddhism, Hinduism, and Islam to be allowed to practice in prison.

Prisoners are guaranteed the right to express themselves through constitutional amendments and various case laws that allow the freedom of religion while incarcerated. However, the applicability and extent of this freedom is limited in scope regarding the safety and security of a correctional facility. Initially, members from our Native group were already discriminated against, from a racial perspective, by some correctional staff and officers. Unlike in jail though, other prisoners viewed us with respect, particularly me, due to the violent nature of my criminal offense against law enforcement and my reputation for fighting other inmates and staff from the county jail. When I first arrived in prison, there was only a large Christian group and a very small but well-established Wiccan group that had access to religious services. I had attempted to gain help and insight from the Wiccan group to better understand how our Native group could establish ourselves within the prison. However, the Wiccan group refused to help us, as they felt that it might infringe upon their territory and they might lose their positive connection to the prison administration. This did not deter me or other individuals in the Native group, and we began researching aspects of the law and asking some of the lifers/long-timers for legal assistance and guidance.

After many months of being denied the ability to have a Native religious group by correctional administrators, they conceded when we drafted and threatened a lawsuit against the facility. This was both a victory and loss, as we now had made enemies with correctional administrators, but we could have group meetings and exercise our religious beliefs. Violations of policy and procedure by staff became frequent through not allowing us to cover up with prayer blankets, or interrupting prayers and opening medicine bag contents. Religious items were supposed to be opened like legal correspondence, only in the presence of the prisoner, but this was often violated by correctional staff. Later a lawsuit was filed against the prison administration for discriminatory practices and the denial of a sweat lodge, which was later granted.

Toward the end of my sentence in prison, I focused heavily upon rehabilitative programs, and I took a college correspondence course in psychology and decided that I would pursue higher education at a local community college upon release. After I left prison, I found that I could practice my religion freely and that higher education was my path to redemption. I was released on parole from the Maine Department of Corrections (MDOC) and sent back to my home in Michigan through an interstate compact agreement in 2007. Since my release from the custody of the MDOC, I have made a 180 degree turn away from my past, from destroying my community to strengthening it and enhancing public policy and community safety. I have also struggled to acclimate to society due to the trauma that I have endured throughout a decade of incarceration. It has also been extremely difficult to navigate the criminal collateral consequences of conviction, which are the policies that allow legal discrimination against formerly incarcerated individuals.

The lack of employment opportunities can lead to the commission of more crimes to provide for the basic needs of offenders. The old expression "desperate times call for desperate measures" seems to be an appropriate analogy for this situation. Bureau of Justice statistician William Sabol conducted a study on the employment conditions for offenders released from Ohio State correctional facilities during 1999–2000.[35] This study concluded that post-prison employment following the first two years after release is affected by the local labor-market conditions. He also found that pre-employment experiences contributed to future employment opportunities for offenders. Sabol concluded that more than one-third of the ex-prisoners in his study had not found employment by the end of the eighth quarter after their initial release. He also found that pre-prison employment experiences increased the likelihood of post-prison employment by approximately 6 percent. Further analysis found that pre-prison employment had a much greater effect on future employment than the trends in local labor markets and increased the probability of future employment during the first two years of release by 10 percent.[36]

I started college in the fall of 2007 and have obtained three college degrees since (AAS, BA, and MPA) and will complete all the requirements for a doctorate with the acceptance of a dissertation proposal in the winter of 2018. I am a rare breed as an educated former prisoner, but I am not the first. Yeager reviewed historical archives and read many of the forgotten books by Frank Tannenbaum, who was incarcerated in the early 1900s.[37] Tannenbaum enrolled in college upon his release and eventually earned a doctorate, with his broadly published dissertation on prisons, while simultaneously becoming a well-known prison reformist of his era. Tannenbaum visited many prisons and earned the respect of various correctional administrators, including warden Thomas Mott Osbourne.[38] I feel that I and a small population of other formerly incarcerated leaders/reformers are living in the shadow of Tannenbaum, who is considered the first convict criminologist and is the hundred-year-old archetype for my current life trajectory and current research project.

I applied to thousands of jobs and was never given a chance of employment until I was offered a teaching position as a non-tenure-track professor shortly after earning my master's degree in the winter of 2013. I taught for nearly three years as an instructor at Western Michigan University and currently teach undergraduate and graduate courses at the University of Michigan-Dearborn as a lecturer in criminology and criminal justice studies. A large part of my pedagogic technique is to teach my students how to identify and fight systemic oppressions such as racism and injustice in public policy. I have worked collaboratively with numerous nonprofit organizations that serve prisoners and parolees from all kinds of racial backgrounds, such as the Prison Creative Arts Project at the University of Michigan, to offer workshops inside correctional facilities. Being critical and pensive about a topic is very important to truly transfer knowledge to our students in an unbiased manner. I never would have thought in a million years that I would ever step foot back inside a prison. However, I recently have done so on numerous occasions across the United States under contract with various organizations or governments, or on a volunteer basis. I want to change the status quo for released prisoners and give them hope and inspiration while they are incarcerated. I have become very active, throughout Michigan and in other states, as an advocate for criminal justice reform. I often speak at community-based events and lobby public officials to embrace progressive public-policy reform measures, and I have offered dozens of professional presentations at multiple colleges/universities.

I have conducted numerous related consulting projects, such as contracts with the U.S. Department of Justice, to train executive-level correctional administrators nationwide on evidence-based best practices. I can easily connect to returning citizens and their families as I have the credibility and knowledge from doing this work for years as a member of their subculture. Beyond all my academic work and professional accomplishments, I am also now a father who is trying his best to instill positive values in my young daughter. I teach her about the importance of education and diversity, and love the fact that she is a bilingual child whose mother is French. Although her mother and I are no longer in a relationship, we both share the same perspective to provide our child with the best educational experiences possible. My daughter was enrolled in a private Montessori school at the age of only one until the age of five. She is now six years old and enrolled in an excellent school in France and exposed to global diversity. Not only is my child also multiracial, like me, but she has two different religious/ethnic backgrounds that further her cultural diversity. Her mother has Jewish lineage and is the grandchild of a survivor of the Holocaust. My daughter can also practice Native beliefs and travel to sacred sites with me that are of cultural and historical importance. I am very pleased that my child has so many protective factors that will hopefully shield her from falling into the trap of the carceral state. Many children who have incarcerated or previously incarcerated parents have a much higher probability of becoming incarcerated themselves. I will continue with everything in my power to break the chains of inequity and generations of poverty that have previously cursed my family, for the benefit of future generations of my offspring.

NOTES

An early version of this paper was presented at the annual meeting for the American Society of Criminology in November 2017 at the Philadelphia Marriott Downtown in Pennsylvania. The theme for the meeting was Crime, Legitimacy and Reform: Fifty Years after the President's Commission. Aaron T. Kinzel is a formerly incarcerated individual who is also a doctoral student in the College of Education, Health, and Human Services, and a Lecturer in Criminology and Criminal Justice Studies at the University of Michigan–Dearborn.

1. C. Ellis, T. Adams, and A. Bochner, "Autoethnography: An Overview," *Forum Qualitative Sozialforschung/Forum: Qualitative Social Research* 12, no. 1 (2010): 1–13.
2. Ibid.
3. G. Newbold et al., "Prison Research from the Inside: The Role of Convict Autoethnography," *Qualitative Inquiry* 20, no. 4 (2014): 439–48.
4. J. Irwin, *The Felon* (Englewood Cliffs, NJ: Prentice-Hall, 1970), 7–36.
5. Ibid.

6. Ibid.

7. Ibid.

8. American Civil Liberties Union, *The Prison Crisis*(2017), https://www.aclu.org/prison-crisis.

9. Ibid.

10. Bureau of Justice Statistics (BJS), *Recidivism* (2017), http://bjs.gov.

11. R. S. Hall and J. Killacky, "Correctional Education from the Perspective of the Prisoner Student," *Journal of Correctional Education* 59, no. 4 (2008): 301–20.

12. J. Gonnerman, "Kalief Browder, 1993–2015," *New Yorker*, June 7, 2015.

13. Michigan Council on Crime and Delinquency (MCCD), Youth Behind Bars (2017), http://www.miccd.org.

14. Ibid.

15. M. Gottschalk, *Caught: The Prison State and the Lockdown of American Politics* (Princeton, NJ: Princeton University Press, 2015), 1–22.

16. Harlow v. Fitzgerald, 457 U.S. 800, 818 (1982).

17. Gottschalk, *Caught*, 79–97.

18. Ibid.

19. W. Tregea, *Prisoners on Criminology: Convict Life Stories and Crime Prevention* (Lanham, MD: Lexington Books, 2014), 109–40.

20. Ibid., 331–48.

21. D. Clemmer, *The Prison Community* (New York: Rinehart, 1958), 294–320.

22. Ibid.

23. J. I. Ross and S. C. Richards, *Behind Bars: Surviving Prison* (Indianapolis, IN: Alpha Books, (2002), 72–74.

24. Ibid.

25. Clemmer, *The Prison Community*, 294–320.

26. Ibid.

27. Ibid.

28. National Institute of Justice, Restorative Justice, *National Institute of Justice: Criminal Justice Research, Development and Evaluation* (2017), https://nij.gov.

29. Ibid.

30. Ibid.

31. E. H. Erikson, *Identity and the Life Cycle* (New York: Norton, 1980), 18–50.

32. Ibid.

33. A. Bandura, D. Ross, and S. A. Ross, "Transmission of Aggression through the Imitation of Aggressive Models," *Journal of Abnormal and Social Psychology* 63 (1961): 575–82.

34. Ibid.

35. W. J. Sabol, "Local Labor Market Conditions and Post Prison Employment Experiences of Offenders Released from Ohio State Prisons," in *Barriers to Reentry: The Labor Market for Released Prisoners in Post-Industrial America*, ed. S. Bushway, M. Stoll, and D. Weimen (New York: Russell Sage Foundation, 2007), 257–64.

36. Ibid.

37. M. G. Yeager, *Frank Tannenbaum: The Making of a Convict Criminologist* (New York: Routledge, 2016), 57–71.

38. Ibid.

Mass Incarceration and Mental Illness

Addressing the Crisis

Carolyn Pratt Van Wyck and Elizabeth Pratt

I ndividuals with mental illness are part of the larger crisis of mass incarceration. They are vastly overrepresented in prisons and jails. As of 2016, there are an estimated 401,000 prisoners with mental illness—196,000 in jails and 205,000 in state and federal prisons.[1] This article reviews the magnitude of this crisis in correctional institutions and discusses health care and criminal justice policies that have contributed to the problem.[2] We illustrate some of these situations through the experience of our family and conclude by exploring a selection of well-studied remedies that can reduce the number of inmates with mental illness.

This crisis came home to our family when my young adult son Greg was arrested in 2010 for felony assault on an officer. When the officer told me about my son's charges, I lay on the floor and wailed. For the past year, the symptoms of Greg's mental illness had become increasingly apparent, but in the immediately preceding days his agitation had grown alarming. When he threw a vase and punched my husband, I called the police and told dispatch that Greg had a mental illness. To our horror, Greg's conversation with the responding officer deteriorated and escalated into a physical conflict.

Greg has since been arrested several times. He pleaded no contest and guilty to some charges and was found not criminally responsible on another. He served time in jails in three different counties. He called us frequently from jail, and from those calls, we were aware of the deterioration in Greg's mental condition. After his last arrest, on a misdemeanor charge that was later raised to a felony, he was found incompetent to stand trial. For over three years he was in the county jail, then the state hospital, then back and forth again.

Prior to his first arrest, we had not adequately understood what we were seeing in Greg's symptoms. He had been in counseling earlier that summer, but had stopped going. We had private insurance, but not the skills to encourage Greg into treatment or an understanding of the treatment system. We now realize that as a young man with psychosis and co-occurring substance abuse disorder, Greg had many risk factors for incarceration.[3] His later homelessness increased this risk. The resulting incarceration and hospitalization were costly for local and state government; for our family, who bore a heavy emotional burden as we learned to cope with the impacts of Greg's illness; and for Greg, who spent several years of his young adult life in institutions.

Untreated severe psychiatric symptoms such as impaired judgment, hallucinations, delusions, paranoia, mania, and inability to recognize one's own illness can lead to behavior that does not conform to social norms and may sometimes be criminal. The resulting encounters with law enforcement and the criminal justice system frequently lead to the incarceration of people with mental illness. Jails and prisons, however, were not designed as mental health treatment centers. The harsh and challenging conditions inside correctional facilities can make mental illness worse. In fact, law enforcement and correctional officials have been among the most vocal advocates for alternatives to prison and jail.[4] Addressing this crisis requires implementing criminal justice reforms and building a comprehensive health care system that supports people with mental illness before incarceration.

In order to tell this story, we have made several stylistic and content choices. First, while we shared in many of these experiences as Greg's sister and his mother, for simplicity the personal stories in this essay are told from the perspective of Elizabeth, Greg's mother. Second, while these stories are our own, and some are a matter of public record, they also belong to Greg. To provide a small measure of privacy for him, we have used a pseudonym. Finally, while the emphasis here is on the problem of mental illness and incarceration, we want in no way to minimize the experiences of individuals who have been the victims of crime or hurt by the behavior of someone with mental illness. The lack of support for individuals with mental illness has negative consequences for the people with mental illness, their families, and society at large.

Measures of the Problem

Across the United States, jails and prisons have become holding places for those with serious mental illness. Serious mental illness can include diagnoses such as major depressive disorder, schizophrenia, and bipolar disorder, which affect 4 percent of adults in the United States.[5] The facilities responsible for housing the most people with mental illnesses are no longer the nation's hospitals, but its jails. There is no psychiatric hospital in the United States that holds more people with mental illness than the Los Angeles County Jail, Rikers Island Jail Complex in New York, or Cook County Jail.[6] Incarceration is not a form of medical care. With limited ability to offer treatment, the strategies used to maintain control of prisoners and manage their behaviors can become punitive and harsh.

There is widespread agreement that mental illness is dramatically more prevalent among incarcerated people than in the general population, that the rate of mental illness is higher in jails than in state and federal prisons, and higher among female than male prisoners; however, determining a specific rate of mental illness among inmates is difficult. Researchers face methodological and ethical challenges in conducting research with incarcerated populations and with people facing mental illness. As a result, the estimated prevalence and severity of inmates' mental illness varies among studies. If mental illness is measured by the presence of symptoms, then decisions follow as to whether the symptoms are current, recent, or within the last year, and what severity of symptoms should be counted. Some studies expand results to include inmates with a history of a professional diagnosis, whether recent or lifetime. Others limit counts to only those inmates currently receiving treatment for a mental disorder. A variety of assessment tools are used, ranging from short surveys to detailed interviews designed to pick up symptoms of depression, mania, and psychosis.[7] Those inmates who are too ill to give consent to researchers and those who appear too incoherent to participate, even though they have consented, are sometimes left out of research studies. This introduces a systematic underestimation of the problem.[8]

Statisticians Doris James and Lauren Glaze from the U.S. Department of Justice, Bureau of Justice Statistics, authored a frequently cited 2006 study which found that 64.2 percent of jail inmates and 56.2 percent of state prisoners self-reported impairment due to a mental health problem.[9] When assessing for severe symptoms, the data showed that 60.5 percent of jail inmates and 49.2 percent of state prisoners had experienced mental illness within the last twelve months. James and Glaze further reported that if the mental health disorder was measured by treatment (professional diagnosis, inpatient hospitalization, use of prescription medication, or professional therapy) within the last twelve months before arrest or since admission, the figures declined to 24.3 percent of state prisoners and 20.6 percent of jail prisoners.[10]

A subsequent 2017 U.S. Department of Justice paper by Jennifer Bronson and Marcus Berzofsky found that 14.5 percent of state and federal prisoners and 26.4 percent of jail inmates had experienced severe psychological distress within the last thirty days. Because they looked at symptoms over a shorter time period and used a different measure of symptoms, their figures are lower than those found by James and Glaze.[11] Bronson and Berzofsky found that 36.9 percent of state and federal prisoners and 44.3 percent of jail inmates reported a prior professional diagnosis.[12]

A 2010 study ordered by the Michigan legislature focused on mental illness among state prisoners.[13] It found that 20.1 percent of male and 24.8 percent of female inmates had significant mental-health problems as assessed by a survey of severe symptoms.[14] For male inmates, the highest rate of mental-health problems occurred in special units where 45.3 percent had a mental-health problem, followed by 37.6 percent in administrative segregation, and 17.7 percent in the general prison population.[15]

The demographic characteristics of inmates with mental illness are difficult to pin down and depend again on the definitions of mental illness used. While there is little data on race and mental illness in the justice system, those estimates that are available suggest that minority men and women with mental illness are more likely to be incarcerated than white men and women who have a mental illness. There are also racial and cultural disparities in access to mental health care, stigma around seeking mental health services, and availability of culturally competent care that might affect the rate of diagnosis and past treatment for mental illnesses among minority populations.[16] Age is also a risk factor, and young people with mental illness are more likely to be in custody.[17] In these patterns, the mass incarceration of people with mental illness mirrors the demographic patterns of the larger crisis of mass incarceration. However, as figure 1 illustrates, compared with the general

FIGURE 1. Race of General Population, Incarcerated Popuations, and Incarcerated Groups with Mental Illness (Estimated Percent Distribution)

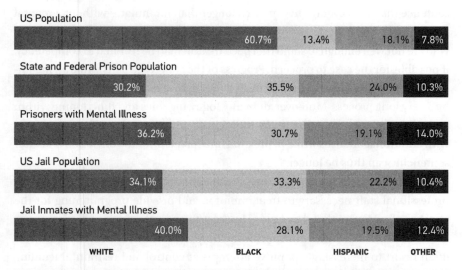

US Population
60.7% | 13.4% | 18.1% | 7.8%

State and Federal Prison Population
30.2% | 35.5% | 24.0% | 10.3%

Prisoners with Mental Illness
36.2% | 30.7% | 19.1% | 14.0%

US Jail Population
34.1% | 33.3% | 22.2% | 10.4%

Jail Inmates with Mental Illness
40.0% | 28.1% | 19.5% | 12.4%

WHITE — BLACK — HISPANIC — OTHER

POPULATION ESTIMATES ARE FOR 2017 FROM "QUICK FACT UNITED STATES," UNITED STATES CENSUS BUREAU, HTTPS://WWW.CENSUS.GOV. PRISON POPULATION AND JAIL POPULATION ESTIMATES ARE FROM BRONSON AND BERZOFSKY, *INDICATORS OF MENTAL HEALTH PROBLEMS REPORTED BY PRISONERS AND JAIL INMATES, 2011–12* (2017), 4, 13. LIKELIHOOD BY RACE OF HAVING SEVERE PSYCHOLOGICAL SYMPTOMS WITHIN THE LAST 30 DAYS WAS COMBINED WITH THESE ESTIMATES OF POPULATION DISTRIBUTIONS IN JAIL TO FIND THE DISTRIBUTION OF PRISONERS WITH MENTAL ILLNESS BY RACE.

prison population, prisoners with mental illness are slightly more likely to be white, because no group is insulated from the effects of mental illness.

The cost of holding individuals in the correctional system is enormous. Spending by states alone on corrections was nearly $45.0 billion in 2015.[18] With an annual budget of over $2.0 billion, the Michigan Department of Corrections calculates that the average cost of a state prisoner is $98.92 per day or $36,106 per year.[19] For the Woodland correctional facility where the prisoners with the most severe mental illness needs are held, the average cost per prisoner is nearly three times higher at $272.52 per day or $99,570 per year.[20] Individuals incompetent to stand trial are moved from jail to state hospitals, where the average daily cost for all patients is $1,044 per day or $380,922 per year per patient.[21] The state hospitals now care for the sickest patients, including those who private hospitals will not accept. Approximately 53 percent of Michigan's 770 public hospital beds are occupied by individuals involved with the justice system, either to be restored to competency in order to stand trial or because they were found not guilty by reason of insanity, crowding out others who might need inpatient treatment.[22]

For people with mental illness, the consequences of an encounter with law enforcement can be more severe than for those without a mental illness. For a similar offense, someone with mental illness is likely to have a maximum prison sentence that is on average five months longer than for inmates without a mental illness, and often their detention is in worse conditions.[23] After arrest, defendants who are not well enough to stand trial need treatment to be restored to competency, if possible, for the case to proceed. Progress of the court case halts while an incompetent defendant waits for treatment, and during the treatment period, which can be a very long process. Moreover, difficulty following rules and functioning within a prison routine means that many individuals with mental illness are charged with additional offenses while in prison. Time served prior to conviction and after sentencing can thus be longer.[24]

While many jails have mental health screening, they generally do not have the professional staff necessary to treat, monitor, and provide programming for the number of prisoners that they hold.[25] In order to prevent suicide and other forms of self-harm, or to control prisoners when they violate rules, correctional officers often resort to increasingly punitive attempts at control and restraint, including solitary confinement. This was borne out by Greg's experience. When correctional officers decided that Greg needed supervision beyond what could be achieved in any of the other units, they held him in an intake cell for over a week where he had no access to the telephone or time out of his cell. He also was held in a maximum security cell for most of the time, where he only had one hour out of his cell per day. One study of Washington's supermax prisoners found that 45 percent had a serious mental illness. This rate was nearly 3.5 times what the researchers had found in an earlier study of the general prison population.[26]

Other attempts to maintain control of prisoners with mental illness have been more disastrous. In Michigan's Ionia Maximum Security Facility, Kevin DeMott, a teenager with bipolar disorder, made several suicide attempts and incurred many disciplinary violations. Instead of going to the hospital, DeMott was held in solitary confinement for four months, during which time he was not always given his medication. In 2011, when he began to bang his head against the wall of his solitary cell hard enough to leave blood stains, he was pepper-sprayed and chained.[27] In a 2006 Michigan case, Timothy Joe Souders, a twenty-one-year-old man with depression, psychosis, and a history of suicide attempts, was moved into a solitary cell with soft restraints for "disobeying orders." When those no longer held him, Souder was shackled to a concrete slab for four days while waiting to be transferred to a psychiatric hospital. He died of heat exhaustion and dehydration, shackled and without medical care. Souder's death prompted an evaluation of prison medical care and policy limits on the use of restraints.[28] Jails frequently fail to prevent suicides. The U.S. annual suicide mortality rate per 100,000 jail inmates is 46, over three times the national suicide mortality rate.[29]

The consequences of the mass incarceration of individuals with mental illness are severe and numerous. There is a loss of freedom for thousands of people who are particularly vulnerable to abuse while incarcerated. But the consequences are not limited to those who are incarcerated. Families face a heavy emotional and financial burden. They watch as their loved one's health declines. They pay the exorbitant rates of jail phone calls and commit time and money to travel for visits. Taxpayers are billed to hold people in custody who often could be treated at a lower cost outside of jail. Individuals who, with treatment, might be able to live and work in the community are instead completely dependent on public funding and held in the most restrictive conditions.

How Did We Get Here?

The extreme overrepresentation of people with mental illness in the criminal justice system is multicausal. People with mental illness often struggle to follow norms. They can be caught up in nuisance violations like loitering, or might simply fail to remember to pay for services. Alternately, untreated psychosis might contribute to more severe criminal behavior. Policies that lead to increased incarceration more generally also tend to expand the incarceration of people with mental illness. Mandatory minimums, aggressive prosecution, and broken-windows policing, which targets minor crimes in efforts to clean up neighborhoods and reduce signs of blight, funnel people with mental illness into prison and jail and extend their stays. Many of these policies are covered elsewhere in this volume. Drug-related crimes are also common, as about half of individuals with severe mental illness have a co-occurring substance-abuse disorder.[30]

Lack of treatment for mental illness can increase the likelihood of offending and incarceration rates. Studies have found that treatment adherence (as measured by medication possession and regular outpatient care) reduces the risk of both arrest and community violence.[31] Those who are not in treatment are approximately 2.5 times more likely to commit serious violence or aggressive acts than those who are in treatment and adhering to it.[32] Recognizing the need for treatment and believing in its efficacy also reduces the likelihood of violence in the community.[33] However, predictors of criminality and violence are complex and include age, gender, and other indicators in addition to substance abuse and mental health status. Individuals with mental illness account for only a small portion (3–5 percent) of violent crime and are more likely to be victims of violent crime than perpetrators.[34]

Despite the efficacy of treatment in preventing or reducing the risk of incarceration, for many it is difficult to begin seeking services in the first place. Admitting to the need for mental health care can be difficult in a society where stereotypes of those with severe mental illness are more common than images of recovery. Mental illness is frequently represented as an excuse or problem that is not real. Friends and relatives might say that it is all "in your head," that it simply requires willpower, and that a better attitude might cure the problem. Other attitudes towards mental illness can be even more pathologizing. Some images of mental illness assume a pathology so deep as to make the individual seem untreatable and nearly inhuman. Mental illness is used as a cheap marker of violence and terror in movies and Halloween costumes.

In contrast, images of successful recovery and ongoing treatment are rare. Without positive images of recovery, it is hard to believe that treatment can be effective. When University of Michigan professor Peter Railton publicly acknowledged his experiences with depression, he was clear about the concerns that had previously prevented his disclosure. He worried that he would seem "tainted, reduced" and that no one would want to marry him or start a family. Friends, he thought, might "start tip-toeing around my psyche," and he wondered, "Would colleagues trust me with responsibility?"[35]

Acknowledging past or current treatment for psychosis can be even more challenging. In her book *An Unquiet Mind*, Kay Jamison, a psychiatry professor at Johns Hopkins University School of Medicine, acknowledged that she "had many concerns about writing a book that so explicitly describe[d] [her] own attacks of mania, depression, and psychosis, as well as [her] problems acknowledging the need for ongoing medication." Sharing her story could jeopardize her work. "Clinicians," she said, "have been, for obvious reasons of licensing and hospital privileges, reluctant to make their psychiatric problems known to others."[36] When fear of professional repercussions, discrimination, and stigma compel people in recovery to remain silent, the prevailing images of mental illness are shaped by stereotypes. For many people, mental illness is an invisible illness. We typically only recognize people with mental illness when their lack of treatment is obvious, when they seem scary and different, and their illness is at its worst.

For severely ill individuals, mental illness can create a lack of insight that makes it difficult to recognize the need for treatment. Symptoms like delusions, hearing voices, mania, or paranoia can prevent the recognition that one's perception is not accurate. Even with mild depression and anxiety, recognizing which perceived risks or attacks on one's self-worth are based in reality and which are the lies of the disease is exceptionally challenging. Recognizing a problem, believing that treatment could help, and finding the energy to follow through can all be major hurdles for people with mental illness.

In cases where severe symptoms of mental illness prevent an individual from seeking help, mandatory treatment can be part of the solution. The standards for involuntary treatment aim to be strong enough to protect an ill person and the community from likely harm while providing due-process safeguards and respect for individual rights. However, depending on state law, the criteria for involuntary treatment may require that there is an immediate threat to self or others. Even when suicidal intent or other tendencies have been expressed, it can be difficult to demonstrate that those threats are imminent. Journalist Pete Earley writes of his experience securing treatment for his son. When his son was in crisis, wandering the streets of Manhattan for five days, Earley drove to New York to bring him home. On the drive back, his son discussed suicide and his special mission from God, and Earley took him directly to the emergency room. When his son declined treatment, Earley "was told to bring him back *after* he hurt himself or someone else." His son was arrested forty-eight hours later.[37]

Even when someone acknowledges the need for treatment and is willing to brave the associated stigma, it can be exceptionally difficult to find care, particularly if inpatient care is required. In 1955, the United States had 558,922 beds in state psychiatric hospitals. In 2014 there were 37,209 psychiatric beds in state and county hospitals. The rate of public psychiatric inpatient beds per 100,000 people fell by 96.5 percent from 337 to 11.7 over that period.[38] By comparison, the thirty-four developed countries in the Organization for Economic Cooperation and Development reported a median rate of public hospital beds in 2014 of 68 per 100,000—nearly six times higher than the rate in the United States.[39] This mass closure of psychiatric hospitals was due to an alignment of various factors including awareness of poor hospital conditions, overconfidence in early antipsychotic medications, social and civil-rights pressures, lawsuits, and budget priorities. The expectation that a network of community treatment facilities would fully support people who were no longer hospitalized was not met.

Psychiatric hospitals in the 1940s and 1950s were not, in too many cases, successful treatment institutions. Overcrowding, poor conditions, and treatments like lobotomy horrified Americans as they read about them and saw pictures in exposés published by *Life* and others.[40] Disgust at the conditions in hospitals combined with anti-authority sentiment in the sixties fueled the antipsychiatry movement. A coalition including Thomas Szasz, R. D. Laing, and former patients crafted a picture of psychiatry where medication, therapy, and hospitalizations were just ways of coercing patients into narrow definitions of normalcy.[41]

Meanwhile, promising new medications offered hope that severely ill people in hospitals could be treated and return to their communities to live normal lives. The prospect of full recovery using medication, avoidance of the problems of psychiatric hospitals, and increased respect for the rights of people with mental illness drove a push for community-based care. President John F. Kennedy signed the Community Mental Health Centers Act in 1963. The act provided grants for the construction of public and nonprofit community mental health centers in order to treat patients in less restrictive settings. The bill originally included money to staff the centers, but the funding was removed prior to enactment.[42] The goal of this legislation was to create an alternative, kinder, and more inclusive treatment system; however, the programs were not as successful as people had hoped and met criticism by the mid-1970s.[43]

While community mental health centers were struggling to establish comprehensive community care, state psychiatric hospitals faced increasing financial and legal pressures. In 1965, when President Lyndon Johnson signed Medicaid into law, it included provisions to further move patients from hospitals into the community. The Institutions for Mental Disease (IMD) exclusion stated that Medicaid dollars could not be used to pay for hospitalization in any facility with more than sixteen psychiatric beds.[44] This meant that state governments were fully responsible for the costs of state hospitals, as opposed to federal Medicaid funding, which could be used for community care.

In the 1970s, a series of lawsuits made it much harder for the state to confine people with severe mental illness. The first of these cases, *Wyatt v. Stickney*, went before the Alabama Supreme Court in 1973. It secured a patient's right to a minimum standard of care, including minimum staffing levels, educational opportunities, and regularly reviewed treatment plans with progress reports for each patient. Notably, the court decided that states would not be excused from the requirements for lack of funding.[45] Two years later, the U.S. Supreme Court ruled in *O'Connor v. Donaldson* that states could not "constitutionally confine . . . a nondangerous individual who is capable of surviving safely in freedom by himself or with the help of willing and responsible family members or friends."[46] After these rulings, states had to provide much clearer reasons for holding patients, had to provide treatment, and had to fund the hospitals if they were to remain open. Many hospitals closed.

It is frequently argued that the deinstitutionalization of people with mental illness caused "transinstitutionalization," with those who might have resided in public hospitals in 1950 now warehoused in jails and prisons. This, they suggest, drives a substantial portion of prison growth. However, the hospital population that existed in 1950 was largely made up of groups who are not presently at high risk of arrest. Approximately half of hospital patients were women, compared to current state prisoners, who are 93 percent male, and jail inmates, who are 87.3 percent male. Thirty percent of state hospital patients were elderly patients sixty-five or older, many with dementia, compared to only 1.8 percent of prisoners and 0.5 percent of jail inmates.[47] For many of these patients, community settings were an improvement. Other former patients were at increased risk of homelessness or incarceration and received too little, if any, care.[48] While lack of hospital beds contributes to high rates of incarceration for people with mental illness, additional factors are at work.

As psychiatric hospitals have largely disappeared and community services remain limited, the available treatment options are fragmented and hard to navigate. The system of care for individuals with mental illness varies greatly depending on an individual's health insurance or eligibility for Medicaid. Both publicly funded community mental health agencies (CMHAs) and private insurance plans have barriers to care, which start with access to coverage and continue with difficulties obtaining effective, comprehensive treatment. CMHAs used to provide mental health care to the general public, but now primarily serve patients with Medicaid, which limits access to the public system to people with relatively low incomes and recipients of Supplemental Security Income.[49] This makes it difficult for CMHAs to fund treatment for those without any insurance and those with private insurance, unless they have alternative grant, state, or local funding for those purposes. Nationwide, 57 percent of patients served through public mental health agencies are funded by Medicaid only.[50] In Michigan, this figure rises to 84 percent.[51] Due to these funding constraints, there are relatively few opportunities for Michigan residents with private insurance to be treated by the public mental health system.

Even for patients with Medicaid, there are limitations on care provided by CMHAs. Michigan public mental health agencies do not bill Medicaid on a fee-for-service basis. Instead, the amount of Medicaid funding available is distributed through a formula to the CMHAs. While having Medicaid may open the door to eligibility for treatment at a public agency, each agency has a limited amount of total Medicaid dollars and must allocate those funds among patients and programs; thus, there are still decisions to make about how best to use the available Medicaid funding and the level of care to provide each patient.[52]

Those with private insurance also face substantial obstacles to care. For many years, plans capped coverage for mental health in ways that did not apply to other types of illnesses. Limits to the length of hospital stays and number of outpatient visits, or outright coverage exclusions for mental health care sometimes applied. Federal parity requirements passed in 2008 reduced the difference between coverage for mental and physical health care for group health-insurance plans.[53] These changes were later extended to Medicare and then Medicaid. With the implementation of the Affordable Care Act, most private health insurance now covers essential mental health benefits, including inpatient and outpatient treatment.[54] Young adults are able to remain on their parents' health insurance until age twenty-six, which allows them to access mental health care during the ages at which serious mental illness often manifests.[55] Although mental health coverage through private insurance is more widely available now, and it has fewer differences from physical health care, it may not cover practices that are a part of a comprehensive continuum of care. These include crisis stabilization, step-down care after hospitalization, case management, nurse office visits, home visits, and other forms of care that encourage staying in treatment.[56] These services can be useful to avoid hospitalization, maintain an individual's stability and connection to the community, and keep people out of jail.

Insurance coverage does not guarantee that a patient will be able to find services. There is a shortage of psychiatrists, and those in private practice might choose not to see patients whose disease is too severe. There is also a severe shortage of private psychiatric hospital beds. Patients who seek emergency mental health care in a hospital emergency department face waits for a hospital bed three times longer than other types of patients.[57] In a survey of emergency physicians, 90 percent reported that patients are boarded in their emergency departments until a bed is found, and it is not unusual for the waits to take days.[58] For patients who are hospitalized, the average length of psychiatric hospitalizations has declined so that hospital stays are shorter than the time it takes for some medications to become effective.[59]

For people with co-occurring disorders, these challenges are magnified. Treatment of mental illness and substance abuse must be integrated; however, individuals seeking treatment for both tend to be caught in a no-access situation. Only 18 percent of substance abuse treatment centers and 9 percent of mental health centers provide dual-diagnosis-capable treatment for people with co-occurring disorders.[60] At one point our family sought inpatient treatment for Greg's substance abuse and were disappointed that some programs that sounded promising refused to admit individuals with co-occurring mental illness.

When patients manage to start treatment, follow-up is often exceedingly difficult. Dropping out of treatment can be precipitated by mundane problems such as missing appointments or not paying bills on time.[61] Expecting an individual with active symptoms of severe mental illness to be reliable in making appointments, filling prescriptions, and following up on referrals after hospitalization is not realistic. About 24 percent of patients with psychosis will miss appointments, and 58 percent of patients do not follow up on care after hospitalization.[62] Young people, men, and members of minority groups are less likely to be engaged consistently in treatment. Lower education, lack of contact with family, and unemployment also are associated with leaving treatment, as is having a co-occurring substance abuse disorder.[63]

Lack of capacity for hospitalization, shortage of comprehensive services including psychiatry and integrated treatment for co-occurring disorders, funding and insurance limitations, and barriers created by lack of insight into one's illness all contribute to the difficulty that ill individuals and their families face when trying to obtain treatment. When these practical issues are amplified by societal stigma, obstacles to seeking and persisting in treatment can be hard to overcome. The criminal justice system is left to deal with the behavior of individuals who are too ill to live in the community without support. Tax dollars that cannot be found for community treatment are made available for the substantial costs of incarceration. Mentally ill inmates and their families suffer the consequences.

Treatment in Custody and after Discharge

The lack of treatment in jail while cases are pending, difficulties with inmates too ill to stand trial, and lack of coordination of services when inmates are released can delay and disrupt care. Jails frequently have less comprehensive mental health treatment available because most inmates have relatively short stays.[64] Prisons typically have more mental health treatment resources than jails. A 2010 study ordered by the Michigan legislature and completed by a team of independent researchers found that many prisoners with symptoms of mental illness were receiving no treatment. The team assessed prisoners for symptoms of mental illness and verified which prisoners were receiving treatment. The study reported that 16.9 percent of prisoners were receiving mental-health treatment and found that an additional 13.2 percent of prisoners had significant symptoms but were not receiving treatment.[65] The percentage of prisoners treated for mental illness has increased since then. The Michigan Department of Corrections now reports that the share of prisoners receiving mental-health treatment has increased to 23 percent.[66]

For those jail inmates who need competency evaluations or are found incompetent to stand trial, the lack of forensic treatment capacity can cause longer incarceration. Defendants must be mentally competent to understand the charge and the trial process, and to participate in their own defense. This is a basic safeguard in the criminal justice system. Limited ability to conduct competency evaluations and mass closure of state hospitals across the country have created a system that is unable to provide timely care for prisoners. There are significant wait times, first for a competency evaluation and then, if competency restoration is necessary, for a hospital bed.

In Michigan the competency evaluation process is marred by delays that frequently have exceeded the statutory time limit, and a defendant who is found incompetent faces a long wait for a bed in the state hospital system. The history of delays in the competency system is well documented. The Michigan Legislative Auditor found in 2013 that 67 percent of competency evaluations were not completed within sixty days of the court order as required by law. Subsequent reporting by MLive in 2017 showed the long waits that incompetent defendants face for hospital beds. As of December 2, 2016, there were 97 defendants (some out on bond) waiting for a hospital bed. Those defendants waited an average of 177 days for admission to a state hospital for treatment. Nearly a year later, on November 2, 2017, the number waiting for admission to a state hospital had increased to 110 defendants.[67]

The Michigan state budget for fiscal year 2016–2017, however, provided funding to open an unused 30-bed unit at the Center for Forensic Psychiatry, increasing the number of dedicated beds for forensic patients.[68] The following year, construction authorization was provided to replace and expand a state psychiatric hospital. The new facility was expected to open in 2020 with an additional 50 inpatient beds; however, construction was delayed in March 2019 by concerns over the planned location of the facility, including difficulty in recruiting staff.[69] Washtenaw County Sheriff Jerry Clayton noted that delays getting people to competency restoration treatment results in a longer period of decline in jail. This increases the risk that the individual cannot be restored to competency.[70]

The first time I visited Greg in jail after his last arrest (an unsatisfying video visit, the only type of visit allowed in that county), staff told me that they were aware of Greg's severe mental health problem at the time he was admitted. They had attempted to have him hospitalized, but were denied. In spite of the agreement that he was ill, there was still a wait of over seven months (214 days) from jail intake to admission to a state hospital. This was divided into several long waits—46 days from the date of incarceration to the order for a competency evaluation, another 66 days for the completion of the evaluation that found him incompetent, then 21 days until the court hearing for the official declaration of incompetency, followed by a wait of 81 days until he was moved to a state hospital for treatment. Throughout this period, our family's impression from speaking to Greg on the phone was that his mental condition was continuing to deteriorate.

These problems are not unique to Michigan. From July 2017 to July 2018, the number of defendants in Colorado waiting for hospitalization increased from 36 to 281 and the average wait time for an incompetent defendant to access hospital care has increased from 28.1 days to 80.6 days. Judges in Colorado have been threatening to hold officials from the Colorado Department of Human Services in contempt of court if treatment is not provided in a timely fashion.[71] Similarly, Michigan judges have been using show-cause orders to demand reasons why defendants are not being moved to hospital care for restoration to competency.[72] In a national survey, 20 of 37 responding states had been either threatened with or held in contempt, primarily due to long waits for treatment to restore competency.[73]

Providing continuity of care for prisoners when they are discharged is a challenge, but it can help to reduce recidivism. Creating a treatment plan is particularly important for individuals with both mental health and substance abuse disorders because of the difficulty of finding care. The main steps in an effective discharge plan are Assess, Plan, Identify, Coordinate (APIC). The recommended procedures start with screening on admission to incarceration to identify those with treatment needs, planning for treatment while incarcerated and upon release, identification of community resources, and a direct coordination of follow-up care among agencies.[74]

Lack of treatment upon release causes severe problems. When Greg was released on bail a month after his first arrest, there was little planning for his care. He had spent three of the four weeks in the state hospital and was subject to a probate court order for involuntary mental health treatment. When he was discharged from the state hospital, there was essentially no discharge planning because the hospital's plan was simply to return him to jail with a prescription. When he was released from jail, he was given about a week of medication. No follow-up appointment was scheduled. The probate court order listed our local CMHA as the service provider, but they found him ineligible for their services because his symptoms did not meet their severity and persistence criteria. We called the private psychiatrist who previously had treated him for years for anxiety, depression, and attention deficit disorder. To our dismay, the psychiatrist said he could no longer see Greg because his private practice did not have the resources to encourage and monitor treatment adherence in someone so ill. He limited his patients to those with insight into their disorders. Many of the private psychiatry practices we contacted had a blanket policy that they would not accept patients on probate court treatment orders. Greg was considered too ill for most private care and too well for public care.

In response to our concerns about having Greg back in our home, his former psychiatrist even suggested that jail might be a good place for Greg at that time. The claim by a physician that jail is a good place for a person with mental illness was a stunning indictment of the state of mental health care. Our society has returned to a place where confinement in the most restrictive setting possible, a correctional institution, has come to seem like a "good option" for a person with severe mental illness. Treatment for mental illness has moved from overcrowded institutions at mid-century, through an underfunded experiment with community services, to penal-system warehouses where hundreds of thousands of people with mental illness are out of the public view and easily ignored.

Criminal Justice Policy Solutions

Addressing the high rates of mental illness in prison and jail is a key part of the solution for high incarceration rates overall. Effective policies can be implemented. Criminal justice interventions to reduce this problem were proposed over twenty years ago.[75] Since then, research has accumulated on program efficacy and the magnitude of the crisis. This argues for urgent implementation and expansion of evidence-based initiatives.

Each step of an individual's contact with the criminal justice system from the first call to law enforcement to possible arrest, charge, trial, incarceration, and release, can be seen as an opportunity for someone with mental illness to connect or disconnect with treatment. The Sequential Intercept Model (SIM), developed by Ohio local official and physician Mark Munetz and GAINS Center for Behavioral Health and Justice Transformation consultant Patricia Griffin, helps to identify the stages of the criminal justice process and community resources that can be accessed at each stage.[76] The SIM exercise is conducted by a coalition of community members who review available treatment and criminal justice practices with respect to mental illness and substance-abuse disorders. The resulting map of existing services illustrates opportunities for interventions to avoid the criminalization of mental illness.[77]

Sequential intercept maps typically look at six stages of involvement with the health care and criminal justice systems, intercepts 0 to 5. Intercept 0 addresses availability of health and outreach services prior to contact with police or the criminal justice system. In an article published by the National Council of State Court Administrators, former chief judge of the Wayne County (Michigan) probate court and current state court administrator Milton Mack recommends that Intercept 0 also include the civil court system, recognizing that probate court judges and the laws that govern their decisions are critical when an individual may need involuntary treatment.[78] The remaining intercepts cover law enforcement and emergency services; initial detention and court hearings; jail, court, and forensic evaluations and commitments; reentry from incarceration and forensic hospitalization; and community corrections and supports such as parole and probation. At every intercept, screening for mental illness and offering services to address health care needs are important. Some interventions that are regularly identified as necessary and that research shows to be useful include Crisis Intervention Teams (CIT) and mental health courts.

Horrifying outcomes of law enforcement encounters with people with mental illness resulted in the development of CIT. Specifically, the program grew from the death of a young black man in 1987. Joseph Robinson's mother called the Memphis police because he was self-harming and in crisis. When the police arrived, they shot him repeatedly.[79] Facing outrage from the community, the next year, local police and other community stakeholders worked together to form a program to educate law enforcement officers to recognize and respond effectively to a mental health crisis.[80] CIT results in better outcomes of these police calls and protects the safety of both the officer and the ill person.[81] When officers can identify a mental health emergency and de-escalate the situation, individuals may be more likely to accept help and avoid incarceration.[82] Where CIT is available, callers to 911 and dispatchers can request a CIT-trained officer for calls that involve a person with mental illness. CIT is a pre-booking diversion program; with effective response and de-escalation, an arrest can be avoided. Depending on the nature of the problematic behavior, the situation might be resolved peacefully onsite, or the ill person can be evaluated and treated in a crisis unit or emergency department and possibly avoid jail completely.[83]

Several Michigan jurisdictions have conducted CIT training. In Clinton, Eaton, and Ingham Counties, the Tri-County Crisis Intervention Team was formed in 2016 through a collaboration of the Lansing Police Department; the Community Mental Health Authority of Clinton, Eaton, and Ingham Counties; and the National Alliance on Mental Illness (NAMI) Lansing to provide CIT training to officers and other first responders from a number of jurisdictions within the tri-county area and around the state. About 200 first responders were trained as of December 2018.[84]

The CIT approach is made more effective by the availability of a secure mental health crisis treatment center where persons who need emergency mental health treatment can be taken. The Memphis psychiatric emergency center, for example, has a no-refusal policy for people brought in by police.[85] In the absence of crisis stabilization beds or sufficient time for an officer to wait for an ill person to be treated at the emergency room, a police officer may have no option but to convey the ill person to jail, where secure custody is available. Miami-Dade County, Florida, has used CIT to divert over 16,000 people to crisis units. The average number of jail inmates per day declined from 7,000 to 3,000. This allowed closure of a jail, which saved $12 million per year in correctional costs.[86]

A community coalition in Clinton, Eaton, and Ingham Counties of Michigan completed the SIM process in August 2017. The resulting number-one priority was development of a crisis services center with a secure unit.[87] This would allow police officers to deliver an individual with mental illness directly to a secure care center for assessment and stabilization. Without such a facility, an officer needs to wait with a detained patient in the emergency department, which can be time-consuming and remove the law enforcement officer from other duties. Long waits at an emergency department can make it more practical for law enforcement officers to take a person with mental illness to jail instead of a hospital.[88]

Mobile crisis units are another option that can be used either in conjunction with police or instead of police calls in a mental health emergency.[89] The mobile crisis team can visit a person at home to assess and potentially stabilize the situation without the need for police intervention or an emergency department visit.[90] Mental illness is a factor in about 10 percent of police calls; thus expansion of mobile crisis units can relieve pressure on police departments.[91] The combined program and health care costs per case of a mobile-crisis-unit response was 23 percent lower than for police responses.[92]

For offenders who are convicted, mental health courts are part of a trend of problem-solving courts that work with a specific class of offender such as veterans or persons with drug and alcohol problems. These courts divert people from incarceration to probation supported by comprehensive services.[93] The thirty-three mental health courts in Michigan include a variety of criminal justice and mental health professionals who screen potential participants and supervise and treat individuals during the period they are under court supervision.[94] Offenders are admitted to a mental health court after conviction; however, any violent offense that results in death or serious bodily harm, and any criminal sexual conduct render an individual ineligible for mental health court. For state fiscal year 2016–2017, some 53 percent of mental health court participants had a co-occurring substance abuse disorder. Successful completion of the mental health court program may result in a one-time discharge and dismissal of a conviction. The average duration of mental health court supervision of adults was 16 months for circuit court and 13 months for district court.[95]

In a mental health court, a primary goal is to connect the ill individual with a variety of treatment options, including medication, but other services are also provided to a participant. These include substance-abuse treatment and educational and vocational opportunities. Securing safe and drug-free housing also is a best practice. For Michigan mental health courts, these are grant-funded services not typically available to other offenders. The Michigan mental health court grant program now requires that mental health courts satisfy statutory certification standards in order to establish consistent, evidence-based practices across jurisdictions.[96] Mental health court participants report regularly to the court and appear frequently before the judge in order to demonstrate progress and compliance. Incentives and sanctions are used to give the individual clear signals as to satisfactory progress. Persons who complete all of the requirements for a mental health court are said to have graduated. In 2016–2017, roughly 52 percent of participants successfully graduated from the mental health court. Unemployment among graduates was reduced by over half, from 57 percent at admission to 25 percent at discharge.[97]

Reduced recidivism over a two-year and four-year period has been demonstrated in Michigan for both mental health court graduates and participants. For graduates from district mental health courts, 15 percent had a new conviction after two years and 25 percent after four years, as opposed to recidivism rates among the comparison group of 28 percent and 43 percent after two and four years respectively. At the circuit-court level, at two years out, 11 percent (vs. 27 percent) of graduates had a new conviction, and at four years 28 percent (vs. 30 percent) had a new conviction.[98] It is possible that recidivism increases over time because individuals who became more stable with the strong support of mental health courts become worse when that level of supervision and treatment is no longer available. If a robust mental health continuum of care is not available in the community, then it is necessary to wait for a new offense to reengage someone in treatment through a mental health court. The court can require individual treatment and behavioral changes in a way that is not possible in the absence of an involuntary treatment order.[99] Unfortunately, mental health courts are an intervention that occurs only after a crime has been committed. The mental health court uses the authority and resources of the court and special grant-funded services to fill gaps in community mental health care and divert people from incarceration.

Health Policy Interventions

There are proven initiatives that can be implemented within the health-care system to improve treatment of individuals with severe mental illness. Early treatment, outreach and engagement techniques to encourage treatment, and additional funding for mental health services are all part of the solution. It is essential to lower the barriers to treatment to prevent the continued suffering and severe consequences of serious mental illness.

There is now compelling evidence that comprehensive treatment beginning soon after psychotic symptoms develop leads to improved outcomes for patients. In the Recovery After an Initial Schizophrenia Episode (RAISE) study, physician and schizophrenia researcher John M. Kane and his colleagues investigated the impact of providing coordinated specialty care to individuals with a first episode of psychosis. The treatment group received the NAVIGATE protocol of services. This consists of four core components: individualized medication management, family psychoeducation, resilience-based therapy, and supported employment and education. The study showed the effectiveness of coordinated specialty care and demonstrated that the interventions were more effective than regular community care and were more effective if started earlier in the psychosis.[100]

Individuals with psychosis in the United States have rarely received early treatment. In fact, the RAISE results showed that the average duration of untreated psychosis for patients in the study was 74 weeks. After two years, patients who received coordinated specialty care were more likely to still be in treatment and were more likely to work or attend school. In terms of health, the comprehensive-care group had improved symptoms, including less depression than the control group. Quality-of-life measures were significantly better in the research group than in the control group. The benefit of coordinated specialty care was higher in patients with shorter duration of untreated psychosis. Research has shown that for serious mental illness, early treatment is more effective than delayed treatment. It results in use of lower effective doses of antipsychotic medication and more significant improvements than when treatment is delayed.[101] Providing coordinated specialty-care interventions costs an estimated $3,674 more per year per patient than typical care; however, the intensity and cost of treatment tends to decline over time. In spite of the modest cost and relatively small population of young adults with first-episode psychosis who would need to be treated, private insurance typically does not cover some effective practices such as family psychoeducation and vocational services.[102] Best-practice treatment also is not available in many areas. Michigan currently has four comprehensive specialty-care practices funded through the federal Mental Health Block Grant set aside for early treatment.[103] As Lisa Dixon, another researcher reporting on the RAISE study, and her coauthors note, the current lengthy delays for individuals to access treatment cause unnecessary suffering and can no longer be defended. They continue, "The stakes are high, with mounting morbidity, premature mortality, and economic costs that only partially measure the true human costs of delayed and inadequate care. This is an important and optimistic moment in U.S. health care policy for vulnerable early schizophrenia patients."[104]

For more long-standing or hard-to-treat cases of mental illness, other treatment delivery systems can be used to bring treatment directly to ill individuals who are most at risk of severe consequences such as incarceration or homelessness. Assertive Community Treatment (ACT) brings mental health treatment to individuals in their homes, including medicine delivery and case-manager visits.[105] An initial refusal to start treatment does not stop the engagement, but outreach continues. Results of ACT include decreased hospital visits and less homelessness for participants.[106] For individuals involved with the justice system, a study conducted in Rochester, New York, combined judicial monitoring and Forensic ACT with group problem-solving between the court and treatment team, use of graduated punishments to create legal pressure for treatment, and treatment plans built with individual risk factors for criminal behavior in mind. This approach reduced hospitalization, time in jail, and emergency-department visits (when one outlier patient with fifty emergency-department visits was excluded from the analysis).[107] While the study did not report specific changes in costs, the improved outcomes imply savings distributed across the justice system, corrections, state hospitals, and local mental health agencies.

For patients whose lack of insight makes seeking or adhering to treatment difficult, presenting a possibly harmful situation for the individual or others, involuntary court-ordered treatment can help. Assisted Outpatient Treatment (AOT) provides this for individuals who meet strict legal criteria, which vary by state. It is a less restrictive option than involuntary inpatient hospitalization. The improved outcomes from AOT include lower rates of homelessness, psychiatric hospitalization, self-harm, and incarceration.[108] In Michigan, Kevin's Law contains the requirements for judges to order involuntary treatment. Recent amendments to Kevin's Law made it easier to obtain an order for involuntary treatment and allowed probate court judges to order AOT either alone or in combination with inpatient care.[109] These changes provide opportunities to order treatment prior to an absolute crisis.

In addition to programs such as ACT and AOT, there are other interventions that can be used as part of a continuum of care to help people stay in treatment. In some cases, less intensive interventions such as peer support, appointment reminders, and assistance filling prescriptions can be helpful. Meeting outpatient providers prior to leaving the hospital can make it more likely that follow-up appointments will be kept. A short-term option is the use of Critical Time Intervention, a special program to connect individuals with more intensive services during a time of transition—for example, from inpatient hospitalization to home. The provision of services including connections with outpatient providers, attention to social supports, and motivating substance-abuse treatment can be effective in encouraging patients to stay in treatment.[110]

Effective integrated treatment of co-occurring substance abuse and mental health treatment is important to reducing incarceration. Among people with mental illness, reducing substance abuse also reduces the risk that those individuals will commit an act of violence that could result in imprisonment.[111] Integration of substance abuse and mental health treatment that addresses the co-occurring disorders together is associated with improved outcomes for patients, including fewer arrests, improvement of symptoms, and greater housing stability.[112]

Studies have found a reduction in the cost of corrections when people have access to outpatient treatment and AOT. In a study of 4,056 Floridians with mental illness on Medicaid, increased use of outpatient treatment resulted in less time incarcerated. Even with increased treatment costs, the study found that those who avoided arrest had lower overall costs.[113] Research has shown that AOT reduces the overall cost of caring for people with serious mental illness by lowering spending for inpatient care and criminal justice involvement. Another study made separate calculations for AOT in New York City and five counties elsewhere in New York State. In New York City, the cost of care for AOT participants declined from the year prior to enrollment to the following twelve-month period by 43 percent, with a further reduction of 13 percent in the second year. The counties outside of New York City registered larger savings of 49 percent in the first year and 27 percent more in the second year, which reduced average per capita costs from $104,284 the year before enrollment in the study to $39,142 in the second year following AOT enrollment.[114]

Even as we highlight the potential cost savings of better mental health care, it is important to acknowledge that many other health conditions require similarly priced forms of care that are typically authorized with less reluctance from insurance companies and taxpayers. Monthly costs for intensive treatment and support for comprehensive specialty care for first-episode psychosis, for example, are comparable with the average monthly health-plan expenses for people with diabetes.[115] Mental health care, despite parity, is still often treated as less important, as a luxury, where other forms of health care are seen as necessities and rights.

When my ninety-one-year-old father left the hospital after having pneumonia, his insurance covered a stay in a residential rehabilitation facility that offered several hours of physical therapy a day to help him recover his strength and return home. When I went to assist him in the transition from hospital to rehabilitation center, I was struck by the enormous contrast between his treatment and that of my son, who had been admitted to a state psychiatric hospital the week before. There was no wait for my father's hospitalization; Greg waited in jail for months. The lovely rehabilitation facilities were a stark contrast to the old facilities where my son stayed. While I was relieved that Greg was out of jail and into the hospital, it was easy to see the distinction between the comprehensive treatment my father was provided as a matter of course and the difficult path to treatment my son faced. The stigma surrounding mental illness does not just impact the way we talk about and seek treatment for mental illness. It has discriminatory effects. It changes the ways in which we are willing to fund and provide basic care.

Challenging Myths and Stigma

A better public understanding of mental illness, what it looks like, and how to help makes it easier for people to recognize symptoms and seek medical help. Mental Health First Aid is an eight-hour class developed to increase recognition of mental illness and substance-abuse problems and teach people how to respond when someone is struggling or in crisis. One goal of the program is to have as many people trained in Mental Health First Aid as know cardiopulmonary resuscitation.[116] This helps us respond to mental-health emergencies as we would to any other, rather than turning away. Mental Health First Aid has been shown to reduce negative attitudes toward mental illness and improve ability to offer support to others.[117]

While our family struggled to cope with Greg's illness, I happened to walk through a health fair on the Michigan Capitol lawn at lunchtime. I stopped at the booth for the NAMI Lansing and told the volunteer that I thought my son was mentally ill. I was near tears when he suggested that I enroll in the NAMI Family-to-Family class (then called Families Helping Families). My husband and I learned to "see the individual not the illness" and not to take problematic behavior personally. This shift in attitude toward our son helped us to stay in a positive relationship with him even during difficult times. We met other families who had seen their loved ones recover and flourish. We heard the NAMI In Our Own Voice presentation where individuals with mental illness spoke about their paths to recovery in a powerful demonstration that mental illness does not need to be a secret and that treatment can work.[118]

In the past, cancer was a fearful and unspeakable condition until patients came forward with their experiences and pushed for better care. Now, mental illness is undergoing a similar transition. As people speak out, myths and stigma are replaced by a more realistic understanding. NAMI programs, Mental Health First Aid, and other awareness efforts can help people both to be more supportive of others and to feel less alone in their own experiences with mental illness. This makes openness and advocacy possible.

Conclusion

When individuals with mental illness are incarcerated, the results can be potentially catastrophic and irreversible. The extraordinary cost of an inmate's custody after an offense has occurred appears to dwarf the resources that were expended prior to the arrest. Stopping the negative trajectory of severe mental illness is key to reversing the numbers of persons with serious mental illness in prison and jail. This requires public financial support, changes in insurance reimbursement practices, and an effective continuum of care for psychiatric illnesses. Most importantly, this requires political will.

We also need more willingness to recognize and address mental illness earlier, and less fear and denial. People can and do recover from mental illness. Relapses may occur or symptoms change over time, but recovery is possible. Many people with a history of severe mental illness live well in the community.

But where is the responsibility for implementing changes that will improve mental health care and outcomes? Families have limited ability to intervene in the mental health care of an adult. In many states, even a legal guardian cannot order mental health treatment or hospitalization for an ill individual, and the illness can end up making treatment decisions.[119] Once there is a crime, state and local governments make resources available for incarceration and increasingly for diversion programs for eligible individuals; however, having to wait for criminal problems to arise to make treatment available is backwards. If effective treatments were available up front, the investments in the mental health system would result in savings in correctional costs; but when public financial resources are limited, finding funds to invest in treatment now that will save money later is unreasonably difficult. Funding for corrections is regarded as essential, while spending for mental health care waits on the back burner. Inadequate and delayed treatment can have severe consequences.

While we cannot know what the course of Greg's illness would have been had jail been avoided, we do know that although he was restored to competency once after a seven-month hospitalization, he was returned directly to jail where his condition again deteriorated. It was then determined that he was not criminally responsible, but by the time he was before the court again, about five months after leaving the state psychiatric hospital, he was again incompetent and was referred for a new competency evaluation. After another wait for a hospital bed, he was in a state psychiatric hospital for seventeen consecutive months. His condition improved, but he was not restored to competency a second time. According to Michigan law, the charge against him was dismissed, and he was discharged from the hospital on a mental health treatment order under the supervision of the local community mental health agency.

We need to continue to improve the response of the criminal justice system to mental illness, but the tools of the correctional system are blunt compared to the potential for interventions such as early treatment with coordinated specialty care and assertive community treatment. We need a health care system that can help people before they are arrested.

NOTES

1. Calculated using rates of a "current indicator of a mental health problem," from Jennifer Bronson and Marcus Berzofsky, *Indicators of Mental Health Problems Reported by Prisoners and Jail Inmates, 2011–12* (Washington, DC: U.S. Department of Justice, Bureau of Justice Statistics, June 2017), https://www.bjs.gov/content/pub/pdf/imhprpjil112.pdf, 3; and Bureau of Justice Statistics, "Correctional Populations in the United States, 2016, Appendix Table 3," https://www.bjs.gov/index.cfm?ty=pbdetail&iid=%206226.

2. We limit the scope of our study to health services and incarceration for adults.

3. The National Institute of Health describes psychosis as "conditions that affect the mind, where there has been some loss of contact with reality . . . a person's thought and perceptions are disturbed and the individual may have difficulty understanding what is real and what is not. Symptoms of psychosis include delusions (false beliefs) and hallucinations (seeing or hearing things that others do not see or hear). Other

symptoms include incoherent or nonsense speech, and behavior that is inappropriate for the situation. A person in a psychotic episode may also experience depression, anxiety, sleep problems, social withdrawal, lack of motivation, and difficulty functioning overall." National Institute of Mental Health, "What Is Psychosis?," https://www.nimh.nih.gov/ health/topics/schizophrenia/raise/what-is-psychosis.shtml.

4. Christina Hall, "Mark Hackel: Jails New Asylums for Mental Health Patients," *Detroit Free Press*, September 28, 2018; National Sheriffs' Association, "National Sheriffs' Association Resolution 2015–6," https://www.sheriffs.org/government-affairs/resolutions; Troy Goodnough, "State Funding for Mental Health Will Reduce Crime and Save Money," *Bridge: News and Analysis from the Center for Michigan*, December 19, 2017.

5. NAMI (National Alliance on Mental Illness), "Mental Health by the Numbers," https:// www.nami.org.

6. Alisa Roth, *Insane: America's Criminal Treatment of Mental Illness* (New York: Basic Books, 2018), 2.

7. A detailed comparison of estimates can be found in Seth J. Prins, "The Prevalence of Mental Illnesses in U.S. State Prisons: A Systematic Review," *Psychiatric Services* 65, no. 7 (July 2014): 862–72.

8. Brant E. Fries et al., "Symptoms and Treatment of Mental Illness among Prisoners: A Study of Michigan State Prisons," *International Journal of Law and Psychiatry* 36 (2013): 316–25.

9. Doris J. James and Lauren E. Glaze, *Mental Health Problems of Prison and Jail Inmates*, rev. ed. (Washington, DC: U.S. Department of Justice, Bureau of Justice Statistics, 2006), https://www.bjs.gov/content/pub/pdf/mhppji.pdf.

10. Ibid.

11. Data for state and federal prisoners were combined in this study. Bronson and Berzofsky, *Indicators of Mental Health Problems Reported by Prisoners and Jail Inmates*.

12. Ibid., 3.

13. Fries et al., "Symptoms and Treatment of Mental Illness among Prisoners."

14. Ibid., 322.

15. Special units consist of acute care, crisis stabilization, detention/punitive segregation, hospital, protective custody, residential treatment programs, residential substance-abuse treatment, and social-skills development units. Fries et al., "Symptoms and Treatment of Mental Illness among Prisoners," 8.

16. NAMI (National Alliance on Mental Illness), "Diverse Communities," https://www.nami. org.

17. Bronson and Berzofsky, *Indicators of Mental Health Problems Reported by Prisoners and*

Jail Inmates, 4; James and Glaze, *Mental Health Problems of Prison and Jail Inmates*, 4.

18. Vera Institute of Justice, "The Price of Prisons: Prison Spending in 2015," https://www. vera.org.

19. State contributions to the juvenile justice system are funded separately. Michigan Senate Fiscal Agency, *FY 2016–17 Appropriations Report: Part II—Initial Appropriations*, July 2016, 76, http://www.senate.michigan.gov/SFA/Publications/Approps/Initial2017. pdf; Michigan Department of Corrections, *Report to the Legislature Pursuant to Article V of P.A. 107 of 2017, Section 904*, https://www.michigan.gov/documents/corrections/ Sec_904_FY17_FINAL_608509_7.pdf.

20. Michigan Department of Corrections, *Report to the Legislature Pursuant to Article V of P.A. 107 of 2017*.

21. Calculated based on gross state appropriations and average hospital population in fiscal year 2016–2017 for state psychiatric hospitals and forensic mental health services in Michigan Public Act 268 of 2016 (House Bill 5294, 2015–2016 session), http://legislature. mi.gov/doc.aspx?2016-HB-5294, 127.

22. Doris A. Fuller et al., "Going, Going, Gone: Trends and Consequences of Eliminating State Psychiatric Beds, 2016," Treatment Advocacy Center, Office of Research and Public Affairs, http://www.treatmentadvocacycenter.org/going-going-gone, 16.

23. James and Glaze, *Mental Health Problems of Prison and Jail Inmates*, 8.

24. Substance Abuse and Mental Health Services Administration, *Guidelines for Successful Transition of People with Mental or Substance Use Disorders from Jail and Prison: Implementation Guide* (Rockville, MD: Substance Abuse and Mental Health Services Administration, 2017), 4, https://store.samhsa.gov.

25. John Counts, "Speedy Trial? Not If You're Mentally Ill in Michigan," MLive.com, https:// www.mlive.com; Goodnough, "State Funding for Mental Health Will Reduce Crime and Save Money."

26. Natasha A. Frost and Carlos E. Monteiro, "Administrative Segregation in U.S. Prisons" (Washington, DC: U.S. Department of Justice, National Institute of Justice, March 2016), https://www.ncjrs.gov/pdffiles1/nij/249749.pdf.

27. Jeff Gerritt, "Mentally Ill Get Punishment Instead of Treatment," *Detroit Free Press*, February 5, 2012.

28. Libby Sander, "Inmate's Death in Solitary Cell Prompts Judge to Ban Restraints," *New York Times*, November 15, 2006.

29. The Bureau of Justice Statistics reports that in 2013, the suicide mortality rate per 100,000 jail inmates was 46. The CDC reported a nationwide suicide mortality rate of 13.42 per 100,000 people in 2016. A number of recent stories show that Michigan jails

continue to struggle to prevent suicide. In one thirteen-month span, Wayne County Jail had eight suicides. Grand Traverse County Jail reported two in a span of eight months. Mecosta County recently settled a wrongful-death lawsuit after an inmate completed suicide. Margaret Noonan, Harley Rohloff, and Scott Ginder, "Mortality in Local Jails and State Prisons, 2000–2013—Statistical Tables" (Washington, DC: U.S. Department of Justice, Bureau of Justice Statistics, August 2015), https://www.bjs.gov/content/pub/pdf/mljsp0013st.pdf; Ross Jones, "Suicide Surge at Wayne County Jail 'Should Be Ringing Alarm Bells All Over,'" WXYZ.com, July 21, 2017, https://www.wxyz.com/news/local-news/investigations/suicide-surge-at-wayne-county-jail-should-be-ringing-alarm-bells-all-over; Kyle Kaminski, "Inmate Suicide Prompts Investigation: Sheriff Withholds Key Details after Woman Found Hanging inside Jail Cell," (*Traverse City, MI*) *Record-Eagle*, March 2, 2018; John Agar, "Inmate Suicide: $160K Settlement, Deputy Allegedly Distracted by Monday Night Football," *Grand Rapids News*, June 22, 2017; Centers for Disease Control and Prevention, "Injury Prevention and Control: Fatal Injury Data," https://www.cdc.gov/injury/wisqars/fatal.html.

30. National Institute on Drug Abuse, "Comorbidity: Substance Use Disorders and Other Mental Illnesses," https://www.drugabuse.gov; James and Glaze, *Mental Health Problems of Prison and Jail Inmates*, 7; William H. Fisher et al., "Drug-Related Arrests in a Cohort of Public Mental Health Service Recipients," *Psychiatric Services* 58, no. 11 (November 2007): 1448–53.

31. Richard A. Van Dorn et al., "Effects of Outpatient Treatment on Risk of Arrest of Adults with Serious Mental Illness and Associated Costs," *Psychiatric Services* 64, no. 9 (September 2013): 856–62; Eric B. Elbogen et al., "Treatment Engagement and Violence Risk in Mental Disorders," *British Journal of Psychiatry* 189, no. 4 (October 2006): 354–60.

32. Elbogen et al., "Treatment Engagement and Violence Risk in Mental Disorders," 357.

33. Ibid., 354.

34. Debra A. Pinals, "Crime, Violence, and Behavioral Health: Collaborative Community Strategies for Risk Mitigation," *CNS Spectrum* 20, no. 3, special issue (June 2015): 241–49.

35. Peter Railton, "Innocent Abroad: Rupture, Liberation, and Solidarity," Dewey Lecture, February 2015, https://leiterreports.typepad.com/files/dewey-lecture-drs.pdf.

36. Kay Redfield Jamison, *An Unquiet Mind: A Memoir of Moods and Madness* (New York: Vintage Books, 2011), 7.

37. Emphasis added. Pete Earley, "Foreword," in Dinah Miller and Annette Hanson, *Committed: The Battle over Involuntary Psychiatric Care* (Baltimore, MD: Johns Hopkins University Press, 2016), xi.

38. Debra A. Pinals and Doris A. Fuller, *Beyond Beds: The Vital Role of a Full Continuum*

of Psychiatric Care, National Association of State Mental Health Program Directors (NASMHPD) and Treatment Advocacy Center, October 2017, 4, https://www.nasmhpd. org.

39. Treatment Advocacy Center, "Psychiatric Bed Supply Need Per Capita," September 2016, 3, http://www.treatmentadvocacycenter.org.

40. Among the most impactful of these was the photo essay and article by Albert Q. Maisel, "Bedlam 1946: Most U.S. Mental Hospitals Are a Shame and a Disgrace," *Life*, May 6, 1946.

41. David Rissmiller and Joshua Rissmiller, "Open Forum: Evolution of the Antipsychiatry Movement into Mental Health Consumerism," *Psychiatric Services* 57, no. 6 (2006); Heather Murray, "'My Place Was Set at the Terrible Feast': The Meanings of the 'Anti-Psychiatry' Movement and Responses in the United States, 1970s–1990s," *Journal of American Culture* 37, no. 1 (2014): 37.

42. Matt Ford, "America's Largest Mental Hospital Is a Jail," *The Atlantic*, June 8, 2015.

43. Lisa B. Dixon et al., "Transforming the Treatment of Schizophrenia in the United States: The RAISE Initiative," *Annual Review of Clinical Psychology* 14 (2018): 239.

44. Pinals and Fuller, *Beyond Beds*, 8.

45. "Wyatt v. Stickney and the Right of Civilly Committed Mental Patients to Adequate Treatment," *Harvard Law Review* 86, no. 7 (May 1973): 1283.

46. O'Connor v. Donaldson, 422 U.S. 563 (1975), https://supreme.justia.com/cases/federal/us/422/563/#573.

47. Steven Raphael and Michael A. Stoll, *Why Are So Many Americans in Prison?* (New York: Russell Sage Foundation, 2013), 124; Bronson and Berzofsky, *Indicators of Mental Health Problems Reported by Prisoners and Jail Inmates*, 13.

48. Pinals and Fuller, *Beyond Beds*, 9.

49. Milton Mack Jr., "Decriminalization of Mental Illness: Fixing a Broken System," Conference of State Court Administrators (COSCA), 2016–2017 Policy Paper, 6, https://cosca.ncsc.org.

50. Substance Abuse and Mental Health Services Administration, "Michigan 2017 Mental Health National Outcome Measures (NOMS): SAMHSA Uniform Reporting System," 11, https://www.samhsa.gov/data/sites/default/files/cbhsq-reports/Michigan-2017.pdf.

51. Ibid., 3.

52. Ellyn Ackerman, John Maxwell, and Steve Angelotti, "Appropriation Line Item and Boilerplate History: Department of Health and Human Services," Michigan Senate Fiscal Agency, June 2018, 21–22, http://www.senate.michigan.gov/sfa/Departments/LineItem/LIhhs_web.pdf.

53. AAA Practice Organization, PracticeUpdate, "Medicare Outpatient Mental Health

Coverage Parity Begins Jan. 1, 2014," November 7, 2013, https://www.apapracticecentral. org; Department of Health and Human Services, Centers for Medicare and Medicaid Services, "Medicaid Fact Sheet: Mental Health and Substance Use Disorder Parity Final Rule for Medicaid and CHIP," March 29, 2016, https://www.medicaid.gov/medicaid/ benefits/downloads/fact-sheet-cms-2333-f.pdf.

54. Some policies can now exclude mental health coverage and avoid some of the other requirements of the ACA. Robert Pear, "New Rule Allows Small Businesses to Skirt Obamacare," *New York Times*, June 20, 2018.

55. Grace Gonzalez, Eric Goplerud, and David Shern, "Coordinated Specialty Care—First Episode Psychosis Programs: Why Specialty Early Intervention Programs Are a Smart Investment," National Association of State Mental Health Program Directors (NASMHPD), 3, https://www.nasmhpd.org; Centers for Medicare and Medicaid Services, "Young Adults and the Affordable Care Act: Protecting Young Adults and Eliminating Burdens on Families and Businesses," https://www.cms.gov/CCIIO/Resources/Files/ adult_child_fact_sheet.html; NAMI, "Mental Health by the Numbers."

56. Henry J. Kaiser Family Foundation, "Facilitating Access to Mental Health Services: A Look at Medicaid, Private Insurance, and the Uninsured," https://www.kff.org; Gonzalez, Goplerud, and Shern, "Coordinated Specialty Care—First Episode Psychosis Programs," 13; Pinals and Fuller, *Beyond Beds*.

57. Pinals and Fuller, *Beyond Beds*, 15.

58. American College of Emergency Physicians, "Physician Poll on Psychiatric Emergencies," October 2016, newsroom.acep.org/download/PsychEmergencyPollOct2016.pdf.

59. Pinals and Fuller, *Beyond Beds*, 21.

60. Mark P. McGovern et al., "Dual Diagnosis Capability in Mental Health and Addiction Treatment Services: An Assessment of Programs across Multiple State Systems," *Administration and Policy in Mental Health* 41, no. 2 (March 2014): 6.

61. Douglas Mossman, "'Firing' a Patient: May a Psychiatrist Unilaterally Terminate Care?," *Current Psychiatry* (December 2010): 18–20, 22, 29.

62. Fifty-eight percent is a median of previous estimates of "failure to attend a first outpatient appointment" after discharge. Julie Kreyenbuhl, Ilana R. Nossel, and Lisa B. Dixon, "Disengagement from Mental Health Treatment among Individuals with Schizophrenia and Strategies for Facilitating Connections to Care: A Review of the Literature," *Schizophrenia Bulletin* 35, no. 4 (2009): 697.

63. Kreyenbuhl, Nossel, and Dixon, "Disengagement from Mental Health Treatment among Individuals with Schizophrenia," 696.

64. Center for Substance Abuse Treatment, Substance Abuse Treatment for Adults in the

Criminal Justice System, *9 Treatment Issues Specific to Prisons* (Rockville, MD: Substance Abuse and Mental Health Services Administration, 2005), https://www.ncbi.nlm.nih.gov/books/NBK64123.

65. Fries et al., "Symptoms and Treatment of Mental Illness among Prisoners," 321.

66. Kyle Kaminski, Michigan Department of Corrections, email, September 21, 2018.

67. Counts, "Speedy Trial? Not If You're Mentally Ill in Michigan."

68. Michigan Senate Fiscal Agency, *FY 2016–17 Appropriations Report: Part II—Initial Appropriations*, 21.

69. Michigan Senate Fiscal Agency, "Senate Fiscal Analysis, Initial Appropriations, Michigan Public Act 107 of 2017 (House Bill 4323, 2017–2018 session)," July 29, 2017, http://legislature.mi.gov/doc.aspx?2017-HB-4323. Kathleen Grey, "Michigan Officials to Re-evaluate New $115M Psychiatric Hospital in Caro," *Detroit Free Press*, March 13, 2019.

70. Counts, "Speedy Trial? Not If You're Mentally Ill in Michigan."

71. Allison Sherry, "Colorado Increasingly in Contempt as More Judges Recognize That Jail Isn't a Mental Health Answer," *Colorado Public Radio News*, September 11, 2018, http://www.cpr.org.

72. Counts, "Speedy Trial? Not If You're Mentally Ill in Michigan."

73. National Association of State Mental Health Program Directors, *Forensic Patients in State Psychiatric Hospitals: 1999–2016*, 50, https://www.nasmhpd.org.

74. Substance Abuse and Mental Health Services Administration, *Guidelines for Successful Transition of People with Mental or Substance Use Disorders from Jail and Prison*.

75. H. Richard Lamb and Linda E. Weinberger, "Persons with Severe Mental Illness in Jails and Prisons: A Review," *Psychiatric Services* 49, no. 4 (April 1998): 483–92.

76. Collaborators Mark Munetz, the chief clinical officer from Summit County (Ohio) Alcohol, Addiction, and Mental Health Services Board, and Patricia Griffin, a senior consultant from the GAINS Center for Behavioral Health and Justice Transformation, were seeking approaches to reduce the criminalization of mental illness. GAINS stands for Gather, Assess, Integrate, Network, Stimulate. Mark R. Munetz and Patricia A. Griffin, "Use of the Sequential Intercept Model as an Approach to Decriminalization of People with Serious Mental Illness," *Psychiatric Services* 57 (2006): 544–49; SAMHSA (Substance Abuse and Mental Health Services Administration), "About the GAINS Center," https://www.samhsa.gov.

77. Mack, "Decriminalization of Mental Illness," 8.

78. Ibid., 9.

79. Tania Woods and Carl Pendleton, "Developing Partnerships: CIT Officers and Providers, Crisis Intervention Team Collaboration," January 10, 2017, https://www.samhsa.gov/sites/

default/files/programs_campaigns/recovery_to_practice/rtp-cit-011017.pdf; Laura Usher, "Saving Lives, Changing Communities," NAMI (National Alliance on Mental Illness), October 4, 2013, https://www.nami.org.

80. Woods and Pendleton, "Developing Partnerships."

81. Melissa Reuland, Matthew Schwarzfeld, and Laura Draper, "Law Enforcement Responses to People with Mental Illnesses: A Guide to Research-Informed Policy and Practice," Council of State Governments Justice Center, 2009, 11, https://csgjusticecenter.org.

82. Mack, "Decriminalization of Mental Illness," 15; Michael T. Compton et al., "A Comprehensive Review of Extant Research on Crisis Intervention Team (CIT) Programs," *Journal of the American Academy of Psychiatry and the Law* 36, no. 1 (November 1, 2008): 47–55.

83. Mack, "Decriminalization of Mental Illness," 15.

84. Tri-County Crisis Intervention Team, "Frequently Asked Questions," http://www.tricountycit.com/faqs.html.

85. Henry J. Steadman et al., "Comparing Outcomes of Major Models of Police Responses to Mental Health Emergencies," *Psychiatric Services* 51, no. 5 (May 2000): 645–49.

86. Mack, "Decriminalization of Mental Illness," 16.

87. Debra A. Pinals and Brian Case, "Sequential Intercept Mapping Report for Clinton, Eaton, and Ingham Counties, MI: Final Report," SAMHSA's GAINS Center, Policy Research Associates, August 29, 2017, 14.

88. Martha Williams Deane et al., "Emerging Partnerships between Mental Health and Law Enforcement," *Psychiatric Services*, January 1, 1999.

89. SAMHSA, *Crisis Services: Effectiveness, Cost-Effectiveness, and Funding Strategies*, HHS Publication No. (SMA)-14-4848 (Rockville, MD: Substance Abuse and Mental Health Services Administration, 2014), 10, https://store.samhsa.gov.

90. Glenn W. Currier, Susan G. Fisher, and Eric D. Caine, "Mobile Crisis Team Intervention to Enhance Linkage of Discharged Suicidal Emergency Department Patients to Outpatient Psychiatric Services: A Randomized Controlled Trial," *Academic Emergency Medicine* 17, no. 1 (January 2010): 36–43; Shenyang Guo et al., "Assessing the Impact of Community-Based Mobile Crisis Services on Preventing Hospitalization," *Psychiatric Services* 52, no. 3 (February 2001): 223–28.

91. Mack, "Decriminalization of Mental Illness," 14.

92. Roger L. Scott, "Evaluation of a Mobile Crisis Program: Effectiveness, Efficiency, and Consumer Satisfaction," *Psychiatric Services* 51, no. 9 (September 2000): 1155.

93. Mack, "Decriminalization of Mental Illness," 16.

94. Michigan Supreme Court, *Michigan's Problem-Solving Courts: Solving Problems, Saving*

Lives, FY 2017 Annual Report on Performance Measures and Outcomes, 3, https://courts.michigan.gov/Administration/SCAO/Resources/Documents/Publications/Reports/PSCAnnualReport.pdf.

95. Ibid., 39.

96. State Court Administrative Office, Michigan Courts, "Guide for Developing a New Problem-Solving Court," https://courts.michigan.gov/Administration/admin/op/problem-solving-courts/Documents/PSC-Guide.pdf; Michigan Association of Treatment Court Professionals, Mental Health Court Advisory Committee, *Adult Mental Health Court Standards, Best Practices, and Promising Practices*, September 2018, https://courts.michigan.gov/Administration/SCAO/Resources/Documents/bestpractice/MHC-BPManual.pdf; Michigan Association of Treatment Court Professionals, Mental Health Court Advisory Committee, *Adult Mental Health Court Required Best Practices*, September 2018, https://courts.michigan.gov/Administration/SCAO/Resources/Documents/bestpractice/AdultMHC-Required.pdf.

97. Michigan Supreme Court, *Michigan's Problem-Solving Courts*, 31.

98. Ibid., 34–37.

99. Mack, "Decriminalization of Mental Illness," 17–18.

100. John M. Kane et al., "Comprehensive versus Usual Community Care for First-Episode Psychosis: 2-Year Outcomes from the NIMH RAISE Early Treatment Program," *American Journal of Psychiatry* 173, no. 4 (April 2016): 362–72.

101. Dixon et al., "Transforming the Treatment of Schizophrenia in the United States: The RAISE Initiative."

102. Gonzalez, Goplerud, and Shern, "Coordinated Specialty Care—First Episode Psychosis Programs," 13.

103. Catherine Adams, owner and clinical director, ETCH (Early Treatment and Cognitive Health), email, September 26, 2018.

104. Dixon et al., "Transforming the Treatment of Schizophrenia in the United States: The RAISE Initiative," 247.

105. Kreyenbuhl, Nossel, and Dixon, "Disengagement from Mental Health Treatment among Individuals with Schizophrenia," 700.

106. Pinals and Fuller, *Beyond Beds*, 23.

107. J. Steven Lamberti et al., "A Randomized Controlled Trial of the Rochester Forensic Assertive Community Treatment Model," *Psychiatric Services* 68, no. 10 (October 2017): 1016–24.

108. Mack, "Decriminalization of Mental Illness," 13.

109. Michigan Legislature, Public Act 320 of 2016 (House Bill 4674 from 2015–2016 session),

http://legislature.mi.gov/doc.aspx?2015-HB-4674; Jenny McInerney, J. Hunault, and Kevin Koorstra, House Fiscal Agency Analysis, Analysis as Enacted, "Mental Health Code: Revise Assisted Outpatient Treatment Program, Legislative Analysis," February 1, 2017, http://legislature.mi.gov/doc.aspx?2015-HB-4674. Ted Roelofs, "Revision to 'Kevin's Law' Means Quicker Treatment for the Mentally Ill," *Bridge: News and Analysis from the Center for Michigan*, January 12, 2017, https://www.bridgemi.com. Michigan Legislature, Public Act 593 of 2018 (House Bill 5810 from 2017–2018 session), http://legislature.mi.gov/doc.aspx?2018-HB-5810.

110. Kreyenbuhl, Nossel, and Dixon, "Disengagement from Mental Health Treatment among Individuals with Schizophrenia," 699.

111. Elbogen et al., "Treatment Engagement and Violence Risk in Mental Disorders," 357.

112. Substance Abuse and Mental Health Services Administration, "Behavioral Health Treatments and Services," September 20, 2017, https://www.samhsa.gov/treatment.

113. Van Dorn et al., "Effects of Outpatient Treatment on Risk of Arrest."

114. Jeffrey W. Swanson et al., "The Cost of Assisted Outpatient Treatment: Can It Save States Money?," *American Journal of Psychiatry* 170, no. 12 (December 2013).

115. Gonzalez, Goplerud, and Shern, "Coordinated Specialty Care—First Episode Psychosis Programs," 12.

116. USA Mental Health First Aid, "Get Involved and Make a Difference," https://www.mentalhealthfirstaid.org.

117. Mental Health First Aid Australia, "MHFA Australia Course Evaluations," n.d., https://mhfa.com.au/research/mhfa-course-evaluations.

118. NAMI (National Alliance on Mental Illness), "NAMI Programs," https://www.nami.org.

119. Mack, "Decriminalization of Mental Illness," 11.

What Works in Prisoner Reentry

Reducing Crime, Recidivism, and Prison Populations

Dennis Schrantz

The United States is the world's leader in incarceration, with approximately 2.2 million people being held in the nation's prisons and jails—a 500 percent increase over the last forty years.[1] The United States currently incarcerates more people than any other developed nation both per capita and in raw numbers.[2]

Lowering the number of individuals incarcerated is becoming a prominent topic among politicians and other policymakers across the political spectrum. The issue of mass incarceration even became the subject of presidential proclamations by Barack Obama; a campaign speech by a major contender for the White House in 2016, Hillary Rodham Clinton; and national debates among that year's presidential candidates.[3] The Right is finally agreeing with the Left, and amazingly Newt Gingrich is on board with the ACLU—causing so much joy that the ACLU exclaimed, "Sing it, Newt!"[4]

For the first time in modern political American history, a focus on justice policies reached the highest levels of agreement across the political spectrum, and there were signs that the combined efforts of state legislatures and executives on improved justice policies were having an impact. By 2015, the number of people in U.S. federal and state prisons was at its lowest since 2005.[5] And while that is certainly eroding as the Trump administration starts to drag the country backward,[6] the past few years have been remarkable.

But speeches and calls for better policies—indeed, even better policies themselves—will not end the era of mass incarceration. Improvements to community supervision, an enormous expansion of human service resources for offenders, and a rethinking of executive branch probation and parole services are needed. Although community-based programs can contribute to some reduction in post-prison crime, the largest contributor to prison growth is often parole failure—not for new criminal acts but for technical violations. That factor has to be addressed or we won't changet our nation's addiction to imprisonment.

The increased academic attention to evidence-based principles and practices, although helpful, will not fix the problem either—unless the folks running the prisons and the supervision agencies can figure out how to apply the research to actual real-life cases that they have to supervise, and they are given the resources to do so effectively.[7]

Despite extensive attention to reforming prisoner reentry approaches in the last decade, the return-to-prison recidivism rates of former prisoners have not changed substantially in most states. The most recent comprehensive study of state-level offender recidivism was performed by the Pew Center on the States for their 2011 report *State of Recidivism: The Revolving Door of America's Prisons.* Pew defined recidivism as a technical violation or a new crime committed by a former prisoner that results in a return to prison. The study showed that out of the thirty-three states that reported recidivism data for both the 1999 and 2004 release cohorts, only seventeen states had a decrease in recidivism and sixteen states had an increase in recidivism. Only six of the thirty-three states achieved a drop in recidivism of greater than 10 percent.

Many reform efforts continue to focus on reducing recidivism among former state prisoners through improvements to prisoner reentry policy within jurisdictions. For example, recently, when the National Criminal Justice Association and the National Governor's Association organized a criminal-justice reform summit under their National Criminal Justice Reform Project in 2017, nineteen of the twenty states at the table stated that prisoner reentry was their most important reform focus. Why? Because at least several states, led by Michigan in the early 2000s, showed they can substantially cut back the size of their prison population by reducing crime and violations by former prisoners, saving millions of dollars by improving the way they assess and respond to prisoners' post-release needs.

The Scope of the Problem

In addition to the 2.2 million people incarcerated in the United States by the end of 2015, an additional 4.7 million people were on probation and parole.[8] Each year, hundreds of thousands of men and women leave prison and return to their communities; during 2015 alone, over 640,000 people sentenced to federal and state prisons were released, making prisoner reentry a major factor in the public-safety arena.[9] The fact is that at least 95 percent of people incarcerated in state prisons will be released back to their communities at some point.[10] And this does not include the nearly 9 *million* people released from local jails each year.[11] So, prisoner reentry is a fact of life affecting millions of citizens and their families.

But being released doesn't mean they are free. The stigma of imprisonment, coupled with a breathtaking inability to secure affordable housing and employment—made more difficult due to low levels of education and high levels of alcohol and drug addiction—creates a nearly impossible set of circumstances for former prisoners. The statistics about former prisoners' education, employment, health, and housing challenges inform the scope of the challenges:

- Only about half of incarcerated adults have a high school degree or its equivalent.[12]
- Employment rates and earning histories of people in prison and jail are often low before incarceration as a result of limited education, low job-skill levels, and the prevalence of physical and mental health problems; incarceration only exacerbates these challenges.[13]
- A three-state recidivism study conducted from 2001 to 2006 found that less than half of people released from prison had secured a job upon their return to the community.[14]
- The American Bar Association has documented 27,254 state occupational licensing restrictions nationwide for people with a criminal record.[15]
- People in the justice system experience chronic health conditions, infectious diseases, substance use disorders, and mental illnesses at much higher rates than the general population.[16]
- In 2005, more than half of all people incarcerated in prisons and jails had a mental illness: 56 percent of state prisoners, 45 percent of federal prisoners, and 64 percent of jail inmates. Of those who had a mental illness, about three-quarters also had a co-occurring substance use disorder.[17]

- In a study of more than 20,000 adults entering five local jails, researchers documented serious mental illnesses in 14.5 percent of the men and 31 percent of the women, which taken together constitutes 16.9 percent of those studied—rates in excess of three to six times those found in the general population.[18]
- In a 2008 study of the U.S. jail population in 2002, about 15.3 percent had been homeless at some time the year before incarceration—up to 11.3 times the estimate for the general adult population—and for those with a mental illness, the rates were 20 percent.[19]
- About 10 percent of people entering state and federal prison had recently been homeless, and at least the same percentage of those who leave prison are homeless for some period of time after release.[20]

With these factors working against former prisoners, one wonders how their children are affected. Generational impacts due to mass incarceration are well documented. Consider:

- Parents with minor children make up 54 percent of people incarcerated in prisons and jails, or 1.2 million people: more than 120,000 mothers and 1.1 million fathers.[21]
- Between 1991 and 2007, the number of children with a parent in state or federal prison grew 80 percent. Today, an estimated 2.7 million children in the United States have a parent in prison or jail—that is, one in every twenty-eight children (3.6 percent of all children).[22]
- Under the Personal Responsibility and Work Opportunity Reconciliation Act (PRWORA), thirteen states fully prohibit anyone with a drug-related conviction from receiving public assistance under the Temporary Assistance to Needy Families (TANF) program; twenty-three other states maintain a partial ban.[23]

Given these dire circumstances, it should be no surprise that most released prisoners fail so frequently and return to prison. In a study that followed 404,638 people released from state prisons in thirty states in 2005, about 67.8 percent were arrested within three years of release, and 76.6 percent within five years of release.[24] About 55 percent returned to prison after three years.[25]

How exactly did we get into this mess? An examination of the history of parole and reentry in the United States sheds some light on the reasons that new frameworks are needed that provide practical and tested approaches to improving prisoner outcomes.

History and Development of Modern Reentry Practices

The concept of parole—French for "word," as in giving one's word—started in 1840 in a penal colony in the South Pacific when the man in charge of the colony, Captain Alexander Maconochie, created what he called the "mark system" that allowed prisoners to progress through a series of stages while imprisoned, leading to their release. According to Joan Petersilia in her breakthrough book on reentry, *When Prisoners Come Home*, "[Maconochie] assumed that prisoners should be prepared for a gradual, conditional release to full freedom."[26] This was a breakthrough approach since up until that time, when prisoners finished their sentences of punishment and harsh conditions, they were simply freed. Maconochie's approach provided the beginnings for work furlough, parole, and indeterminate sentencing as his efforts produced positive results. However, as a harbinger of the politics to come, Maconochie was eventually released from service in 1849 because his approach was seen as too lenient.

Sir Walter Crofton tried the mark system in Ireland in 1854, but added a reporting requirement through the police department, and beginning in Dublin, a new position of a civilian officer was added to the police force to help former prisoners find jobs, visit them, and supervise their activities. This new position found some success and became the genesis for the modern parole officer. In 1876, the so-called "Irish System" was brought to the United States, ironically enough by a Michigan penologist, who began using the system as the newly appointed superintendent of the Elmira Reformatory in New York.

From that point on, this "indeterminate" approach to imprisonment where prisoners' conduct was used to determine the point of release began to spread, and by 1907 the State of New York adopted the approach; by 1927, only three states were without a parole system. By 1940, about 44 percent of all prisoners were released on parole as part of the indeterminate structure, which rose to 72 percent by 1977. By 1942, all states and the federal government had systems for earning release and post-release supervision. But by 1999—after years of criticism of leniency and failure echoing Maconochie's plight one hundred years earlier—only 24 percent of prisoners were paroled, as the nation replaced the system of mandatory release that Petersilia calls, "a profound change in the way that inmates are returned to the free community [that has] gone unnoticed and undebated by the U.S. public."[27]

Regardless of the approach—determinate or indeterminate—social scientists agree that parole has been used primarily as a way to reduce prison populations and control former prisoner behavior, as opposed to providing rehabilitation, and parole has never garnered much public approval. Gallup polls taken in 1934 and 1998 each found that about 80 percent of the general public had a poor opinion of the public policy, thinking it too lenient. Over time, beginning in the 1960s, parole began to be associated once again with assistance and rehabilitation—in addition to punishment—and this had the effect of at least some regenerated public support for indeterminate terms, decided by parole boards, followed by a term of supervision when additional rehabilitation is expected to occur. One would think that good public policy would dictate that if citizens are concerned about public safety, some follow-up from prison is needed, and yet, many states either have parole boards who do not parole—citing the risk of the prisoner and wanting to keep them behind bars as long as possible—but then release them without any supervision or supports as they end up "maxing out" of prison. As Petersilia aptly points out,

> Common sense and empirical evidence call for reinstating discretionary parole release for inmates. Parole release decisions should be made by a professional parole board, which should be guided by objective risk prediction instruments or parole guidelines to make release decisions. Inmates should be given incentives to participate in prison programs, since research shows that regardless of their initial incentive to become involved, some positive effects will accrue for some people. No one is more dangerous than a criminal who has no incentive to straighten himself out while in prison and who returns to society without a supervised transition plan.[28]

As the current approach to prisoner reentry developed, the work of Petersilia in 2003 and the subsequent publication in 2005 by Jeremy Travis of *But They All Come Back: Facing the Challenges of Prisoner Reentry*[29]—which delved deeper into the services needed to support effective reentry—stand out as they help practitioners who struggle with the interpretation of research into practical applications in their day-to-day work. Subsequently, organizations such as the National Institute of Corrections, the Center for Effective Public Policy, and the Center for Justice Innovation began assisting local and state jurisdictions by guiding the interaction between science and practice, building on the excellent advice of reentry leaders like Petersilia and Travis.

Petersilia suggested four principles in 2003 to improve reentry: alter the in-prison experience, change prison release and revocation practices, revise post-release services and supervision, and foster collaborations with the community and enhance mechanisms of informal social control.[30] Travis suggested five principles in 2005: prepare for reentry, build bridges between prisons and communities, seize the moment of release, strengthen the concentric circles of support, and promote successful reintegration.[31] They are quite consistent and form the basis—in all of their rich detail in their books—for the subsequent work by national think tanks and technical assistance providers as practical applications, models, and frameworks were developed that could help interpret their advice into practical applications for the work in the field.

But as a final point in the historical context of improving prisoner reentry, one of the most complex and difficult facing advocates deserves special attention: the disparate nature of the justice system, which treats persons of color so discriminately that it defies imagination.

The Racist Underpinnings of the United States Penal System

The racist underpinnings of the United States criminal justice system is well documented, with research dating back many decades.[32] But beginning in 1991, with the publication of the shattering examination of race and justice by Marc Mauer of the Sentencing Project in *The Race to Incarcerate*, a new dedication to the issue took hold.[33]

Since then, no other publication captured the history, sentiments, and facts of the racially biased justice system like Michelle Alexander's 2010 publication, *The New Jim Crow*, which provides an exhaustive and pivotal examination of the issue.[34] Her book and its companion *Study Guide and Call to Action* has spurred more discussion in America's churches, learning institutions, and public forums than during any time in modern history.

Her narrative, which begins here with the 1877 Reconstruction Era, needs little explanation:

> The backlash against the gains of African Americans in the Reconstruction Era was swift and severe. As African Americans obtained political power and began the long

march toward greater economic equality, whites reacted with panic and outrage . . . vagrancy laws and other laws defining activities such as "mischief" and "insulting gestures" as crimes were enforced vigorously against blacks . . . [and] opened up an enormous market for convict leasing, in which prisoners were contracted out as laborers to the highest bidder . . . tens of thousands of African Americans were arbitrarily arrested during this period.

Death rates were shockingly high, for the private contractors had no interest in the health and well-being of their laborers, unlike the earlier slave-owners who needed their slaves . . . to be healthy enough to survive hard labor. Convicts had no meaningful rights at this time and no effective redress . . . the U.S. Constitution had abolished slavery but allowed one major exception: slavery remained appropriate as punishment for a crime.[35]

Jump ahead one hundred years and the political climate repeated itself. Alexander writes:

The shift to a general attitude of 'toughness' toward problems associated with communities of color began in the 1960s, when the gains and goals of the Civil Rights movement began to require real sacrifices on the part of white Americans, and conservative politicians found they could mobilize white racial resentment by vowing to crack down on crime. In the early 1990s, resistance to the emergence of a new system of racialized social control collapsed across the political spectrum. A century earlier, a similar political dynamic had resulted in the birth of Jim Crow. . . . Now a new racial caste system—mass incarceration—was taking hold, as politicians of every stripe competed with each other to win the votes of poor and working class whites, whose economic status was precarious, at best, and who felt threatened by racial reforms. . . . The results were immediate. As law-enforcement budgets exploded, so did the number of people behind bars. In 1991, the Sentencing Project reported that the number of people behind bars in the United States was unprecedented in world history, and that one fourth of young African American men were now under the control of the criminal justice system. . . . More than 2 million people found themselves behind bars at the turn of the 21st century . . . where discrimination in employment, housing, and access to education was perfectly legal, and where they could be denied the right to vote. . . . The New Jim Crow was born.[36]

Lest one be demoralized by the sheer magnitude of the historical and complex challenges facing the criminal justice system, Alexander gives hope and buoyancy to reform efforts—as can be read at the close of the chapter—but not without admonishing us to understand the need for a complete rethinking of the system. She writes:

> Those who believe that advocacy challenging mass incarceration can be successful without overturning the public consensus that gave rise to it are engaging in fanciful thinking, a form of denial. Isolated victories can be won—even a stream of victories—but in the absence of a fundamental shift in public consciousness, the system as a whole will remain intact [or] . . . the system will rebound. The caste system will reemerge in a new form, just as convict leasing replaced slavery, or it will be reborn, just as mass incarceration replaced Jim Crow.[37]

Reducing Prison Populations through Improved Prisoner Reentry

As stated earlier, many criminal-justice reform efforts over the past decade have focused on reducing recidivism among former state prisoners through improvements to prisoner-reentry policy within jurisdictions. More specifically, beginning in 2003, the National Institute of Corrections (NIC) and the National Governors' Association (NGA) sponsored multistate academies and provided a year of onsite technical assistance to improve prisoner-reentry strategic planning within seventeen participating states.[38] Both NIC and NGA emphasized the development of high-level strategic plans. These high-level plans, they believed, would enable jurisdictions to take immediate and short-term steps to improve former prisoner outcomes while they worked to complete the enormous long-term system changes that are required for a lasting impact on crime and recidivism reduction.

The two national academies used the NIC Transition from Prison to Community (TPC) Model, which was—and still remains—the operative high-level model for prisoner-reentry reform and has helped foster much of the change witnessed in the United States over the past ten years.[39] The 2003 TPC Model has had enormous value as a foundation for effective strategic planning that helps prepare jurisdictions for tactical or implementation planning—that is, how to put those strategies into action. Beyond the TPC Model, the Re-Entry Policy Council developed in 2005 a virtual encyclopedia about how to improve prisoner reentry, *The Re-Entry Policy Council Report*. It includes policy statements and recommendations to assist with planning through the development of sound, evidence-based policies and provides guidance on how to put those policies into action.[40]

Meanwhile, beginning in 2008, the federal Second Chance Act (SCA) required that participating jurisdictions develop and implement comprehensive strategic plans to reduce recidivism.[41] But most SCA grants fund program-level efforts designed to reduce recidivism for relatively small, targeted numbers of program participants, rather than system-change efforts. The work of moving from strategic planning to small-scale implementation to large-scale, system-wide replication requires an extraordinary level of coordination and capacity building. Without additional tools and resources to support effective implementation activity, the lessons learned from the NIC and NGA efforts and from SCA programs will not be taken to scale, and major statewide reductions in recidivism will continue to fall well short of state and national goals.

Researchers have established the need to achieve a better link between what research evidence shows works and how to implement that research on the ground—particularly on the issue of recidivism reduction.[42] Clearer guidance is needed in the field on how to implement research findings and how to successfully replicate well-performing programs—specifically in prisons and parole agencies and their affiliated human-service delivery partners in the community.[43] In essence, there is a call to arms for better connections that help build evidence through applied research that allows researchers and practitioners to work together as active partners with joint ownership of the research process and outcomes.[44] What has been needed is implementation guidance to translate planning into action and achieve statewide reductions in recidivism.

The Nexus between Research and Practice

Some states—such as Arizona, Delaware, Georgia, Louisiana, Michigan, and Montana—have been using a new approach and an innovative tool that will improve the practical application of evidence-based practices to reduce recidivism. The Strategic Planning for Prisoner Reentry Framework (the Framework), developed by the Center for Justice Innovation in cooperation with the National Reentry Resource Center and the Northpointe Institute for Public Management, adapts the Re-Entry Policy Council Report and TPC Model by taking specific targets for

THE STRATEGIC PLANNING FOR PRISONER REENTRY FRAMEWORK

Phase 1: Getting Ready
1 Assessment and Classification
   1.1   Development of Intake Procedures
2 Returning Citizen Behavior and Programming
   2.1   Development of Programming Plan
   2.2   Physical Health Care
   2.3   Mental Health Care
   2.4   Substance Abuse Treatment
   2.5   Children and Family Support
   2.6   Behaviors and Attitudes
   2.7   Education
   2.8   Technical Training
   2.9   Work Experience

Phase 2: Going Home
3 Returning Citizen Release Preparation
   3.1   Development of Parole and Reentry Plan (TAP2)
   3.2   Housing
   3.3   Continuity of Care Planning
   3.4   Working with Potential Employers
   3.5   Employment upon Release
   3.6   Identification and Benefits
   3.7   Release Preparation for Families
   3.8   Release Preparation for Victims
4 Release Decision Making
   4.1   Advising the Releasing Authority
   4.2   Release Decision

Phase 3: Staying Home
5 Supervision and Services
   5.1   Design of Supervision and Treatment Strategy (TAP3)
   5.2   Implementation of Supervision and Treatment Strategy
   5.3   Maintaining Continuity of Care and Housing
   5.4   Job Development and Supportive Employment
6 Revocation Decision Making
   6.1   Graduated Responses
7 Discharge and Aftercare
   7.1 Development of Discharge/Aftercare Plan (TAP4)

Source: Dennis Schrantz, Center for Justice Innovation

change to a highly specific implementation level in ways that can be monitored and measured. The targets for change are categorized within the three TPC Model phases and seven primary decision points that constitute the reentry process.

The innovative elements and training in the use of the Framework push jurisdictional reentry planning beyond high-level strategy to focus on detailed actions needed to implement and sustain recidivism reduction through improved policy and practice. Both the tool and the training to support its use are grounded in established principles of successful strategic planning and change management. The Framework has helped several states to meet their goals for policy change.

The Framework identifies twenty-six "targets for change" with goals and operational expectations provided for each target. These targets for change have been distilled from the policy statements of the Re-Entry Policy Council Report, as well as the work being done in several states around the issue of family reunification. Practical activities are provided within the Framework to help guide a state's strategy to meet their recidivism reduction goals, as well as references to research and publications for each targeted policy area. Importantly, intermediate performance measures are embedded in the tool to help monitor progress toward the primary goal of recidivism reduction.

The Framework, augmented by tools and resources currently available through a variety of public domain resources, focuses on the "science of implementation," which in criminal justice is a relatively new frontier, although with a unique history that has established a dedication to this emerging discipline. Over the past decade, the science related to *developing and identifying* evidence-based policies, practices, and programs has improved. However the science related to *implementing* these policies, practices, and programs with fidelity (particularly on a large scale) that results in good outcomes lags behind.

The Strategic Planning for Prisoner Reentry Framework

The Framework's vision of improved reentry is that returning citizens released from prison will have the tools and support needed to succeed in the community. In order to make this vision a reality, the mission embedded in the Framework is to improve public safety by reducing crime through implementation of a seamless plan of services and supervision developed with each returning citizen—delivered through state and local collaboration—from the time they enter prison through their successful transition, reintegration, and aftercare in the community.

The fundamental goals of reentry articulated in the Framework are to (1) promote public safety by reducing the threat of harm to persons, families, and their property by citizens returning to their communities from prison; and (2) increase success rates of returning citizens who transition from prison by fostering effective, evidence-based risk and need management and treatment, returning citizen accountability, and safe family, community, and victim participation. Performance measures to determine the degree to which these goals are met include measurements of increased public safety through the reduction of recidivism (as measured by reconviction and return to prison) and successful completion of community supervision.[45]

The Framework builds on approaches for reentry improvement developed by the National Prisoner Re-Entry Council, as outlined in its *Re-Entry Policy Council Report*, and the National Institute of Corrections through its Transition from Prison to Community (TPC) Model (see sidebar).[46] These approaches provide guidance for specific justice policies that will be considered by states as the "Targets for Change" to improve prisoner reentry. These targets for change are categorized within the three TPC Model phases (Getting Ready, the Institutional Phase; Going Home, the Pre-Release Phase; and Staying Home, the Community Supervision and Discharge Phase) and seven primary decision points that constitute the reentry process.

For each target for change, goals and operational expectations are included, as well as references for further reading to specific pages within the voluminous *Re-Entry Policy Council Report* and other publications that pertain specifically to the target for change that is being addressed. Thus, the Framework provides a practical guide to help direct a state's plan to meet the policy goals and operational expectations of prisoner reentry reform—increasingly as a result of legislation or executive order. The Framework also frees state agencies to begin to focus immediately on implementation.

Importantly, the Framework underscores the three overarching policy and practice considerations that must be in place to truly reform a returning citizen's behavior: Transition Accountability Planning, Case Management, and Evidence-Based Practices. The Framework also provides state agencies and local partners with the tools to move from planning to implementation and to accurately measure changes in recidivism. By moving reentry planning beyond high-level strategy to a focus on carefully scripted actions, states can more effectively reduce recidivism. The priorities for implementation of the Framework include an improved transition accountability planning process with each returning citizen, from the point of

imprisonment through successful discharge from post-release community supervision, with an emphasis on safe, affordable housing and employment.

The Framework also includes recommendations for state governance of reentry
reforms that include justice agencies (corrections, probation, parole, the parole
board, etc.) and other state departments that govern behavioral health, developmental disabilities, community health and other human-service agencies, statewide
human-services organizations, business representatives, law enforcement, victims'
advocates, local reentry coalition members, and faith-based leaders.

The Framework suggests state agency management for this "Implementation
Steering Team" (IST) that guides prisoner reentry reforms through local work groups
and department-based resource teams throughout the state in a unique, diverse,
and robust state/local partnership.

States should first focus on the highest priorities embedded in the Framework,
including

- the development of state and local organizational structures,
- the development and implementation of the Transition Accountability
  Planning (TAP) process,
- the identification of moderate to high risk/moderate to high needs prisoners
  who will return to their communities, and the development of community
  assessments that catalog current reentry services for each community
  (assets),
- the barriers that prevent or diminish access to the services by returning
  citizens, and
- gaps in those services.

The major points of emphasis in the TAP process are assuring safe, affordable housing and employment (and/or education) driven by actuarial risk/needs offender
assessment. States should pilot these new approaches so that the reforms have time
to gel and add local jurisdictions incrementally. Eventually, once the Framework is
shown to be effective, the focus can turn to taking the effort statewide and then up
to scale. Staffing must be sufficient in order to expand the effort step by step and
so that the lessons learned in other states are taken into account.

The Michigan Experience: Impact of Prisoner Reentry Reforms

By connecting research to practice, Michigan achieved notable reductions in recidivism of former prisoners. According to a 2012 report from the Council of State Governments' Justice Center, between 2005 and 2007, Michigan reduced returns to prison by 18 percent, one of the largest reductions in recidivism of former prisoners in the United States.[47] The Justice Center report observed that "over a longer period, Michigan's decline in recidivism is even more significant, with a 28% reduction in returns to prison between 2000 and 2008."[48] According to more recent data (2013) from the Michigan Department of Corrections, the recidivism rate improved for these offender cohorts by 38 percent through December 2011.[49]

As a result of the improved outcomes of parolees, Michigan's prison population declined over 12 percent in just three years (2006–2009), and has continued to decline to 17 percent (2006–2013)—the steepest reduction in the shortest period of time of any state in the nation.[50] Subsequently, Michigan has also led the nation in prison closings with an astonishing twenty-one facilities closed, saving nearly $350 million annually. Since the efforts to control and reduce the prison population began in 2002, it is estimated that cost avoidance for prison operations is nearly $1 billion.[51] Michigan's accomplishments represent the most rapid and massive decarceration effort in United States history. And the crime rate has not increased.[52]

> While it may seem obvious that locking up more people would lower the crime rate, the reality is much more complicated. Sentencing and release policies, not crime rates, determine the numbers of persons in prison. . . . Michigan has undertaken what may be the currently most effective changes to reduce incarceration in any of the states. . . . As a Michigan Department of Corrections official bluntly stated in testimony to the Michigan legislature, these steps "have broken the political logjam that has consistently stymied many prior justice policy reform proposals," by providing incentives for various stakeholders to support the initiatives and without requiring politically-sensitive reductions in statutory penalties for criminal offenses. . . .
>
> The history of over-incarceration in Michigan illustrates why the fact that over-incarceration results from deliberate policy choices about punishment rather than directly from crime rates is actually good news. As a persuasive body of evidence demonstrates, with an effective criminal justice policy, public safety can be improved, crime rates lowered, and our massive over-incarceration reduced.

Michigan's experience is important because it demonstrates that common sense can in fact beat demagoguery and that smart-on-crime policies can actually triumph.[53]

Lessons Learned

There is much to be learned from the experiences in Michigan on how to use improved prisoner reentry approaches to reduce recidivism and, ultimately, the size of a state's prison population. To begin with, elected officials in Michigan, beginning with the governor, understood the political context of the work. And since elected officials will ultimately make the decisions to allow executive-branch agencies to act "tough *and* smart" on crime issues, they need incentives and early successes.

When focusing on the goals of crime reduction and fewer victims, working with offenders is easier to support. Secondly, high-level decision makers focused on budget issues and how the hugely expensive prison system simply could not be sustained—particularly since it was clear that the number of people in prison had very little impact on crime. Michigan officials understood that the work on offender crime and recidivism reduction is directly related to the national recognition that we cannot sustain the high budget levels for corrections, and we must reduce incarceration.

There was a growing recognition that the science of research and evaluation, a dedication to what is called "evidence-based strategies," provided ample evidence that new and smarter approaches were proving successful. Beginning with the governor, supported by the legislature, the Michigan Department of Corrections realized that it is impossible for major system reform to take shape without highly disciplined strategic planning based on research and evidence about what works when implementing targeted changes to policy and practice. Four cornerstones of the collaboration between justice and non-justice agencies are essential (see addendum 1 for more detail):

- Start with accurate offender risk and need assessment.
- Focus on improved offender case management, driven by accurate risk and need assessment, and work with one offender at a time to improve outcomes.
- Implement "success-driven" offender supervision that stresses the role of the supervising officer as a coach rather than merely a surveillance officer.

- Focus on agency-wide staff development and "change management," not merely training. Justice agencies must become "learning organizations" and embrace the need to learn new approaches to reduce crime and recidivism.

Since "system change" within corrections parole agencies is complex, it is difficult for leaders and staff to wrap their arms around the myriad of issues needed for sustainable system change. So, during the years when Michigan introduced reentry reforms, the leaders in the agency focused on specific core areas of functions that are critical to the ability to sustain reforms over time. And since it was clear that the capacity and competency within the department was needed, outside assistance was funded with private foundation dollars and federal grants to help provide the skills and time needed to execute the needed changes.

To begin with, the department had to improve its mid-level organizational structure, so the department developed and promoted mid-level managers who were competent and capable of overseeing the facility, and field and community work required to improve offender success. High-level leadership was critical, but changes must come from within the existing management structure. Champions were identified who were willing to get in front of the initiatives and help develop them and then guide them through the trenches.

The mid-level managers in turn had to make certain that there were additional resources for their staff. Managers were committed to do all they could for line staff to have the tools and resources necessary to improve offender success. This included providing staff with incentives, rewards, technology, and training that were needed to conduct business in the new ways required by the system changes for recidivism reduction. Technology became critical to free staff to work more closely with offenders so that their attitudes and beliefs are adjusted.

In order to make these changes "stick," the department began to integrate the changes into policy and procedures to reflect that offender success and recidivism reduction was not just a "pilot" program or "initiative" but standard operating procedure. It was emphasized that these reforms were not be about programs, although programming is important, but about fundamental changes in policy.

To ensure that the allocation of resources is consistent with policies and procedures, the department's annual budgets were analyzed to determine if expenditures were supportive of the new vision of improved offender success. And with a nearly $2 billion budget, it could not be argued that the agency did not have enough funding. The key was not to find more money, it was to spend the money the agency had more efficiently and in ways that were more effective at improving offender outcomes.

To ensure that as the department developed and implemented new and innovative ways to measure offender success and failure, more resources were dedicated to evaluating and implementing evidence-based practices, such as risk- and need-assessment tools that drove case management and then were evaluated to determine the impact on violations, crime, and returns to prison.

The department also dedicated a great deal of attention to internal and external collaboration. Effective and strategic collaboration with probation personnel, prison staff, parole agents, and community-based agencies was critical in determining the short-, intermediate-, and long-term success of former prisoners. Community, faith, law-enforcement, and victim leaders were not to be an afterthought; they were brought to the table as equal partners in the process. Sustained and long-term former offender success happens in communities, not in justice agencies.

State and local agencies outside the justice system were broadly represented on both state and local policy teams and included in the state's efforts to promote offender success, especially because some of these agencies presented barriers that worked against recidivism reduction efforts by way of funding and eligibility restrictions. Offenders can only succeed when their needs are viewed holistically; planning and implementation committees and councils reflected that in their memberships. Leaders in housing, addiction services, training and employment, and mental health were at the table.

Much attention was dedicated to working with community leaders who eventually "owned" prisoner reentry as full partners in the process, and this ownership had explicit expectations for engagement. Local steering teams were responsible for developing and reaching consensus in a collaborative manner on local, community-based "Comprehensive Community Plans" for both diversion from prison to probation on the front end and prisoner reentry on the back end. To be funded by the state, the local plans had to address specific service areas, such as housing, employment, substance abuse services, mental health, transportation, victim services, and the involvement of local law enforcement and faith-based institutions.

For each of these service areas, the comprehensive community plan described the local assets in place to increase the potential for success for former prisoners, barriers that impede maximum use of these assets, gaps in services, and proposed solutions to address the barriers and gaps. Thus, the plans built upon existing services and embedded their use within the context of comprehensive service delivery.

Plans must focus on both policy and procedure that is critical to implementation: Who does What and When.

Local community coordinators were essential to both local diversion efforts and the prisoner reentry process at each of Michigan's eighteen regional sites, as they were responsible for staffing the steering team and managing the development and implementation of the comprehensive plans. They coordinated and monitored the use of funds, the effectiveness of service delivery, community outreach and education, and collaboration with service providers and justice system professionals.

Finally, in Michigan, nothing was more important to prison diversion efforts and prisoner reentry efforts than continual public education. Taxpayers must recognize recidivism reduction services as public protection strategies, not as "coddling convicts." This required a disciplined dedication of purpose that was carefully developed, implemented, and managed. Local diversion and reentry steering teams comprised of elected and other officials offered many avenues to educate the public and special stakeholder groups.

Fundamental to full community support, for example, was the support of law-enforcement officials such as chiefs of police, sheriffs, and prosecutors who dedicate their careers to fighting crime. Their involvement in the local process as partners in the development and the execution of the public education plan was essential to gain and sustain their ongoing support.

Approaches and successes in Michigan were the subject of many reports, articles, and editorials,[54] and the state's story about improving prisoner reentry is one of several in the nation that show how improvements in policy and practice, anchored in research and proven over time, can pave the way for other states to "improve the odds that released offenders will not reappear at the prison gate. That outcome benefits everyone, saving public funds and keeping communities safe."[55] If states will apply with fidelity the many lessons learned in Michigan, they have great potential to reduce mass incarceration.

Other Views

Criminal justice reformers promote multifaceted approaches to reduce mass incarceration. Some suggest improvements on the front end with more diversions from prison. Others, as is suggested throughout this chapter, recommend back-end improvements in prisoner reentry. Both are correct and shouldn't be viewed

| *Dennis Schrantz*

as an either-or. Beyond the applications of practical approaches that are within our grasp are deeper considerations that offer another view. For example, a very thorough analysis of societal prejudice and political realities is provided by Marie Gottschalk, who offers a sobering critique of what she deems an approach that "shuns state-led solutions aimed at addressing deep-seated structural problems" in her treatise on crime and punishment, *Caught: The Prison State and the Lockdown of American Politics.*[56]

> The three-R solution (reentry, recidivism and justice reinvestment) promises to give people a second chance, never acknowledging that many of the people cycling in and out of prison and jail were never really given a first chance, let alone an equal chance. . . . Jeremy Travis defined reentry a decade ago in a very open-ended way. It was simply the "process of leaving prison and returning to society." . . . The surge in enthusiasm for reentry has not fundamentally changed the discourse over punishment and has further entrenched certain punitive tendencies.
>
> The reentry solution as currently conceived has several serious shortcomings. Reentry charts a very narrow path to a better life that many ex-offenders have trouble navigating due to factors that are not under their control or even the control of corrections departments. Many champions of reentry portray successful reentry largely as a matter of helping ex-offenders acquire the right individual skills to become employable. They ignore or downplay the enormous structural obstacles that stand between ex-offenders and full economic, political, and social membership in the United States. . . . Framing reentry in narrow human capital terms focuses public attention on correcting the reported inadequacies of offenders and ex-offenders. It deflects public policy away from correcting the deeper structural problems in the U.S. economy . . . defending reentry, treatment and rehabilitative programs in terms of their potential to reduce recidivism rates, trim penal budgets, and cut the prison population is an extremely risky and ultimately self-defeating strategy. The very best treatment and reentry programs are capable of making only modest contributions to reducing recidivism rates, and prison-based ones are the most ineffective on this score . . . recidivism is an extremely slippery concept, and crimes by ex-offenders are not the main drivers of crime rates.

For those reentry advocates who are doing what they can to decrease mass incarceration—with some very positive and notable results—this opinion provides an important context for the work, rather than a call to stop, and public and private discourse on the subject of reentry needs to include a focus on the high-level political realities of racism and the need to change "the discourse over punishment." This is articulated quite poignantly by Michelle Alexander who stated,

> The relevant question is not whether to engage in reform work but how. There is no shortage of worthy reform efforts and goals. Differences of opinion are inevitable about which reforms are most important and in what order of priority they should be pursued. These debates are worthwhile, but it is critical to keep in mind that the question of how we do reform work is even more important than the specific reforms we seek. If the way we pursue reforms does not contribute to the building of a movement to dismantle the system of mass incarceration . . . none of the reforms, even if won, will disrupt the nation's racial equilibrium . . . We run the risk of winning isolated battles but losing the larger war.[57]

So, we soldier on, as we must. One cannot look at the accomplishments in a state like Michigan—that positively affected tens of thousands of prisoners and their families—and not believe that there is a role to play for prisoner reentry reforms even as we acknowledge that a broader focus on racial disparity and the deep rooted economic policies in this country have created a virtual caste system for the poor and disenfranchised.

■ ADDENDUM 1

The Importance of Evidence-Based Practices

The fundamental goal of offender reentry is to improve public safety by increasing offender success and, thereby, reducing the threat of harm to people and property in the communities to which offenders return. Data indicating that almost two out of every three offenders released from state prisons return to prison within three years, the experience of communities and families that have been victimized, and the soaring costs of re-incarcerating offenders that fail in the community show us that achieving this goal requires a new approach. It is not enough to *monitor and contain* risk. Instead, the corrections system should aim to *reduce* risk.

Fortunately, research conducted over the past thirty years has provided substantial evidence of the policies and practices that are effective for reducing offender risk. Evidence-Based Practice (EBP) is the application of this evidence to the functions of the corrections system, its partners, and the professionals within those systems.

Definition

Evidence-based practice (EBP) is the use of scientifically supported techniques to reduce offender risk and recidivism:

- EBP describes the individual programs and curricula that have been rigorously tested and proven to be effective.
- EBP also describes a broader, more fundamental shift in the policies and procedures that guide how a criminal justice agency, its personnel, and other reentry-related professionals interact with offenders, on a daily basis, to engage them in the process of change.

The Critical Elements of Evidence-Based Practice

An evidence-based practice approach to offender reentry includes the following critical elements:

- Practice is guided by the principles of effective intervention: The accumulation of decades of research on offender risk reduction and behavior change points to a set of core principles of EBP. The best outcomes are achieved when these principles are reflected consistently across policies, procedures, and day-to-day interactions with offenders.
- Interventions are grounded in research and delivered with fidelity: Although EBP is about more than individual programs, it requires that offenders have access to programs and interventions that have been proven, through rigorous evaluation, to be effective. Moreover, the programs are delivered with fidelity to the original, evaluated design and are evaluated regularly to ensure the intended outcomes are achieved.
- Corrections professionals and their partners from other service delivery systems establish and maintain effective relationships with offenders: By employing specific skills and techniques, such as building rapport, balancing enforcement with treatment, and affirming the offender's role in the change

process, corrections staff and other professionals involved in the reentry process enhance the offender's desire and ability to change.

Evidence-Based Practice Policy and Practice

How do the elements of EBP translate into more specific policy and practice guidelines for improving reentry outcomes? This section lists and describes recommendations for implementing EBP.

Assess Actuarial Risk and Need

At the time of intake, a comprehensive assessment process should be conducted with each offender to measure individual risks and needs. The assessment should identify static (unchangeable) risk factors and dynamic (changeable) risk factors. Some common risk factors include age at first arrest, current age, gender, and criminal history. Criminogenic needs are dynamic risk factors that, when changed, impact the offender's risk for recidivism. These include:

- Antisocial attitudes, cognitions
- Antisocial associates, peers
- Antisocial behavior
- Family, marital stressors
- Substance abuse
- Lack of employment stability, achievement
- Lack of educational achievement
- Lack of pro-social leisure activities

The tool(s) used to conduct the assessment should be validated for use with similar populations and administered by trained staff. Assessments should be readministered throughout the transition process to monitor progress.

Enhance Intrinsic Motivation

The external motivation applied by the criminal justice system through the use of sanctions and penalties can effectively influence behavior change, particularly in the short term. However, in order to sustain change over time, the motivation to change needs to come from the offender. Staff should interact with offenders in ways that enhance internal motivation and support change.

Target Interventions Based on Risk, Need, and Responsivity

To maximize risk reduction, each offender should be assigned interventions based on the following considerations:

- Risk: The level of intervention should match the level of risk. Focus supervision and treatment resources on the offenders who are most likely to commit crimes without the intervention. Lower-risk offenders should receive less intervention and supervision.
- Need: Interventions should address the offender's greatest criminogenic needs, which are the dynamic factors that contribute to the offender's likelihood of committing another crime.
- Responsivity: The types of interventions and the methods of delivery should match the offender's learning style, motivation, culture, gender, and other factors that are likely to impact how the offender responds to an intervention.

Skill Train with Directed Practice

Interventions should emphasize a cognitive-behavioral approach that challenges antisocial thinking patterns and teaches new skills that are practiced by the offender and reinforced by staff. Again, these approaches should not be limited to program settings. They should shape the daily, routine interactions between the offender and staff.

■ ADDENDUM 2

Michigan Prison System—Statistics

From 1980 until its peak in 2009, the total federal and state prison population of the United States climbed from about 330,000 to more than 1.6 million—a nearly 400 percent increase—while the total general population of the country grew by only 36 percent, and the crime rate *fell* by 42 percent. The national crime rate declined consistently throughout the thirty-seven-year period, except for a gradual uptick of just 17 percent between 1985 and 1991 (during which the rate remained lower than in 1980). The catalyst of this prison expansion was policy changes that prioritized "getting tough" on crime.

During this time period, from 1980 to 2006, when the Michigan prison system was at its highest, the population grew by 36,330 prisoners to 51,454, a 240 percent increase. But since that peak year, the population has witnessed massive reductions, with the end result in 2015 of a prison population 20 percent lower, a reduction of 10,332 prisoners. Most of the net drop (82 percent of it) occurred during five consecutive years (2007–2011) of greater than 2.3 percent decline each year, led by 2009 (–6.7 percent [–3,260]). The population rebounded in 2012–2013 (+1.9 percent) and then decreased in 2014–2015 (–2.6 percent), followed by another larger decline in 2016 (–3.5 percent).

The 2007–2011 prison population decline (–17 percent) was due to progressively fewer prison admissions (–22 percent from the peak prison population year across all admission types) and more annual prison releases (+15 percent on average compared to the peak prison population year, with a record spike in 2009).

The 2014–2015 prison population decline (–2.6 percent) was due to fewer annual prison admissions (-10 percent across all admission types). DOJ BJS data for Michigan for calendar year 2016 are not available yet, but Michigan's latest prison-population projection report indicates that a 2016 prison population decline (–3.5 percent) was primarily due to more paroles, and to a lesser degree fewer prison admissions.

Significant and consistent declines in all crime rates, total arrests, and new felony court dispositions following the peak prison population year were among the major drivers of the prison population decline in Michigan. From the peak prison population year (2006) through 2015:

- Index crime rate: –39 percent
- Violent crime rate: –26 percent
- Property crime rate: –42 percent
- Total arrests: –23 percent
- New felony court dispositions: –20 percent

It is important to note that other states whose crime rates also declined were unable to take advantage of that as their prison populations continued to increase.

The Michigan Prisoner Reentry Initiative (MPRI)—as designed and implemented by the executive branch, and facilitated by some enabling legislation and funding from the legislature—has been credited with much of the decrease in both crime and the prison population, especially during the extended 2007–2011 years of most noteworthy prison population decline. The MPRI contained numerous elements that reformed many aspects of the criminal justice system in the state, affecting both prison admissions and prison releases. Given the prison population reductions, Michigan has closed more than twenty-six facilities and camps, saving $392 million in operating costs annually and likely millions of dollars more in cost avoidance since population projections had been even higher than the peak population before the MPRI began.

Current five-year projections expect that the prison population will continue to decline gradually. Prisoner population reduction was greater among the white population (white: -20 percent; black: -15 percent), but that change yielded only a 1 percent shift in the racial proportions within the prison population.

NOTES

1. The Sentencing Project, *Trends in U.S. Incarceration*, updated April 2015, 2, http://sentencingproject.org/doc/publications/inc_Trends_in_Corrections_Fact_sheet.pdf.

2. R. Walmsley, *World Population List*, 10th ed. (Essex, UK: International Centre for Prison Studies, 2013), http://www.prisonstudies.org.

3. The 106th NAACP National Convention (Whitehouse.gov broadcast, July 14, 2015). President Barack Obama stated, "Mass incarceration makes our country worse off, and we need to do something about it." Columbia School of International and Public Affairs: 18th Annual David N. Dinkins Leadership and Public Policy Forum (Columbia Media Services 2015) https://sipa.columbia.edu/forums/dinkins. In Democratic presidential hopeful and former secretary of state Hillary Clinton's speech, she called for body cameras in every police department in the country, as well as an end to an "era of mass incarceration." Inimai Chettiar, "Republicans and Democrats Agree: End Mass Incarceration," *Aljazeera America*, September 26, 2015, http://america.aljazeera.com/opinions/2015/9/republicans-and-democratics-agree-end-mass-incarceration.html. Republican presidential candidates Jeb Bush, Carly Fiorina, Rand Paul, Chris Christie, and Democratic candidates Hillary Clinton, Bernie Sanders, and Martin O'Malley have all called for criminal justice reforms in their runs for president.

4. Inimai Chettiar and Rebecca McCray, "Sing it, Newt! Gingrich and Allies Promote Criminal Justice Reform," American Civil Liberties Union, January 13, 2011, https://www.aclu.org/blog.

5. E. Ann Carson, *Prisoners in 2015* (Washington, DC: Bureau of Justice Statistics, 2016), https://bjs.gov/content/pub/pdf/p15.pdf.

6. Marc Mauer, letter, general appeal for funding for the Sentencing Project, November 29, 2017: "President Trump and Attorney General Sessions are doing all they can to sustain mass incarceration. Almost weekly the Administration has been contending that crime is out of control and that it's time to revive the War on Drugs."

7. See, e.g., Brad Bogue et al., *Implementing Evidence-Based Policy and Practice in Community Corrections*, 2nd ed. (Boston: Crime and Justice Institute, Community Resources for Justice, 2009), 11–21.

8. Danielle Kaeble and Thomas P. Bonczar, *Probation and Parole in the United States, 2015* (Washington, DC: U.S. Department of Justice, Bureau of Justice Statistics, 2016), https://bjs.gov.

9. Carson, *Prisoners in 2015*.

10. Timothy Hughes and Doris James Wilson, *Reentry Trends in the United States* (Washington, DC: U.S. Department of Justice, Bureau of Justice Statistics, 2002), https://bjs.ojp.usdoj.gov/content/pub/pdf/reentry.pdf.

11. Allen J. Beck, "The Importance of Successful Reentry to Jail Population Growth," PowerPoint presentation at the Urban Institute's Jail Reentry Roundtable, June 27, 2006, urban.org/sites/default/files/beck.ppt.

12. Caroline Wolf Harlow, *Education and Correctional Populations* (Washington, DC: U.S. Department of Justice, Bureau of Justice Statistics, 2003), https://bjs.ojp.usdoj.gov/content/pub/pdf/ecp.pdf.

13. Harry J. Holzer, Steven Raphael, and Michael A. Stoll, *Employment Barriers Facing Ex-Offenders* (Washington, DC: Urban Institute, 2003), https://urban.org.

14. Christy Visher, Sara Debus, and Jennifer Yahner, *Employment after Prison: A Longitudinal Study of Releasees in Three States* (Washington, DC: Urban Institute, 2008), https://urban.org.

15. Margaret Colgate Love, Jenny Roberts, and Cecelia Klingele, *Collateral Consequences of Criminal Convictions: Law, Policy and Practice* (New York: Thomson West, 2013).

16. National Commission on Correctional Health Care, *The Health Status of Soon-to-Be-Released Prisoners: A Report to Congress*, vol. 1 (Chicago: National Commission on Correctional Health Care, 2002), ncchc.org; David Cloud, *On Life Support: Public Health in the Age of Mass Incarceration* (New York: Vera Institute of Justice, 2014), https://vera.org/publications.

17. Doris J. James and Lauren E. Glaze, *Mental Health Problems of Prison and Jail Inmates* (Washington, DC: Bureau of Justice Statistics, 2006), https://bjs.gov/content/pub/pdf/mhppji.pdf.

18. Hank J. Steadman, Fred Osher, Pamela Clark Robbins et al., "Prevalence of Serious

Mental Illness among Jail Inmates," *Psychiatric Services* 60, no. 6 (2009): 761–65, https://csgjusticecenter.org.

19. Greg A. Greenberg and Robert A. Rosenheck, *"Jail Incarceration, Homelessness, and Mental Health: A National Study,"* Psychiatry Services (2008), https://ps.psychiatryonline.org.

20. Caterina Gouvis Roman and Jeremy Travis, "Where Will I Sleep Tomorrow: Housing Homelessness, and the Returning Prisoner," *Housing Policy Debate* 17, no. 2 (January 2006), 389–419.

21. Pew Charitable Trusts, *Collateral Costs: Incarceration's Effect on Economic Mobility* (Washington, DC: Pew Charitable Trusts, 2010), https://www.pewtrusts.org.

22. Ibid.

23. Rebecca Beitsch, "States Rethink Restrictions on Food Stamps, Welfare for Drug Felons," *Stateline,* July 30, 2015, https://www.pewtrusts.org.

24. Matthew R. Durose, Alexia D. Cooper, and Howard N. Snyder, *Recidivism of Prisoners Released in 30 States in 2005: Patterns from 2005 to 2010* (Washington, DC: Bureau of Justice Statistics, 2014), https://bjs.gov/content/pub/pdf/rprts05p0510.pdf.

25. Ibid.

26. Joan Petersilia, *When Prisoners Come Home: Parole and Prisoner Reentry* (New York: Oxford University Press, 2003).

27. Ibid., 57.

28. Ibid., 74.

29. Jeremy Travis, *But They All Come Back: Facing the Challenges of Prisoner Reentry* (Washington, DC: Urban Institute Press, 2005).

30. Petersilia, *When Prisoners Come Home,* 171.

31. Ibid., 324.

32. See, for example, Kenneth Stampp, *The Peculiar Institution: Slavery in the Ante-Bellum South* (1956; New York: Vintage, 1989); Ira Berlin, *Many Thousands Gone: The First Two Centuries of Slavery in North America* (Cambridge, MA: Belknap Press, 1998); C. Vann Woodward, *The Strange Career of Jim Crow* (1955; New York: Oxford University Press, 1989); Leon Litwack, *Trouble in Mind: Black Southerners in the Age of Jim Crow* (New York: Penguin, 1999); Allan Spear, *Black Chicago: The Making of a Negro Ghetto, 1890–1920* (Chicago: University of Chicago Press, 1967); Kerner Commission, *1968 Report of the National Advisory Commission on Civil Disorders* ([1968] 1988), https://www.hsdl.org/?view&did=35837; B. Pettit and B. Western, "Mass Imprisonment and the Life Course: Race and Class Inequality in U.S. Incarceration," *American Sociological Review* 69 (2004): 151–69.

Loïc Wacquant, "From Slavery to Mass Incarceration:, Rethinking the 'Race Question' in the US," *New Left Review* 13 (January/February 2002): 44. "Not crime, but the need to shore up an eroding case cleavage, along with buttressing the emergent regime of desocialized wage labour to which most blacks are fated by virtue of their lack of marketable cultural capital, and which the most deprived among them resist by escaping into the illegal street economy, is the main impetus behind the stupendous expansion of America's penal state."

33. Marc Mauer, *The Race to Incarcerate* (New York: New Press, 2006).

34. Michelle Alexander, *The New Jim Crow: Mass Incarceration in the Age of Colorblindness*, rev. ed. (New York: New Press, 2012).

35. Ibid., 30, 31.

36. Ibid., 55–58.

37. Ibid., 234–35.

38. Georgia, Idaho, Indiana, Iowa, Kentucky, Massachusetts, Michigan, Minnesota, Missouri, New Jersey, New York, North Dakota, Oregon, Rhode Island, Tennessee, Texas, and Virginia.

39. National Institute of Corrections, *TPC Reentry Handbook: Implementing the NIC Transition from Prison to the Community Model* (Washington, DC: Department of Justice, 2008).

40. Council of State Governments, *Report of the Re-Entry Policy Council: Charting the Safe and Successful Return of Prisoners to the Community*, 2005, https://csgjusticecenter.org.

41. 110th Congress, *Second Chance Act of 2007: Community Safety through Recidivism Prevention* (Washington, DC: U.S. Government, 2008). http://www.govtrack.us/congress/bills/110/hr1593.

42. D. L. Fixsen, S. F. Naoom, K. A. Blase et al., *Implementation Research: A Synthesis of the Literature* (Tampa: University of South Florida, Louis de la Parte Florida Mental Health Institute, National Implementation Research Network, 2005).

43. T. E. Feucht and C. H. Innes, "Creating Research Evidence: Work to Enhance the Capacity of Justice Agencies for Generating Evidence," in *Contemporary Issues in Criminal Justice Policy*, ed. Natasha Frost, Joshua Freilich, and Todd Clear (N.p.: Cengage Learning, 2009), 7–16.

44. T. E. Feucht, *Cultivating Evidence: Linking Knowledge from Innovation to Program Evaluation and Multi-Site Replication* (San Francisco: American Society of Criminology Annual Meeting, 2010), xx.

45. The intention is to determine changes in the reconviction and re-imprisonment rates for returning citizens that are stratified to allow analyses for differing rates based on level of risk. As a result, the risk levels of prisoners are expected to change over time and will be measured by a new "prison population risk tool" being developed.

46. Re-Entry Policy Council, *Report of the Re-Entry Policy Council: Charting the Safe and Successful Return of Prisoners to the Community* (New York: Council of State Governments, January 2005). Peggy Burke, *TPC Reentry Handbook: Implementing the NIC Transition from Prison to the Community Model* (Washington, DC: U.S. Department of Justice, National Institute of Corrections, August 2008).

47. CSG Justice Center, "States Report Reductions in Recidivism," September 25, 2012, https://csgjusticecenter.org.

48. Ibid.

49. Michigan Department of Corrections, "Michigan Prisoner Reentry: A Success Story," 2013, https://www.michigan.gov/documents/corrections/The_Michigan_Prisoner_Reentry_Initiative__A_Success_Story_334863_7.pdf.

50. Ibid. From 2006 to 2009 the prison population dropped from 51,577 to 45,478—a 12 percent drop in three years. The decline continues today; through February 2013, the population has dropped by 17 percent.

51. Nicole D. Porter, "On the Chopping Block: State Prison Closings," The Sentencing Project, August 2011, https://www.sentencingproject.org.

52. See Luke Mogelson, "Prison Break: How Michigan Managed to Empty Its Penitentiaries While Lowering Its Crime Rate," *Washington Monthly* (November/December 2010), https://www.questia.com/magazine/1G1-259077645/prison-break-how-michigan-managed-to-empty-its-penitentiaries. See addendum 2.

53. Elizabeth Alexander, *Michigan Breaks the Political Logjam: A New Model for Reducing Prison Populations*, American Civil Liberties Union, November 2009, https://www.aclu.org.

54. See, for example, Judith Greene and Marc Mauer, *Downscaling Prisons: Lessons from Four States*, The Sentencing Project, 2010, https://www.sentencingproject.org; Porter, "On the Chopping Block: State Prison Closings"; Alexander, *Michigan Breaks the Political Logjam*; "Prison Break: How Michigan Managed to Empty Its Penitentiaries While Lowering Its Crime Rate," *Washington Monthly* magazine, November/December 2010; CSG Justice Center, "States Report Reductions in Recidivism."

55. Susan K. Urahn et al., *State of Recidivism: The Revolving Door of America's Prisons*, Pew Center for the States, April 2011, https://www.pewtrusts.org. See also Greene and Mauer, *Downscaling Prisons*.

56. M. Gottschalk, *Caught: The Prison State and the Lockdown of American Politics* (Princeton, NJ: Princeton University Press, 2015), 79–97.

57. Michelle Alexander, *The New Jim Crow: Mass Incarceration in the Age of Colorblindness* (New York: The New Press, 2010), 236.

CONCLUSION

I t has been our purpose to educate the lay reader about mass incarceration, especially as it is manifested in Michigan. While mass incarceration is a national problem, the vast number of incarcerated people are held in state prisons and local jails. To understand what factors are driving mass incarceration as well as how to address the problem requires not only an examination of national trends, but a close look at state and local laws and policies at all levels of the criminal justice system. We wish to reiterate that mass incarceration is about more than the sheer number of people behind bars; it is also about the ripple effect on the families and communities of incarcerated and formerly incarcerated citizens. By combining current research with the stories and perspectives of those most directly affected, we hope we have deepened the readers' understanding and given the problem a human face.

Michigan's record of addressing the incarceration crisis is mixed. The good news, as noted in the introduction to this volume, is that the prison population in Michigan has declined to just below 40,000 from an all-time high of 51,500 in 2007. As of April 2018, the state had closed or consolidated twenty-six prisons since 2005 and is anticipating another closure.[1] Furthermore, as Dennis Schrantz has shown in his article in this volume, Michigan has been a national leader in reducing recidivism.

At 29.8 percent, the recidivism rate in Michigan is near historic lows and one of the lowest in the country.[2] In recent signs of progress, the state has set aside $84 million in its 2019 budget for indigent defense. This comes a decade after a report from the Sixth Amendment Center that ranked Michigan's indigent defense system among the worst in the nation. It has been estimated that inadequate defense was the cause of 50 percent of overturned convictions.[3]

As noted in the introduction to this volume, Michigan leads the nation in the length of time people spend behind bars; thus parole reform is critical to reducing the state's prison population. Some progress has been made in this area. In September 2018, Governor Snyder signed "Objective Parole" into law, which will require the parole board to use evidence-based standards and provide a compelling reason to deny parole when prisoners are first eligible. Although more modest than the initial "Presumptive Parole" bills, it represents some success for groups that have been advocating parole reform in Michigan for years. It is anticipated that Objective Parole will reduce the prison population by about 2,000 in five years.[4] Although poor conditions in prisons have been an ongoing issue, one bright spot is a recent announcement that after reports of serious food contamination, the privatized prison food service has been discontinued and food service in state prisons will once again be supplied by state workers.[5]

Even though there has been progress, much needs to be done. As of this writing, the campaign to Raise the Age of criminal responsibility to eighteen is stalled in the state legislature, and Michigan remains one of four states to automatically try seventeen-year-olds as adults and house them in adult facilities. Michigan also needs sentencing reform and would benefit from the reinstatement of a sentencing commission to set guidelines that ensure punishment is proportional to the crime, and that people with similar prior records who have committed similar offenses are similarly treated.[6]

As prisons have closed and the prison population has declined, the conditions of incarceration have deteriorated in the drive to save money. Serious staffing shortages in Michigan prisons have increased safety concerns. As of March 2018 there were about 740 vacancies for corrections officers; more than 10 percent of guard positions were vacant.[7] In 2016 female corrections officers at Women's Huron Correctional Facility brought a federal lawsuit alleging they were forced to work excessive overtime as a result of staff shortages, which made conditions unsafe in the prison. A proposed settlement of the suit would require the State of Michigan to pay $750,000 to female officers, allow female officers to transfer to other prisons, and possibly open up positions in the all-women's prison to male guards; male guards have been banned in women's prisons in Michigan as the result of a prior sexual abuse settlement.[8]

The increased incarceration of women and the problems plaguing Women's Huron Valley Correctional Facility, now the only women's prison in Michigan, is an area for further research that we were not able to address in this volume. In Michigan between 2006 and 2016, the numbers of female prisoners incarcerated, admitted, and released increased, while the numbers of male prisoners incarcerated, admitted, and released decreased over the same period.[9] The causes for this increase still need more analysis, but harsh sentencing policies for nonviolent offenders and drug offenses are contributing factors. While the numbers of incarcerated women in Michigan increased, the conditions of their incarceration deteriorated, largely due to the 2009 closing of the Robert Scott Correctional Facility because of budget cuts, and the transfer of women to the Women's Huron Valley Correctional Facility. The *Detroit Free Press* has reported extensively on overcrowding at Huron Valley as well as other problems, and in fall 2018 a proposed class action lawsuit was filed in federal court claiming that many prisoners have been "packed into former closets and other converted rooms," that they are confined to their cells most of the time because of a lack of recreation areas, and that they lack adequate clothing and medical treatment.[10] Between 2010 and 2015 a dramatic spike in violent incidents and suicide attempts at the facility has been documented.[11] There has been a long, unpleasant history of problems in women's prisons in Michigan. Between 1993 and 2009 more than nine hundred women prisoners alleged sexual misconduct by guards. A class action lawsuit against the Michigan Department of Corrections ended in a record $100 million settlement in 2009 and banned male guards from working in female prisons in Michigan.[12]

Ending mass incarceration will require us to reckon with the legacy of racism, which continues to shape our criminal justice system. From arrest to sentencing to incarceration, people of color are treated more harshly than whites are treated for comparable crimes. As Michelle Weemhoff and Jason Smith have shown in their article in this volume, even though there has been a reduction in the incarceration of young people nationwide, the racial disparities in youth confinement have increased, and they've increased in Michigan by a dramatic 73 percent. In Michigan, black youths account for 40 percent of all juvenile arrests. And as Darryl Thomas noted in his article, while we are witnessing a gradual decline in incarceration rates, police use of deadly force is on the rise.

Ending mass incarceration will require a better understanding of the relationship between crime and incarceration, and a change in the public image of incarcerated people. Too often criminal justice policy is driven by fear and political expediency rather than reason. Recently, there has been a bipartisan effort to reduce the prison population in Michigan (and other states) because of the considerable cost to state and local governments of locking up so many people. But fiscal arguments alone are insufficient to bring about the changes that are needed. Fundamental change will require a broader rethinking about how to increase the safety and prosperity of our communities. Many of the articles in this book conclude with specific recommendations for changing laws and initiating programs and policies that have been shown to be successful in reducing incarceration and deterring crime. Some of the recommendations discussed include training officers in de-escalation, improving data collection, developing racial impact statements prior to adopting new criminal justice legislation, expanding alternatives to incarceration, reforming sentencing policies, investing in local solutions such as violence prevention programs, substance abuse treatment, crime survivor services, restorative justice practices, and making mental health treatment accessible to keep the mentally ill out of the criminal justice system.

In conclusion, it is the editors' hope that this collection of essays, stories, and art will help readers to better understand the facts of incarceration, its ripple effects, and the people who are living and have lived behind bars. Ending mass incarceration is perhaps the key civil-rights issue of our time.

NOTES

1. Kahryn Riley, "Three Criminal Justice Proposals before Michigan House This Week," Mackinac Center for Public Policy, April 13, 2018, https://www.mackinac.org.
2. Brad Devereaux, "Michigan Prisons Short 740 Corrections Officers, Paying $70M in OT," MLive.com, March 2, 2018, https://www.mlive.com.
3. Justin A. Hinkley, "Michigan Approves 84M to Give the Poor a Fair Fight in Court," *Lansing State Journal*, June 19, 2018.
4. "New Law Reforms Parole Guidelines in Michigan," *Click on Detroit*, September 13, 2018, https://www.clickondetroit.com/news/governor-snyder-signs-objective-parole-bill-into-law.
5. Riley, "Three Criminal Justice Proposals."
6. "Reforming Sentencing Policies," Safe and Just Michigan, 2018, https://www.

safeandjustmi.org/our-work/reforming_sentencing_policies.

7. Devereaux, "Michigan Prisons Short."

8. Paul Egan, "State of Michigan to Pay $750K to Settle Women's Prison Federal Lawsuit," *Detroit Free Press*, August 31, 2018.

9. Pamela R. Smith, PhD, "Incarcerated Women in Michigan," unpublished manuscript.

10. Paul Egan, "Women Say Conditions at Crowded Michigan Prison 'Cruel and Unusual,'" *Detroit Free Press*, September 6, 2018.

11. Ibid.

12. Kyle Feldscher, "Looking Back: How High-Profile Complaints about Prison Conditions Were Investigated and Resolved," *Ann Arbor News*, September 8, 2014, https://www.mlive.com.

CONTRIBUTORS

Bette Avila received a doctoral degree in sociology at Michigan State University; her dissertation is titled "Importance of Motherhood and/or Social Stigma of Infertility: What's Driving Infertility-Related Outcome?" Generally, her research areas have included obesity prevention and intervention, rural health concerns, infertility, decisions about medical treatment, social support and illness, and the social construction of health and illness.

Charles Corley is an associate professor of criminal justice at Michigan State University who has written widely on race, juveniles, and the criminal justice system. His current research focuses on children of incarcerated parents.

Rand Gould has been incarcerated in Michigan prisons for more than twenty years. He is a longtime radical who was involved in protests against the War in Vietnam and fought in the unions against corporate exploitation of workers and the planet. He has been widely published in the radical press, including recent articles in *San Francisco Bay View* such as "The Lesser Threat" (October 2016), "Michigan Prisoners Rise Up! Overcrowded and Underfunded State Prisons Spawn Resistance" (November 2016), and "New Mail Policy in Michigan Prisons: Billionaires Profit at the Expense of Prisoners, Their Families and Friends, and the U.S. Postal Service" (January 2, 2018). Almost all of his writing, including "Know Your Enemy: The New COINTELPRO and the Slippery Slope of Identity Politics," can be found at his website, www.freerandgould.com. His writing can be found as well at Lois Ahren's Real Cost of Prisons Project website, www.realcostofprisons.org.

Reuben Kenyatta is an art curator at the Prison Creative Art Project, College of Literature, Science and Arts, University of Michigan. He is also a veteran of the Vietnam War era and a formerly incarcerated citizen. In an effort to recover from post-traumatic stress disorder during military service, Reuben began utilizing art therapeutically as a means of stress management, and he discovered that the creative process of art making was healing and restorative. Being self-taught in the durable medium of acrylic, he now specializes in turning proposed ideas into visual images for practical application and to encourage positive solutions about social concerns. His work can be found at https://www.kenyatta-art.com.

Aaron Kinzel is a formerly incarcerated person as well as a doctoral student in the College of Education, Health, and Human Services, and a lecturer in criminology and criminal justice studies at the University of Michigan-Dearborn. Kinzel is not a typical college professor, due to his diverse roles and interests. Despite having three degrees under his belt, Kinzel found it immensely hard to find an appropriate job. He is a true believer that a person's past mistakes in society should not define the rest of their lives, and his story is one of persistent determination and struggle to change the system. He has conducted training seminars for upper-level personnel for the Department of Justice, has completed contracts with the DOJ and Federal Bureau of Prisons, and routinely does speaking engagements.

Barry Lewis received his Master of Social Work from the School of Social Work at MSU and recently obtained the Limited Licensed Master Social Worker. Originally from Denver, Colorado, he moved to Michigan in 2009 to pursue his dual bachelor's degrees at Wayne State University, where he graduated with a degree in journalism and another in urban studies. His special focus is on juvenile and criminal justice systems and reform.

Rubén O. Martinez is professor of sociology and director of the Julian Samora Research Institute at Michigan State University. His research interests include neoliberalism and Latinos, diversity leadership in higher education, institutional and societal change, education and ethno-racial minorities, youth development, Latino labor and entrepreneurship, and environmental justice. Martinez is the editor of the Latinos in the United States book series with Michigan State University Press. He has numerous publications, including three coauthored books: *Chicanos in Higher Education* (1993), *Diversity Leadership in Higher Education* (2007), and *A Brief History of Cristo Rey Church in Lansing, MI* (2012); one edited volume, *Latinos in the Midwest* (2011); and two coedited volumes: *Latino College Presidents: In Their Own Words* (2013), and *Occupational Health Disparities among Racial and Ethnic Minorities: Formulating Research Needs and Directions* (2017).

D. Quentin Miller is professor of English at Suffolk University in Boston. He is the author and editor of numerous books and articles on American literature, including *Prose and Cons: Essays on Prison Literature in the United States* (2005); *A Criminal Power: James Baldwin and the Law* (2012); *The Routledge Introduction to African American Literature* (2016); *American Literature in Transition: 1980–1990* (2018); *Understanding John Edgar Wideman* (2018); and the twelfth edition of *The Bedford Introduction to Literature*, coedited with Michael Meyer.

Elizabeth Pratt retired in 2018 after nineteen years as a fiscal analyst with the nonpartisan Michigan Senate Fiscal Agency, where she worked on a wide variety of state budget and tax issues. She is an officer and past president of the National Alliance on Mental Illness (NAMI) Lansing, which provides education, support, and advocacy for individuals living with mental illness and their families. Elizabeth is married to Scott Pratt. They have two children: "Greg," whose experience with mental illness and incarceration is included in "Mass Incarceration and Mental Illness: Addressing the Crisis," and coauthor Carolyn Pratt Van Wyck.

Phillip "UcciKhan" Sample is the founder/executive director of RAHAM (Response Able Hands and Minds) Inc. He is a circle member of the Criminal Justice Initiative (CJI) and is a formerly incarcerated person who served 15 years of hard time in the Michigan Department of Corrections. Phillip attended the 2011 Race Conference with Buzz Alexander from the Prison Creative Arts Project, discussing his experience and performing spoken word. Since his release, Phillip has published the first part of his autobiography, *The Passion of The Life: The Life, Death & Resurrection of Phillip A. Sample*, and *To My Unborn Seed (Thoughts, Fears, Feelings & Hopes)*.

Phillip was also the assistant director for prison reenactments for the film *Natural Life*, a documentary about five juveniles sentenced to life in prison without parole.

Dennis Schrantz is director of the Center for Justice Innovation. For over four decades, he has succeeded in developing and implementing policies that have reduced prison and jail costs while enhancing public safety. He has played high-level roles in corrections policy in Michigan, Louisiana, Alaska, Montana, Georgia, and other states. As chief deputy director of the Michigan Department of Corrections, he led the creation and implementation of the groundbreaking Michigan Prisoner ReEntry Initiative, which contributed to substantial reductions in the prison population without an increase in crime by parolees. He has published numerous articles about ending mass incarceration and the lessons that have been learned to assist states in safely and effectively reducing the numbers of persons incarcerated through the use of evidence-based practices and community engagement.

Lynn Scott is a retired professor from James Madison College and the Residential College in Arts and Humanities at Michigan State University, where she taught courses in writing and research, including a research writing course on prisons and punishment in the United States. In retirement she identifies as an activist working toward criminal justice and prison reform. Lynn's doctoral work was in American and African American literature, and she has published widely on the author James Baldwin, including *James Baldwin's Later Fiction* (2002) and *James Baldwin and Toni Morrison: Comparative Critical and Theoretical Essays* (2006), coedited with Lovalerie King.

Jason Smith, LMSW, is the director of Youth Justice Policy at the Michigan Council on Crime and Delinquency. He leads MCCD's legislative advocacy efforts and serves as the coordinator of the campaign to raise the age of juvenile jurisdiction in Michigan 18. Additionally, Jason is responsible for managing several of MCCD's projects that aim to reduce the use of out-of-home placement through the statewide expansion of effective, community-based programming for justice-involved youth. In the past, Jason served as the lead researcher and coauthor of "Restoring Kids; Transforming Communities," a report that details the use of juvenile court diversion programs in Michigan.

Curtis Stokes is a professor of political theory as well as Marxist and radical thought in James Madison College at Michigan State University. He was founding director of the doctoral program in African American and African studies at Michigan State University and has been the lead organizer of the biennial conference Race in 21st Century America. His publications include articles, review essays, and six books, including *The Evolution of Trotsky's Theory of Revolution* (1982); *The State of Black Michigan, 1967–2007* (2007), coedited with Joe T. Darden and Richard W. Thomas; *Race and Human Rights* (2009); and most recently *Malcolm X's Michigan Worldview: An Exemplar for Contemporary Black Studies* (2015), with Rita Kiki Edozie.

Megan Sweeney is an associate professor of the Department of English Language & Literature and the Department Afroamerican and African Studies at the University of Michigan, Ann Arbor. Her publications include an award-winning monograph, *Reading Is My Window: Books and the Art of Reading in Women's Prisons* (2010); an edited collection, *The Story Within Us: Women Prisoners Reflect on Reading* (2012); numerous articles and book chapters about African American literature, reading, and incarceration; and creative nonfiction in *Brevity*, *Entropy*, and *Bennington Review*. Sweeney has received fellowships from the Radcliffe Institute for Advanced Study, UM's Institute for the Humanities, the Ford Foundation, and the Woodrow Wilson Foundation, and in 2014, she was awarded an Arthur F. Thurnau Professorship, UM's highest honor for outstanding undergraduate teaching.

Darryl C. Thomas is an associate professor in the Department of African American Studies at Penn State University. He has published widely on the international politics of the Third World, African/Africana studies, globalization, Global Africa/ African Diaspora, and the USA/China contestation over Africa and the Global South. He is a member of the Chinese in Africa/Africans in China Research Network, and the Black Curriculum Development Project. Thomas is currently completing a text that is entitled *Global Africa, Black Internationalism and the Challenges to Neoliberalism in the 21st Century*, and *African Americans and the Shifting Boundaries of Freedom in the 21st Century*.

Carolyn Pratt Van Wyck received a doctorate in history in 2018 from Michigan State University. Her dissertation, "'Type-C': Empowerment, Blame, and Gender in the Creation of a Carcinogenic Personality," explores alternative and popular beliefs about cancer and personality. While at MSU, she advocated for improved campus mental health resources, taught courses on the history of medicine, and worked as program administrator for the Social Science Scholars Program, where exceptional students research a wide variety of social issues and related policies.

Martin Vargas entered the Michigan prison system in 1972 to serve a parolable life sentence for an offense committed at age seventeen. For forty-five years he journeyed through Michigan prisons until his release in February 2018. He obtained his associate degree at the Michigan Reformatory and in 1990 earned a bachelor's degree from Spring Arbor college. While at the Ionia Correctional Facility (ICF), using a workbook created by Deni Elliott, of the University of Southern Florida, Martin created and taught an ethics course called "Core Values." Over six-hundred men voluntarily completed the course in thirteen years. In 1994 he became an art tutor at the only recognized art program funded by the Michigan Department of Corrections. He exhibited for twenty-three years in the largest juried prisoner art exhibit in the world, created by the Prison Creative Arts Project (PCAP) and hosted by the University of Michigan. PCAP provided many opportunities for Martin, including a 2017 presentation of his painting *Veritas—The Lifer* (which is reproduced in this volume) to United States Supreme Court Justice Sonia Sotomayor when she visited the University of Michigan. Martin's signature-style "Pudgies" became popular after he created them for donation to a hurricane-survivor fundraising event in 1998. For years he has donated paintings to nonprofit organizations, friends, and family, and his work has won numerous awards. Since his release Martin has had three successful solo exhibits; remains in his long and loving relationship with his wife, Barbara; and continues creating and exhibiting art. His work can be found at http://martinvargasarte.com/.

Michelle Weemhoff, MSW, is the founder and lead strategist of Next Generation Justice Consulting, LLC and part-time instructor at Western Michigan University's School of Social Work. Over the past decade, she has held various roles at the Michigan Council on Crime and Delinquency, including deputy director and senior policy advisor, leading initiatives to improve court proceedings and quality legal representation for youth, expand the use of alternatives to detention and incarceration, and end the prosecution of youth in the adult criminal justice system. Michelle has coauthored numerous reports, including *Youth Behind Bars: Examining the Impact of Prosecuting and Incarcerating Kids in Michigan's Criminal Justice System* (2013) and the Youth Transition Funders Group's *Blueprint for Youth Justice Reform* (2016).

INDEX